Virginia's Western War
1775–1786

Virginia's Western War
1775–1786

Neal Hammon and Richard Taylor

STACKPOLE
BOOKS

Published by
STACKPOLE BOOKS
5067 Ritter Road
Mechanicsburg, PA 17055
www.stackpolebooks.com

Printed in the United States of America

10 9 8 7 6 5 4 3 2 1

FIRST EDITION

Library of Congress Cataloging-in-Publication Data

Hammon, Neal O.
    Virginia's western war : 1775-1786 / Neal O. Hammon and Richard Taylor.
      p. cm.
    Includes bibliographical references and index.
    ISBN 0-8117-1389-X
    1. Virginia—History—Revolution, 1775-1783—Campaigns. 2. Frontier and pioneer life—Virginia. 3. Pioneers—Virginia—History—18th century. 4. United States—History—Revolution, 1775-1783—Campaigns. I. Taylor, Richard, 1941- II. Title.

E263.V8 H36 2002
973.3'3—dc21
                                                         2002020592

Dedicated to Barbara and Elizabeth

CONTENTS

PREFACE

VISITORS TO LOCUST GROVE IN LOUISVILLE ARE SHOWN THE SMALL ROOM in the house where Gen. George Rogers Clark died in 1818. During my last visit, after pointing out the only portrait of Clark made during his lifetime, the guide told the visitors that "had it not been for Clark, everything north of the Ohio River would now be Canada." This is an oversimplification of the facts but one commonly held today.

It has long been the opinion of the authors that most contemporary books on early frontier history, even those by noted historians, often miss the mark. Some are too class oriented, while others go to the opposite side of the road and are too politically oriented. A few past historians stress the military aspects of the frontier struggle, omitting the hardships of the struggling civilian population. Only four individuals who moved west in 1775—Daniel Boone, George Rogers Clark, Benjamin Logan, and James Harrod—have received special attention. Many frontier leaders, including such men as James John Floyd, Dr. William Fleming, William Whitley, John May, Isaac Hite, Abraham Chaplin, John Todd, and Levi Todd, have been ignored by biographers.

The early histories of Kentucky tell some of the story but generally miss the point because the reader's attention is directed, as a whole, at Kentucky rather than Virginia. Virginia histories, on the other hand, tend to treat the Westerners as mostly ignorant people, too stupid to stay in the Piedmont where they could have led a blissful and cultured existence. After all, neither George Washington, Thomas Jefferson, James Madison,

Henry Lee, nor any other important Virginian ever considered moving to Kentucky. Only a few of their less famous relatives went west.

For secondary source material, one of the best books written on the frontier experience during the Revolutionary War is Charles Gano Talbert's biography of Benjamin Logan, published in 1962. Although Talbert has passed away, his work was of great assistance during the preparation and checking of our text. We attempted to find similar, original, and detailed research that complements his book, but his is a hard act to follow.

The *History of Kentucky* by Temple Bodley was helpful, especially for its notations on land dealings by Virginia and other colonies. His other book, *Our First Great West,* was probably more in keeping with our theme than any other history. In preparing our epilogue, the 1985 work of Wiley Sword, *President Washington's Indian War,* was most informative.

In collecting material, the staff at the Filson Club in Louisville and the Kentucky Historical Society in Frankfort were very efficient and assisted us in every way possible. As the endnotes reveal, much of the research was from the Draper manuscript, which is available on microfilm at both places. For the illustrations we especially thank Martin F. Schmidt, who allowed us to use drawings from his book, *Kentucky Illustrated.*

Some may feel we used too much minutiae, but details make true stories interesting.

INTRODUCTION

ON THE EVENING OF DECEMBER 16, 1773, A GROUP OF WHITE MEN gathered together, removed their hats and coats, and began painting their faces and donning headdresses to disguise themselves as Indians. Completing their preparations, they marched along the streets of Boston to the harbor where they proceeded up the gangplanks of British ships, three newly arrived frigates loaded with tea shipped to America by the East India Company. Although the royal government in London had repealed all import taxes in America except for a tax on tea, many New Englanders were still offended by the symbol of British oppression.

The large crowd of onlookers congregated on the docks to watch as about forty "Indians" boarded the ships. Most had some foreknowledge of what was about to happen though the officers and sailors on the ships were taken completely by surprise, soon realizing that they were greatly outnumbered. The Indians quickly started hauling boxes of tea from the ship's hold. At first, the spectators looked on quietly. The first cheers arose when one of the Indians pried open the lid of the first box with his tomahawk and dumped the contents overboard. When the first containers of tea struck the water, the crowd roared in approval.

Some began shouting, "Throw the tea into the sea." In two hours, 340 chests were staved and emptied into Boston Harbor. The raiding party did not stop until all of the tea had been dumped into the bay. The next morning one witty citizen referred to the event as the Boston tea party. There is a tradition that one young wife discovered, to her dismay, that the shoes beside the bed she shared with her husband were filled with tea.

The Boston Tea Party signaled the resolution of at least some Americans to determine their own affairs. Since the first English settlers had touched landfall at Jamestown in 1607, critical decisions affecting the colonies in almost every sphere originated from abroad. In all thirteen colonies the king still appointed royal governors. Exercising his unquestioned authority, he also granted large tracts of colonial land to his friends and associates.

But the British had not always exercised complete control in North America. Their greatest rival, France, had founded Quebec in 1608 and later established a network of trading posts and villages along the Great Lakes and the Mississippi River. They also controlled New Orleans, the most important port on the Gulf of Mexico. The continuous friction between the French and the English had resulted in two major wars. After what the Americans called the French and Indian War, the French relinquished their claims to the region along the Great Lakes and east of the Mississippi River. By 1763 all of the French-speaking people in Canada and on the east side of the upper Mississippi were compelled to fly the British flag.

Because the war depleted England's resources, the English Parliament decided to shift some of the costs to the Americans. Taxes were imposed, but demands for payment met, as might be expected, with strong resistance. By 1770, many fourth- and fifth-generation Americans no longer felt any loyalty to the overseas government of their ancestors. The expanse of seemingly endless terrain and waterways bred a sense of boundless freedom, which reinforced Americans' resolve to practice self-determination. In many ways Americans had more freedom than their peers ever experienced in England or France. And they wanted to keep it.

A number of factors contributed to the conditions that sowed the seeds of revolution in Virginia. For most Virginians, a republican government was a balanced and traditional arrangement under which the wealthy assumed aristocratic leadership. Visionary but practical-minded Virginians like Jefferson and Washington had more confidence in representative government than had many of their thoughtful contemporaries from other parts of the country. John Adams, Alexander Hamilton, and Gouverneur William Morris were products of colonies where "the people" were regarded as a bothersome mob consisting of poor farmers and lower-class rabble.

By contrast, those ruling in Virginia had always emulated the ideal of the moderate English gentleman. They did not despise tradesmen and laborers, nor did they admire idle aristocrats. They had grown up living in small, isolated, nearly self-sufficient communities. Long-held customs of the Virginia countryside caused most of the planters with sizable holdings to develop into men of responsibility. Everything that made Virginia's elections favor aristocrats, especially the tendency to inherit posts in the House of Burgesses as well as the self-assurance that seemed the birthright of the large planters, encouraged the burgesses to be reasonable and independent in their judgment. Once in the legislature, they seldom glanced over their shoulders for the smile or frown of their constituency, a habit that now makes our elected representatives only a fragile mirror of those who elect them.

By 1775 upper-class Virginians held a traditional, prescriptive right to office so long as they earned the good opinion of their less substantial neighbors. This was a delicate and troublesome balance but a condition that generally produced sound and independent judgment. Officeholders were not worried about reelection or responding to the whims of the electorate. As a result, the House of Burgesses became a place of deliberation and intellectual exchange rarely found among modern legislatures. Though Virginia's leaders were not especially eloquent, persuasive argument was of first importance, and demagoguery held little influence. Such leaders were in a position to have the best knowledge of the larger economic and political problems of the community, and generally they put individual or factional interests aside to act in the best interest of the colony.

If Virginians had a collective fault, it was their abuse of the land. Both the large plantation owners and yeoman farmers overplanted their cash crop, tobacco, a practice that eventually resulted in worn-out parcels of land incapable of supporting either their families or their large labor force. As a consequence, they were often forced to look farther west for the acquisition of new land. Soil exhaustion, combined with fluctuating tobacco prices and the exorbitant prices charged by London merchants, often turned planters into land hunters. This explains why Virginia, more than any other colony, looked west for its future.

In some respects, Virginians regarded the French and Indian War as the solution to their land problems. The "Royal Proclamation of 1754" declared that officers and soldiers were to be paid for their military service with Western land. After the peace treaty had been signed, influential planters engaged in a series of political maneuvers to obtain the reward of

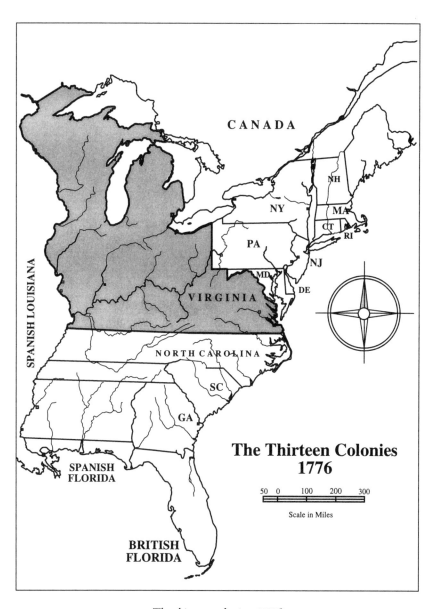

The thirteen colonies, 1776.

land promised by Governor Dinwiddie and the king. Much of George Washington's "public business" during his early years consisted of securing parcels of land for himself and his fellow veterans. Eighteen years passed before he was able to register his first warrant, but eventually he filed 18,500 acres with the county surveyor. Even after he had selected a tract on the Ohio River, he entered another tract on Coal River below present-day Charleston, West Virginia. John Floyd surveyed the land for him, sending the surveys to Col. William Preston, the surveyor of Fincastle County. As soon as Preston received this survey, he wrote Washington and offered to have Floyd survey additional tracts in Kentucky, a favor he had performed for other prominent citizens.

By the spring of 1774, the so-called Fincastle surveyors, under orders from Preston, were surveying military tracts as far west as the Falls of the Ohio. They worked in the interest of such notable Virginia gentlemen as Hugh Mercer, William Byrd, William Christian, Patrick Henry, Alexander Spotswood Dandridge, William Russell, Andrew Lewis, Alexander McKee, Robert McKinzie, John Connolly, William Fleming, James Taylor, Henry Harrison, John Ashby, and the surveyor himself, William Preston. Many of these men would make names for themselves in the Kentucky country during and after the Revolutionary War.

As early as 1768 the Kentucky country had been explored by the Long Hunters, so named because these seekers after valuable skins and pelts traveled long distances from their homes across the mountains in Virginia and North Carolina. "Long" also applied to the extended periods for which they were absent from their families. Passing through the Cumberland Gap in southeastern Kentucky, they ranged over much of the Kentucky country accumulating vast quantities of pelts and valuable furs. Among them were such men as Squire and Daniel Boone, James Knox, Gasper Mansker, Abraham Bledsoe, Joseph Drake, Uriah Stone, and the Skagg brothers. John Finley, the McAfee brothers, and James Harrod may be added, but neither their interests nor their primary motives were confined to hunting for profit. Though all had visited this country, none had made any effort to settle this part of Virginia before 1773.

Daniel Boone, William Russell, and some other frontier families attempted to make the first settlement in Kentucky during the fall of 1773. Russell, a member of the House of Burgesses and a leader in opening up southwest Virginia, possessed land warrants for his military service. These warrants entitled him legally to preempt land for himself and his followers. The ill-fated party departed from Castlewood, Virginia, and had traveled only one day when Indians ambushed the rear of the caravan, which had become separated during the journey. Indians killed one slave as well as the sons of both leaders, a tragedy so disheartening to the surviving members that they turned back.

Boone, the man who has most securely entered the pantheon of American heroes, was born to Quaker parents in Berks County, Pennsylvania, on October 22, 1734. His family moved to North Carolina when he was a young man. As with many others, his introduction to the West came during the French and Indian War when he served as a wagoneer during Gen. Edward Braddock's campaign. Afterward, with his brother Squire, he became a Long Hunter, making his first trip to Kentucky in 1768. On one occasion he lived alone in Kentucky for nearly a year.

Despite the loss of his eldest son, James, Boone remained undeterred in his plan to make either preemption claims or legal surveys in the Kentucky country. After the governor's "order of council," Virginia veterans of the French and Indian War began to apply for Western land entries at the office of the Fincastle surveyor. Col. Andrew Lewis made the first entry on December 15, and five more entries followed him on December 17. By the beginning of 1774 John Floyd, Robert Doack, Robert Preston, and Daniel and Francis Smith—all regular deputy surveyors of Fincastle County—were making preemption surveys on the Holston River. Some entries had a notation at the bottom: "Surveyed in proportion to the improvements according to the order of council the 16th Day of Dec'r 1773." These local preemptions usually contained about 200 acres. The smallest was only 23 acres, the largest 1,345 acres.

In December 1773, the year of the Boston Tea Party, the big topic at Virginia's homesteads and crossroads taverns was not the tax on tea but the availability of land and the opening of the West for settlement. This Western land called Kentucky was then only a vaguely defined part of Virginia. The exact meaning of this Indian word has never been properly defined, assuming it had a specific meaning in the first place. The only reliable definition for Kentucky is that it was a particular place, an area adjacent to the river by the same name. In pioneer times this Kentucky (or Kentucke) consisted of the area extending about eighty miles in all directions from Lexington.

The early mapmakers always had difficulty delineating Kentucky. John Patten's untitled manuscript map made in 1752, for example, shows two rivers in central Kentucky. One is labeled Salt Lick Creek. The other, obviously the present Kentucky River, has no name. Even more misleading, the

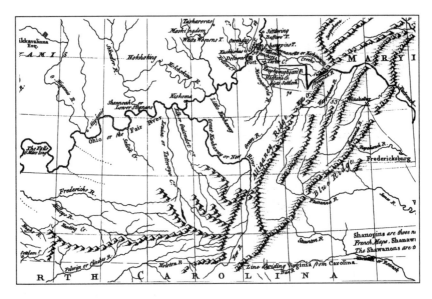

The western parts of Virginia from Washingon's published journal, 1752, showing the part containing the Ohio River down to the Falls.

map from Washington's journal also shows "Saltlick" Creek, but the Kentucky River is left out entirely. By 1775, when Dr. John Mitchell printed his work, *A Map of the British and French Dominions in North America,* the name assigned to the Kentucky River was Cuttawa or Catawba. Lewis Evans' published map and Pownall's revision, 1776, show five watercourses in Kentucky. Moving from east to west across the Kentucky country, they are Totteroy or Big Sandy Creek, Little Totteroy, Great Salt River (now the Licking), Kentucke or Cuttawa River, and Rotten or Beargrass Creek. The north fork of the Kentucky, possibly the present Red River, is called the Warrior's Branch, and the lower part of the Big Sandy is called Frederick River. On the "Great Salt River" we find the "Great Buffalo Lick," "limestone," and "white clay." This map, originally published in 1775, was the first to use the name "Kentucke."

In the fall of 1773 Capt. Thomas Bullitt had returned from Kentucky with a company of adventurers who had explored this faraway country. Bullitt, a native of Prince William County, had distinguished himself serving under George Washington as an officer in the French and Indian War. Virginia's governor, Lord Dunmore, had approved his surveying trip to the Kentucky country to claim land as payment for veterans of the war. And during the summer of 1773 Bullitt and company had surveyed some of the most desirable sites, mostly along the Ohio River as far as what was to become Louisville. Some of the surveys they made for themselves, others on promissory warrants for war veterans. Upon their return, Col. William Preston, the official surveyor of Fincastle County (of which the Kentucky country was a part) would not permit the surveys to be entered on the county survey books because they had not been made by his deputies. This legal technicality invalidated the work of an entire summer for Bullitt and the members of his party. Furthermore, Preston pointed out that some of the surveys were west of the Kentucky River on land beyond Donelson's treaty line in an area still owned by Indians.

Thomas Bullitt must have been disappointed after all of his efforts, but he and his associates used their influence to have some of the surveys legitimized. They appealed to the royal governor, their sympathetic friend Lord Dunmore. On December 15, 1773, members of the Virginia council debated the issue before the governor. Among the interested parties was Dr. Thomas Walker, a physician and explorer, who had led the first expedition through Cumberland Gap into the Kentucky country in 1750, writing a journal that detailed his journey. Speaking on behalf of himself as well as other members of the Loyal Land Company and Andrew Lewis, the agent for the Green Brier Company, he petitioned that land located for veterans not be allowed to interfere with their companies' rights under royal grants. In response, Hugh Mercer submitted a petition on behalf of the veterans. Although this request was not recorded, it most likely proposed that their warrants could be located on any vacant land in Virginia, an area that encompassed the whole of the Kentucky country. The next day the governor and other members of the council announced that officers and soldiers who had served against the French and Indians should:

> be at Liberty to Locate the Grants [they claimed under the Royal Proclamation of 1763] wherever they should desire, so as not to interfere with Legal Sur[veys] or actual Settlements; that every officer be allowed a distinct survey for every thousand Acres. That those are to be deemed Settlers who resided [on] any Tract of Land before last October and Continue to do so, having cleared some part thereof whereby their Intention to reside is Manifested; And that every Settler shall have fifty Acres at least, and also for every three Acres of Cleared land fifty Acres more and so in proportion; which is to be taken as part of the Grants to the said

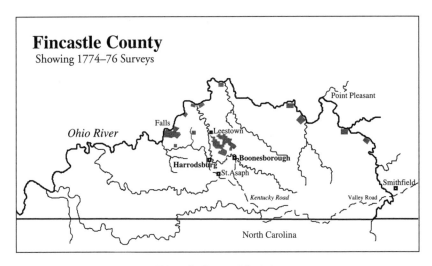

Fincastle County, Virginia.

Companies respectively, when the land Office shall be open to them, unless such Settlers shall chuse [*sic*] to hold under the Officers, or Soldiers or any of them rather than under the said Companies.[1]

That same day Governor Dunmore awarded land grants for Bullitt's surveys performed for Dr. John Connolly and Charles Warranstaff. Their land was situated south of the Falls of the Ohio. At the Falls, Bullitt's surveyors had already laid out streets for a town, and Bullitt had awarded lots to some members of his company. Some in Bullitt's party, including James Harrod, Matthew Bracken, Jack Drennon, John Mann, Willis Lee, Hancock Taylor, John Wollper, John Cowan, and Michael Tygret, would be remembered by creeks named for them. Strangely enough, the land grants to Connolly and Warranstaff were issued even before the land was entered with the Fincastle surveyor, indicating that the royal governor was not obliged to follow rules that applied to ordinary citizens.

The process of acquiring land in Kentucky would change during the summer of 1774, when parties of surveyors would survey large segments of the most desirable land in the central part of the state. While John Floyd was still running the nearby surveys on preemptions, his boss, Col. William Preston, was preparing for him to lead another party to Kentucky. Preston also appointed three men who had been to Kentucky the year before—

Profile of Dr. John Connolly, the Tory who obtained the land grant at the Falls of the Ohio in 1773. His was the first land grant on Western waters.

THE FILSON HISTORICAL SOCIETY, LOUISVILLE, KENTUCKY

Hancock Taylor, James Douglas, and Isaac Hite—as deputy surveyors of Fincastle County when they agreed to return to Kentucky with John Floyd.

Col. William Preston, chief organizer of this venture, was born in Ireland in 1729 and brought to Virginia as a child. He served as an officer during the French and Indian War and later held various offices in several frontier counties. During the time he served as the Fincastle County surveyor, his home was Draper's Meadows near the New River. John Floyd, later to gain prominence in Kentucky, was born in 1751 in Amherst County, Virginia. After the death of his first wife, he moved west and began working as a deputy surveyor for Preston.

Two of the other deputy surveyors were young men from influential families. Hancock Taylor (1738–1774) was born in Orange County, Virginia, the son of Zachary Taylor and uncle of the future president of that name. In the spring of 1769, he and his brother Richard, along with Abraham Haptonstall and another man named Barbour, had left Orange County, descending the Ohio to the Falls and then continuing their explorations to the Mississippi River and 100 miles up the Arkansas River before returning home by sea. Trained as a surveyor, Taylor accompanied Capt.

Thomas Bullitt in 1773 on his journey down the Ohio, making surveys for his father Zachary and the McAfee brothers along the Kentucky River.

Isaac Hite, born in Hampshire County, Virginia, in 1752, was the son of Col. Abraham Hite and a grandson of Joist Hite, an early German settler in the Virginia valley. Hite had also joined Captain Bullitt on his trip to Kentucky in 1773, exploring down the Salt and Kentucky Rivers but not in company with Taylor. Isaac Hite played an active role in early Kentucky; he was a member of the Transylvania legislature in 1775 and part of the Kentucky court in 1781. He later moved to Jefferson County and served in the state senate from 1800 to 1803.

On the expedition these deputy surveyors hired friends and associates to act as boatmen, hunters, and chainmen. Within the first three months of 1774, numerous military warrants, some plotted at designated sites marked in 1773, were filed at the surveyor's office. Most of the warrant holders entered their tracts in Kentucky. In April 1774, these surveyors and their assistants left Preston's office at Draper's Meadows and hiked through the mountains to the Falls of the Kanawha River, where they obtained some dugout canoes for the trip downriver. Their first survey, on April 18 at the mouth of the Coal River, was for George Washington. The next day they were informed of a serious encounter on the upper Ohio in which both white men and Indians had been killed.

According to Thomas Hanson's journal, when John Floyd reached Point Pleasant, where the Kanawha joins the Ohio, he found an encampment of whites:

> At our arrival we found 26 people there on different designs—Some to cultivate land, others to attend the surveyors. They confirm the same story of the Indians. One of them could speak Indian language, therefore Mr. Floyd & other Surveyors offered him 3 [pounds] per month to go with them, which he refused, and told us to take care of our scalps.[2]

At Point Pleasant, Floyd also learned that earlier in the spring, a company of men led by James Harrod had gone down the river to Kentucky with the intention of making improvements to obtain land. Many in Floyd's company who had been to Kentucky with Bullitt in 1773 were acquainted with Harrod, who had also accompanied the surveyor. At Point Pleasant about a dozen other men joined Floyd for his journey down the Ohio. Their intention was to join James Harrod.

On April 22 the party began their journey down the Ohio in four canoes. Four days later, they encountered three men who had been down the
river but had been driven back by Indians. Because Floyd's company contained thirty-four men, the strangers decided to accompany them to Kentucky. Their report of hostile Indians farther downstream, however, caused
four of the surveyors' own men to turn back. Though Floyd's party observed several Indians along the way, there was no trouble. As they traveled
down the river, they stopped to survey the best bottomland under authority of officers' warrants. They also visited an abandoned Indian town but
floated past Big Bone Lick, famous for mastodon bones, without stopping.
Most of company had camped there in 1773.

On May 14, 1774, they reached the mouth of the Kentucky River,
where eleven of the party left to find James Harrod, who was thought to be
"one hundred miles up the Kentucky or Louisa River. . . . Capt. Harrod
has been there many months building a kind of Town &c."[3] Among the
company were two brothers, Jacob and James Sodowski. James left to join
Harrod, and Jacob stayed with the surveyors to earn money as a chainman.
Floyd and Hite explored the countryside, visited Drennons Lick near the
Kentucky River about fifteen miles below the mouth, made a few surveys,
and then proceeded down to the Falls of the Ohio, which they reached on
the twenty-ninth.

James Harrod, the founder of the first permanent settlement in Kentucky, was early seduced by the wonders of the Western country. He was
born in Great Cove, Pennsylvania, some time between 1742 and 1746. An
Indian uprising when he was a child had forced his family to flee their
home. During the French and Indian War he and his older brother
William were members of Col. Henry Bouquet's regiment, serving in 1763
during the Forbes campaign. After the war he and William both settled on
Ten Mile Creek, a branch of the Monongahela, though they also made several trips to the Illinois country. Though having little formal education, he
was intelligent and a natural learner; he was able to speak several Indian
languages as well as French, skills he acquired as a hunter and scout in the
Old Northwest. Explorer, hunter, veteran of the French and Indian War, he
was to become a key leader in the early settlement of Kentucky. In 1773 he
joined Captain Bullitt's company on the trip to Kentucky. During that
summer, accompanied by John Smith, he explored south of the Ohio,
making some tomahawk claims on the Kentucky River near the present
town of Burgin.[4] Returning to the East, he had collected about thirty men
at Graves Creek on the upper Ohio and journeyed to what is now central

Kentucky to preempt land. The party selected a campsite between the Salt and Kentucky Rivers where the present town of Harrodsburg is now located. From this base they explored the surrounding country.

Most of the men who came to Kentucky with Harrod in 1774 were young bachelors from northern Virginia or southern Pennsylvania. Whenever they found a tract of land that appealed to them, they would cut a few trees and start construction of a cabin, believing these acts would suffice to establish a preemption claim. They agreed among themselves that the boundaries between their claims would be halfway between their cabins. Stealing a page from Captain Bullitt, they also laid out lots for a town, awarding one lot to each member of the company. Inside the town, they also erected a few cabins. As strange as it may now seem, James Harrod did not make his preemption claim on land at the proposed town of Harrodsburg but instead at a big "boiling spring" about seven miles to the south.

When they reached the Falls of the Ohio, John Floyd's men split into two groups, one headed by Floyd himself, the other by Hancock Taylor. This was done not only to lay the surveys more efficiently but to stop the continuous quarreling between Isaac Hite and Willis Lee. One of the first surveys at the Falls was made for John Connolly, who had already received a land grant from the governor. For about ten days the men surveyed at the future site of Louisville, then Floyd headed south for Bullitts Lick. In that time the parties had run the borders for thirty tracts, covering about 40,000 acres, or sixty-five square miles. These surveys ran from the river on the north and west sides of the present city of Louisville southwest past where the Watterson Expressway is now and eastward to the present-day suburbs of Anchorage and Prospect. Surveys were made for William Byrd, Alexander Spotswood Dandridge, William Fleming, William Peachey, Henry Harrison, William Preston, Hugh Mercer, William Christian, and other prominent Virginians. John Floyd and Hancock Taylor also managed to survey land for themselves on military warrants they had purchased.

These men ran their surveys wasting little time, but the methods were uniform and produced generally accurate results. Their lines were straight enough by frontier standards, usually staying within two degrees of the intended direction. Along Floyd's major baseline, for example, there was no deviation on either side more than 500 feet in eighteen miles. To run the surveys, they used a large open-faced compass equipped with movable sighting slits. This instrument was mounted on a wooden leg or legs, and after being leveled, the sights were turned to match the desired direction. One would presume that the marker advanced (clearing vegetation as re-

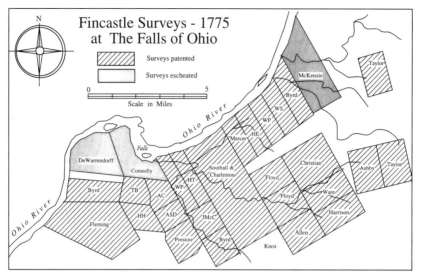

Fincastle Surveys, 1775, at the Falls of Ohio.

quired) as far as practical from the compass but keeping in its sights. After the marker had traveled as far as possible, the compass was moved to his position and the procedure repeated. At the Falls the surveyors used the odd directions 37 and 53 degrees for many of the tracts, but in the Bluegrass the most common directions were 20, 45, 60, 70, and 90 degrees. Most of the boundaries were off less than 5 degrees of true north.[5]

The chainmen traditionally used a sixty-six-foot chain (four poles) consisting of 100 links joined together with "eyes," or flexible loops. The leading chainmen carried pebbles or similar markers, which he dropped at the end of the chain. These were collected by the rear chainman in lieu of recording notes of distance. This seems to be the method used by the surveyors working close to home, but one frontier chainman said that as late as 1781 they were making measurements "either with a Tug or a Grape Vine supposed to be the right length."[6]

The distances of the boundary lines in the 1774 surveys were not as accurate as the directions. Some were so much larger than allowed by the warrant that the surveyors must have increased their size on purpose. For example, when Floyd made the 2,000-acre survey on Beargrass Creek for his friend William Christian, the alleged boundary of 550 by 600 poles turned out to be 648 by 667 poles, for a total of 2,700 acres. (The pole measurement used at the time was the same as the modern rod, or 16.5

feet.) The large Southall and Charlton tract, supposedly 640 poles across, was 706. In between the two was the land Floyd surveyed for himself; supposedly 400 poles square, it was actually 485 poles. This tendency was carried over to the Bluegrass surveys; the tracts along his baseline, measuring northward, instead of being 800 poles, averaged 940 poles.

By early June the surveyors had finished their work at the Falls. Hancock Taylor's last surveys on Beargrass Creek were dated June 8, so he probably left for Harrodsburg sometime soon after. Since Taylor, Lee, and Haptonstall had traveled between the headwaters of Salt River and the Falls in 1773, they were familiar with the country and probably reached Harrodsburg by the thirteenth or fourteeth.

Tradition holds that the town of Harrodsburg was staked off on June 16, 1774. There is nothing to indicate that James Harrod or anyone else in his company was either trained as a surveyor or capable of making a survey. If no one in the party was a surveyor, it is unlikely that anyone carried a compass or chains to Kentucky. How then could they have laid out the town of Harrodsburg? According to all reports, during the two and a half months before Taylor arrived, they had spent most of their time exploring and building themselves outlying lottery cabins.

The only reasonable conclusion is that when Hancock Taylor and his company reached this new settlement carrying their compass, the men at Harrodsburg requested them to lay out the boundaries for a new town, and Taylor and his chainmen obliged.[7] The baseline is said to have run a half mile west from what later became the town spring, with thirty-one inlots and some ten-acre out-lots. Taylor's men then hiked northward along the buffalo road, crossed the Kentucky River, and began making surveys on military warrants in the vicinity of Leestown and along the Elkhorn up to the present Midway, Kentucky. The 200-acre survey he had made for his father, Zachary Taylor, in 1773 at Leestown, was resurveyed and dated June 17, 1774.[8]

Floyd's men, in the meantime, hiked to Bullitts Lick, which they surveyed for Col. William Christian. They then followed the Salt River eastward, Floyd and several others falling ill. When the party reached Elk Creek, two of the men left Floyd and headed for Harrodsburg. One who parted company was James Knox, their guide and Long Hunter, who was apparently bored with the slow progress made by the explorers. The other was Hugh Allen, a veteran of the French and Indian War who had accompanied Floyd to locate his survey personally. Since Floyd had already surveyed his tract on Beargrass Creek, Allen decided to accompany Knox to Harrodsburg.

Floyd's party correctly decided that since the unnamed Brashears Creek was the larger of the two forks, it was the main branch of the Salt River. During the two days that Floyd was recuperating, Isaac Hite and William Nash explored the area. They hiked northward for about fifteen miles and discovered some choice land. Here they lingered to make a few more surveys, eventually reaching the Kentucky River on June 25. For this period Hanson makes the following entry in his journal:

> We traveled about 17 miles different courses, which brought us to the Kentucky on a small creek. We heard the Voice of one man calling to another, which made us imagine there were Indians about therefore as soon as night came on we went about 3 miles up the river & lay without fire. The land was broken that we traveled over this day. [The next day] [we] traveled 7 miles up the river & made a bark Canoe by which we crossed the river. As soon as we had crossed it we heard the report of a gun, we therefore traveled a little way up the river & then took off into the country. We traveled about 12 miles E.S.E. which brought us to Elk-Horn Creek, where we found some good land.[9]

Floyd and his party had reached the Elkhorn near where it intersects present-day Peaks Mill Road about six miles northeast of Frankfort. On the very day that Floyd's company reached the Kentucky River, a party of Indians was making its way southward from the Ohio. They continued southward along the Kentucky, passing the large buffalo fording place at Leestown near present-day Frankfort where Hancock Taylor had made a survey for his father. Not finding anyone there at the time, they kept following the river generally southeast toward Harrodsburg.

In the meantime, Floyd and his men could not resist surveying the bottomland along the Elkhorn. Hanson records their enthusiasm as they appraised its desirability:

> The land is so good that I cannot give it its due praise. Its under growth is Clover Pea vine Cane & Nettles—intermixed with Rich weed. Its Timber is Honey Locust, Black walnut, Sugar tree, Hickory, iron wood, Hoop wood, Mulberry, Ash, & Elm, & some Oak.[10]

The company unpacked their instruments and ran various surveys along the creek for four days. Near the forks of the Elkhorn they discovered some of Hancock Taylor's newly marked survey lines, prompting Floyd to go looking for him. He found Taylor within a short time, and together all the men hiked up to Taylor's base camp (south of the present-day Midway), which was eight miles away.

Back in Virginia, Col. William Preston was anxious about the safety of the surveyors. If a general war with the Northern Indians broke out, they would be in great danger. Though some of the leaders considered the possibility of sending troops to bring them home, it was finally decided to dispatch two good woodsmen for this task. Daniel Boone and Michael Stoner, both accomplished woodsmen, were selected. The son of German immigrants, Stoner was born in 1748 in southeastern Pennsylvania, and, like Boone, had a creek named after him (in present-day Bourbon County). They rode out of Castlewood on June 26 with instructions to cross the Cumberland Mountains at Pound Gap and proceed down the Kentucky River to the Ohio, warning any surveyors and other whites they encountered of the impending danger.[11]

At this time, the Indian war party was moving toward Harrodsburg. On June 13, one of Harrod's men, Jacob Lewis, left camp alone to hunt. It is very likely that he was captured by the Indians about July 1 and made to tell the whereabouts of his companions before he was killed.

At their camp on the upper Elkhorn, the surveyors began making plans to complete their surveys. They decided to split up into three groups under the surveyors Floyd, Taylor, and Douglas/Hite. Preferring to keep his party small, Floyd worked only with Thomas Hanson, William Nash, and Roderick McCra. Hancock Taylor's party consisted of his cousin Willis Lee, his old friend Abraham Haptonstall, and three others—John Green, James Strother, and John Willis. James Douglas and Isaac Hite, both deputy surveyors, were left with Jacob Sodowski, Mordicai Batson, John Ashby, John Bell, and Lawrence Darnell.[12] Thinking the two surveyors needed more men, Douglas recruited William Ballard from Taylor's party by promising to lay out a private survey for him. Two of the men, Thomas Glenn and Benjamin Tutt, had already left the surveyors and returned to Harrodsburg.

Having over fifty more military warrants to survey, the surveyors needed more time to complete their work. Taylor's men had been to Harrodsburg, or "Harrod's Cabins" as it was then known, so they proposed it as a point of rendezvous when the surveys were completed. Anticipating that their work would be finished in about two or three weeks, the others agreed to meet at Harrod's by August 1.

Elkhorn Creek has two main branches, and Taylor had been surveying along the south fork. He took Floyd out and showed him his northernmost boundaries so their lines would not overlap. Floyd proposed to survey along Elkhorn's north fork. Douglas and Hite chose to survey south, starting on the Elkhorn headwaters but locating most of their tracts along Hickman and Jessamine Creeks. While working in their respective areas, both Floyd and Douglas discovered springs that they admired and claimed for themselves. Using the 1,000-acre military warrant that he had purchased, John Floyd claimed the land around Royal Spring (at present-day Georgetown). James Douglas found a spring at the head of Jessamine Creek, which he named for his daughter Janet, who was fondly known as Jessamine. The creek took its name from this spring.

Though the Indian war party did not immediately locate the isolated surveying parties, it soon discovered one of the groups that had accompanied them down the Ohio. James Knox, James Sodowski, James Cowan, James Hamilton, and several others were relaxing at a place north of Harrodsburg known as Fountainbleau Springs. Suddenly, twenty Indians appeared out of nowhere and attacked their camp, killing James Cowan and James Hamilton.[13] Fleeing, the others took shelter in the woods, eventually managing to make their way back to Harrodsburg. Alerted, Harrod immediately sent out parties to locate any of his men who were wandering about making improvements. Within a short time, everyone in his company was back at the camp. Some of the men with Harrod later claimed to have gone back to Fountainbleau Springs to bury the dead. When James Douglas and his men arrived at the springs, however, they reported finding the bodies of the dead men.[14] In any event, on the following day, July 9, 1774, everyone in the vicinity had assembled and started for home. James Knox, who as a Long Hunter was familiar with the trails, probably acted as the guide. The men vacated the country using the old Skaggs' hunting path that led to the Rockcastle and Cumberland Rivers and through Cumberland Gap. Exhausted but relieved, they reached the settlement at Castlewood on July 29.

In vacating the country, James Harrod failed in one important respect. He did not warn the surveying parties of their danger. John Floyd and his companions continued their work, surveying north of present-day Lexington until July 18. They rested at Floyd's spring on July 19, then headed south to rejoin the other parties. Douglas's party had finished its surveys about the same time and headed for Harrodsburg, unaware that it had been evacuated. Closer to Harrod's settlement than Floyd, they arrived first and found the town deserted. Not long afterwards, they found the bodies of Cowan and Hamilton. In the words of Jacob Sodowski, the party spent little time debating how to react to the killings: "We found two men lying dead [at Fountainbleau Springs] and much fresh Indian sign, which induced the party to retreat to their canoe and ran down to the Falls, and from thence to New Orleans."[15]

As Hanson reports, Floyd and his men finally reached Harrodsburg on the morning of July 24:

> At our arrival we were surprised to find every thing squandered upon the ground & two fires burning. Mr. Floyd & Nash went down to the landing place & found these words wrote on a tree, "Alarmed by finding some people killed—we are gone down this way" Mr. Hite's and Mr Douglas party that arrived here 2 days before us, which we knew by a note found there. We took a canoe we found here & crossed the river, & traveled 8 miles north into the country.[16]

The exact location of Hancock Taylor's surveying party between July 8 and 26 is unknown. The following day, Taylor, accompanied by Abraham Haptonstall and James Strother, was paddling a canoe along the Kentucky River when they were fired upon by Indians. Strother was killed instantly. Taylor received two wounds in the body. His old friend Haptonstall managed to get the canoe ashore and helped Taylor make his escape. They joined their companions further upriver and immediately began the long journey back to the settlements to the East.

In spite of what proved to be mortal wounds, Hancock Taylor was able to walk for two days on his own. On the third and fourth days he was helped and carried along by his men. Finally, on the evening of August 1, 1774, John Green advised the dying surveyor to sign all of his surveys in order to validate them. All of them knew the end was near. Taylor, only thirty-six, finished his paperwork and died soon after. His men buried him at the confluence of two creeks at what is now called Taylor's Fork of Silver Creek in present-day Madison County.

By this time John Floyd had passed the Middle and North Forks of the Kentucky River, using an obscure Indian trail that eventually led over the mountains to the Clinch River. Douglas's men had by then recovered their dugout canoes left at the Falls of the Ohio and were well on their way to the mouth of the Mississippi River. Daniel Boone and Michael Stoner also traveled down the Ohio River on horseback and reached the Falls, where Boone observed "petrified buffalo dung" attached to the rocks. In Kentucky "he discovered that some of the surveyors had been attacked and dispersed by the Indians. He also found some of the surveyors and gave them notice of their danger."[17]

Several years later, Boone gave this brief account of his marathon to the frontier, a time during which he and Stoner constantly expected to be attacked themselves:

> [O]n the 26th June the same year I was employed by Governor Dunmore to go out to that country and give the surveyors notice of the breaking out of the Indians War and I took with me Michael Stoner and on the creek that goes by the name of Hickman about 2 or 3 miles below Colonel Levi Todd's I cut the two first letters of the said Hickman's name on a large water oak, with a large stone grown fast in the fork of said tree, in presence of Stoner, and finding the surveyors well drove in by the Indians, I returned home.[18]

John Filson, creator of the Boone myth and the frontiersman's first biographer, published Daniel Boone's "autobiography" in 1784 as part of his *The Discovery, Settlement, and Present State of Kentucke.* In reference to the trip, Boone was quoted as saying, "and [we] conducted in the surveyors, compleating a tour of eight hundred miles, through many difficulties, in sixty-two days."

Other evidence from correspondence of the time indicates that Boone reached Blackmore's fort on the Clinch River on August 27, 1774, in company with John Green and four others, among them probably Willis Lee, Abraham Haptonstall, and John Willis. Though the point is stretched somewhat, it is accurate to say that he conducted (a few of) the surveyors.

Later accounts record that these Indian raids in Virginia, especially in its westernmost counties and in the Kentucky country, were a result of Shawnee policy to "rob the Pennsylvanians and kill the Virginians." In part they resulted from the infamous slaughter of the family of Chief Logan, a Mingo who previously had been friendly to the whites. The murders were committed by a party of "border ruffians" led by a Daniel Greathouse. On April 30 they lured a party of Indians to their camp at the mouth of Yellow Creek about fifty miles below Pittsburgh on the Ohio. They plied them with drink, challenging several to a shooting match. When the Indians' muskets had been fired and they were practically defenseless, Greathouse and his company then murdered eight of them, including Logan's brother and a pregnant sister. Logan retaliated by launching his own vendetta against whites in the Ohio River valley, personally killing thirteen in the ensuing weeks and inducing other Indians to attack the unoffending settlers. This event, in large part perhaps, accounts for the sudden increase in Indian attacks during the spring and summer of 1774. Its cold-blooded brutality, combined with the volatile political climate on the frontier, also precipitated Lord Dunmore's War. Among the Northern Indians there was a growing awareness that the parties invading their hunting grounds were not hunters but surveyors who preceded widespread settlement. The Indians were determined to stop the incursions before a foothold was gained.

In the fall the conflict came to a head when Governor Dunmore of Virginia mobilized the militia and advanced on the Shawnee towns on the Scioto River. This was a unique little war, almost a prelude to the one that was to follow, involving only one Indian tribe and one British colony, Virginia. Pennsylvania had been asked to participate but had refused. At the site of the conflict, the Virginia militia was formed into two armies, Lord Dunmore leading the force that advanced from Pittsburgh and Gen. Andrew Lewis bringing up another army over the mountains and along the Kanawha River. The Shawnee chiefs headed by Cornstalk decided to attack Lewis at Point Pleasant, located at the junction of the Kanawha and the Ohio in what is now West Virginia.

In the early morning of October 10, 1774, four hunters, belonging to Capt. Evan Shelby's and Capt. William Shelby's companies of Virginia from Fincastle County were moving along the Ohio River near the mouth of the Kanawha River when they spotted Indians. In the ensuing exchange of fire, one of them, a man named Hickman, was shot, becoming the first casualty in what some regard as the first battle of the American Revolution. The survivors returned to camp where the officer in command of one wing of the army, Col. Andrew Lewis, a member of the House of Burgesses from Botetourt County, alerted the camp and ordered his troops forward. Lewis was an experienced commander, having served under Col. George Washington and Col. Henry Bouquet during the French and Indian War. What he confronted was an army of determined Indians under the direction of Cornstalk and such other capable leaders as Logan, Red Hawk, and Bluejacket.

When Gen. Andrew Lewis learned of the incident, he organized two divisions, one under his brother Col. Charles Lewis and the other under

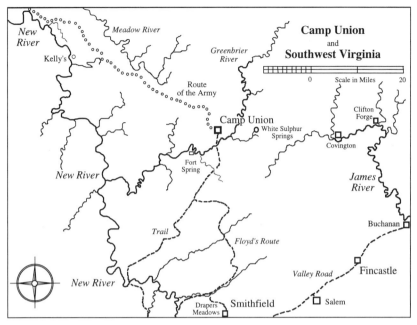

Camp Union and southwest Virginia.

Col. William Fleming, veterans of the French and Indian War. Each of the units consisted of about 150 troops. The small size of his initial deployment suggests that Lewis did not fully appreciate the size of the Indian army confronting him. Fully half of the Virginia troops, it was later said, never participated in the fight. Charles Lewis had fought as a company commander of Augusta troops in combat during Pontiac's Rebellion. His troops marched to the right some distance from the Ohio, Colonel Fleming's troops to the left along the Ohio. Lewis had proceeded no farther than a half-mile from camp when, about sunrise, an attack was made "in a most vigorous manner" his front by the "united tribes" of Indians, including Shawnee, Delaware, Mingo, and several others—the number estimated to be between 800 and 1,000. Along his entire line his troops were fired on. As others have pointed out, wounds decimated the officers, leaving the initiative in the hands of the Indians.

Charles Lewis, mortally wounded, and a number of his Augusta troops fell in the first fire, and many of the others gave ground under the heavy fire of the Indians. A minute or so later, Colonel Fleming's troops came under fire, and Fleming himself was wounded with two balls, one through

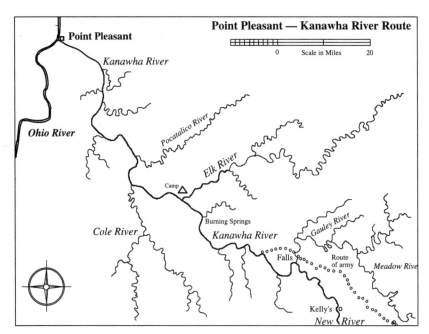

Point Pleasant—Kanawha River route.

his left arm and one in the chest. Casualties were particularly high among the officers. Reinforcements arrived at a critical moment, forcing the enemy to give up the ground it had gained. Though there were lulls, heavy firing continued until after one o'clock in the afternoon. Col. John Field, who led the reinforcements earlier in the day, found his troops isolated on the bank of the Ohio. He was shot fatally as they retreated to join the main body. In their own retreat, the Indians held advantageous positions and gave ground only reluctantly. The battle was fought along a line that extended for a mile and a quarter. Back in camp, Andrew Lewis with some difficulty organized a defense though many of the troops would take orders only from their own leaders, some of whom had been casualties. When sufficient order was restored in camp, Lewis was able to send another body of reinforcements to the front. Toward the end of the day, Lewis' troops pressed forward, forcing the Indians, who had fought bravely as a unified force, into an orderly retreat toward the Ohio.

Sporadic firing continued until nightfall when the Indians effected a safe withdrawal. To prevent the colonials from scalping their dead, many of the Indian dead were scalped by their comrades, but about twenty Indian scalps were taken by the troops. No accurate account of the Indian losses was determined, though one participant believed theirs "far exceeded ours, which is considerable." There were reports that the Indians shouted taunts at the Virginians that they would return the next the day with 2,000 warriors. Among the killed were Cols. Charles Lewis and John Field as well as fifty-one other officers and men. The wounded, including Colonel Fleming, numbered a total of eighty-seven men. These losses in dead and wounded represented about 15 percent of the total force.

After the battle, Cadet John Todd assumed responsibility of keeping the official orderly book of the army, formerly the job of Col. William Fleming. Cadet Todd, a member of Capt. Phillip Love's Botetourt volunteers, was born in Pennsylvania but was orphaned at an early age. He was then sent to Virginia to be educated at a classical school owned by his uncle, John Todd. Prior to volunteering for this campaign, he had practiced law in Fincastle County.

On the day of the battle Lord Dunmore and his force of 1,200 men were a considerable distance upriver at the mouth of the Hocking River. They marched westward toward the Indian villages, and a few days later the Shawnee made peace and agreed to let the Virginians settle south of the Ohio River.

Many of the men who had been to Kentucky during the summer were involved in the campaign, and one, Hugh Allen, was killed in the battle. Daniel Boone, who held the rank of captain, was prepared to march north with his company but was instead ordered to take charge of the defense of the Clinch River settlements. Col. William Christian's force contained several men who later became well known on the frontier. John Floyd raised a company, and most of James Harrod's men also volunteered to serve. Lt. Benjamin Logan raised a company and served under Capt. William Cooke. Because these companies arrived at Point Pleasant on the evening of the battle, they were not engaged in the actual fighting. However, Isaac Shelby, a future governor of Kentucky, together with his father, Evan, and brother James, participated in this hard-fought battle. Another veteran who would become well known and respected on the frontier was Capt. Matthews Arbuckle.

The leader of the Botetourt division, wounded at the battle, later to be involved in Kentucky affairs, was William Fleming. He was born February 18, 1729, of English ancestry in Jedborough, Scotland, graduating from medical school at the University of Edinburgh. Joining the British navy as a surgeon, he came to America after Braddock's defeat and served as a surgeon with the rank of ensign in George Washington's militia regiment. He then accompanied the Forbes campaign with the rank of lieutenant and later as captain in Col. Adam Stephens's regiment on frontier duty. In 1763 he married Anne Christian, settling on a farm in Augusta County until moving to land that became Montgomery County. At the battle of Point Pleasant he had the rank of colonel and led a regiment in the Botetourt militia. Later, he became one of the land commissioners and sat as a public account commissioner in Kentucky.

With the defeat of the Shawnee, the door to the vast expanse of land in Virginia's westernmost counties was not only officially open but regarded by many as safe. Because there were no Indians living in "the plains of Kentucky," many Virginians planned to take the opportunity to immigrate to the new, and, so they thought, peaceful paradise.

There are several myths and misconceptions about Kentucky's first generation of settlers that merit amendment and a few words of clarification. The thousand or so people who extended the Western frontier in 1775 and 1776 were not all Virginians, but those who entered the Kentucky country, however they thought of themselves, technically became Virginians by virtue of jurisdiction and geography. Daniel Boone, for example, was born in present Berks County, Pennsylvania, and later lived in Rowan County, North Carolina, but prior to moving to Kentucky he lived in Fincastle County, Virginia. James Harrod, another early settler on the Western frontier, was born in Great Cove, Pennsylvania, but prior to moving permanently to Kentucky served in the Virginia militia. Though a few came west from Maryland and South Carolina, the majority of the frontiersmen were, or thought they were, Virginians.

Some contend that the people who extended the Western frontier were crude, uneducated pioneers, who moved west without money or credit in order to plant crops on unclaimed land and raise their families. This view is not accurate since a large percentage of those who moved to the western Virginian counties were educated men who possessed basic skills in reading, writing, and arithmetic. Surviving journals and land records of the pioneers confirm this fact. Very few were required to sign their names with an "X." Abraham Chaplin, for example, was certainly a young man without wealth or property in 1774 when he joined James Harrod's adventurers to preempt Western land, but he could, however, read and write. He also knew the basic facts of the Virginia land laws then in effect and conformed to the laws and social customs of the community. Obviously tough, and by our standards very brave, he was required to work hard to obtain the basic necessities of life. Without fame or wealth, Chaplin typified the average frontiersman who immigrated to Kentucky. His journal is the only contemporary written account of the initial settlement of Harrodsburg. Serving as an officer under George Rogers Clark, he was captured by Indians, escaped, and became a prosperous farmer after the war.

A few of the new arrivals on the frontier were what must be described as members of well-to-do, influential families. Mostly they came west to preempt large tracts of lands with warrants issued by Virginia to officers who had fought in the French and Indian War. Men such as George Rogers Clark, John Floyd, William Christian, Levi Todd, John May, William Fleming, and Isaac Hite, though perhaps not in the same class as George Washington, Thomas Jefferson, Patrick Henry, and James Monroe, were reasonably well educated and entirely capable of handling the affairs of government.

The ethnic makeup of the Western frontier during the American Revolution has been the source of much misinformation and propaganda about those who crossed the mountains. Many historians have stated that "independence-loving, Scotch-Irish patriots" predominated on the frontier. One even said that Daniel Boone, whose ancestors emigrated from Devonshire, England, was Scotch-Irish. This idea seems to have been circulated by a few Scotch-Irish descendants, perhaps to compensate for the fact that so many Tories with Scotch or Irish names sided with the British during the war. In North Carolina, Scottish loyalist sentiments were so strong that a sizable army was formed to fight for the king. After a hard-fought battle American "rebels" finally defeated this army on February 26, 1776, at the battle of Moore's Creek Bridge. Neighboring South Carolina was so split by Scotch-Irish citizens who favored King George that troops were sent into the back country to arrest thousands of them. Many were kept in jail until they "confessed their errors [and] united in the American Cause."

Three of the most infamous turncoats in northern Virginia were Alexander McKee, John Connolly, and Simon Girty. When Connolly defected to the British, he proposed to lead two companies of the Royal Irish to capture Fort Pitt. Farther south on the Holston and Watauga, many of the leading patriots were men with common English or Welsh surnames— William Christian, Evan Shelby, James Robertson, William Cooke, Jacob Brown, William Bean, Robert Lucas, and John Carter. They were opposed by John Stuart and Alexander Cameron, both Scotchmen, who attempted to secure the alliance of the Cherokee for the British cause. These examples notwithstanding, there were many loyal Americans of Scotch-Irish descent.

The best study of the ethnic origins of Virginians in Kentucky County, formed in 1777, gives the percentage of Scotch-Irish and Scots at 14 percent and Irish at 5 percent, compared to 71 percent with English origins.

There were also a good many Anglo-Irish and even some Welsh-Irish on the frontier. Just as the Tudor kings encouraged fourteenth-century Presbyterian Scots to settle in Ulster, they also encouraged a similar course for Englishmen and Welshmen who worshiped in the Church of England. The English government even settled Germans in Ireland. In 1709, about 3,800 Protestant refugees from Palatine were induced to Munster and there awarded land.[19] Seventeenth-century Irish immigrants to America with names like Preston and Jackson could more accurately be described as Anglo-Irish. Those with names such as Todd were Welsh-Irish, and those with the name of Strickler were German-Irish. One clue to the ethnic background of Celtic names is the use of "Mac," "Mc," and "O." The former are almost exclusively Scotch while the latter is Irish. Whenever a so-called Scotch-Irishman has a name followed by "son," such as Johnson or Robertson, then the name is either Anglo-Irish or has been anglicized.

Those ill-informed historians who affirm that most people on the frontier were Scotch-Irish Presbyterians obviously discount the fact that in 1774 only one Presbyterian church existed in Virginia. Virginia law prior to the Revolution did not recognize any religions other than the Episcopal church. Thomas Gist, one of the early frontier magistrates, stated that he conducted marriages "according to the rights and ceremonies of the Church of England." As late as 1774, a number of citizens calling themselves "Descenders [sic] bearing the Denomination of Baptist" petitioned the Fauquier court to be allowed to "meet together for the worship of God in our way."[20] The court gave them no answer. Even worse, in Caroline County, two men were brought before the court for teaching and preaching the Gospel, without having Episcopal ordination or a license from the general court:

> Ordered, that they remanded back to gaol of this county and there remain till they give security, each in the sum of twenty pounds and two securities each in the sum of two pounds, for their good behavior twelve months and a day.[21]

Obviously, all Virginians, including those with Scotch names such as McAfee and Campbell, who may have come from a Presbyterian background, were required to pay tithes to the state church.

These same ethnic studies almost without exception excluded the black slaves. In 1777, there were eighty-five men and twenty-four women in the fort at Harrodsburg. Twelve of them were slaves, a population of about 10 percent Negroes. By the time the first tax rolls of Fayette County, Virginia, were made in 1788, the total "Negroes over 12" was 224 in proportion to 1,424 white "Tithables," or about 14 percent. Of the Fayette County families, about 16 percent had slaves. Only five of these families owned more than ten slaves, the maximum number being sixteen. The majority of these slave owners had only one or two blacks living with them.

When William Fleming went through St. Asaphs in 1780, he reported that the station contained 119 people, 25 men, 74 women and children, and 20 blacks, which means that about 17 percent were black.

Early journals, letters, depositions, and various other legal documents also confirm that some of those migrating to Kentucky also brought "white slaves" known as indentured servants. These people sold themselves into bondage for specified periods of time, usually three to seven years, sometimes exchanging their service for passage from England to America. The small population of Virginia made it difficult for these white people to escape their obligations by taking flight. Several indentured people who were brought west to make improvements for their owners applied for land in Kentucky in 1779–80 but were refused on grounds that they were acting as servants for others. Records indicate that, on average, 500 indentured servants were sold each year between 1622 and 1732, an average that probably held to 1775. More indentured servants than slaves were brought to Virginia.

Of those indentured servants and slaves compelled to take up life on the frontier, a few, not finding the dangers to their liking, ran away from their masters with the intention of returning to the older, established settlements in the East. The majority soon decided that the hazards of traveling alone in the woods far outweighed any unpleasant feelings they had about living in Kentucky. The few who did not return voluntarily were usually recaptured within a month or two because the descriptions of these runaways were usually printed in the local newspapers.

Regardless of their feelings and personal inclinations, most black slaves and indentured servants fought side by side with their owners to defend their homes. In many instances, Indians killed slaves who fought with their masters, including one who was captured and tomahawked during Daniel Boone's first attempt to move west in 1773. Another black man, named Sam, was shot when Indians attacked Boone's camp in the spring of 1775 while he was blazing a trail to the Kentucky River for the Transylvania Company. Other blacks accompanied Boone on that trip, including the cook, who was probably the first non-Indian female to settle in what is now Kentucky.

Although there are records of several blacks allying themselves and fighting with the Indians, the majority remained loyal to their masters and regarded Indians as their enemies. When captured, they normally became the slaves of their captors, who generally treated them more harshly than did their white masters. Indians frequently tomahawked captive slaves when their new masters felt they were shirking their duties.

By the time of the Revolutionary War, slavery had been practiced in Virginia for 150 years. Many regarded the peculiar institution as quite normal since it had existed during all of recorded history. In England, the practice had ended during the reign of William I, but prohibition of slavery in the mother country did not extend to the colonies. Colonists first attempted to use captured American Indians as slaves, but the experiment failed because the Indians persisted in running away.

During the Revolutionary War blacks usually assisted their masters in farming, and the records also indicate that many fought alongside them, in some cases protecting the master's wife and family after the master had been killed. Very few blacks left home in 1775 to join Governor Dunmore's Ethiopian Regiment, even though he promised them their freedom if they served in his army. Regardless of their situations on the plantations, most decided that risking their lives for the king was not preferable to farming for their old masters. Since the slaves left almost no written records, their opinions and emotions can be fathomed only through imaginations too easily colored by the preconceptions of the imaginers.

Historian Lewis Collins relates one of the most interesting stories of slaves fighting against the Indians. Maj. George Stockton owned a slave named Ben, who volunteered to chase a war party that had taken horses in the neighborhood. When the pursuers finally overtook the Indians, they found themselves outnumbered by the pursued. Though the leader gave an order to retreat, Ben instead rushed the Indians' line and shot the first Indian he encountered. This prompted the Indians themselves to retreat. As Ben afterward described their exodus, Indians "skipped from tree to tree thick as grass-hoppers." As they fled, Ben yelled to them, "Take that to remember Ben—the black, white man!"

By and large, white people on the frontier hated all Indians, generally regarding them as cruel and dirty savages beyond help or redemption.

They reasoned that the sooner the Indians were killed or driven away the sooner that peace would ensue. Many frontier families had experienced the loss of loved ones from Indian raids during the French and Indian War, Pontiac's War, or Dunmore's War. A person in western Virginia who was twenty years old when the Revolution began had never known a time when all the neighboring tribes had been at peace.

To make matters worse, Indians who killed a person almost always removed his scalp, sometimes lifting it before the man was dead. They often cut their victims to pieces, sometimes removing embryos from pregnant women and displaying them on poles. Similarly, to shock those who might attempt to pursue them, they often chopped off human heads and exhibited them as warning signs. To amuse themselves, warriors often tortured the wounded for hours before killing them. Though they usually killed the weak, the sick, and the old, they often adopted many of the captives who were young. Native American culture was so different from white culture that only a few individuals, such as Daniel Boone, ever tried to coexist with them as equals.

Although the Revolutionary War in the East involved the thirteen original states and the British government, practically all of the fighting in the West was between white Americans and the Indian tribes led and supplied by the British. The Virginia frontier was molested mainly by the Northern tribes, whose warriors were supplied and directed from Detroit or Niagara. These tribes included the Shawnee, Wyandot, Mingo, Miami, and Delaware. Frequently, members of the closest Southern tribe, the Cherokee, would invade Virginia counties, especially Washington, Montgomery, and Kentucky. Thus the war was conducted on two fronts, one adjacent to the Southern mountain area, the other against an enemy invading from across the Ohio River.

In dealing with tramontane politics, the national attitude of the former colonies varied greatly. Virginians had always considered their boundary to lie somewhere west of the Appalachian Mountains. For this reason its leaders generally supported the Western movement. When early settlers needed gunpowder for defense, Virginia supplied it. When they needed additional manpower, Virginia ordered militia to the frontier. By 1779 a permanent or "regular" Virginia army was recruited for use in George Rogers Clark's campaign in Illinois.

Virginia's neighbor to the north, Pennsylvania, also fighting a frontier war, on occasion cooperated in campaigns against the Indians. Because the original charter of the Keystone State limited its Western boundary, Pennsylvania's leaders were less inclined to support conquests across the Ohio. Maryland, having no land interests in the West, opposed migration along the frontier beyond the Appalachian Mountains. Marylanders were envious of Virginia's charter, which allowed Virginians to claim all the Western land above latitude 36 degrees 30 minutes as far as the Mississippi River. Congressmen representing Maryland would gladly have exchanged all the Western settlers and their land for the independence of the seaboard colonies. Many other leaders in the Northern states shared these sentiments.

In the South, matters were different. Like Virginia, Georgia and the Carolinas had charters that extended their boundaries westward indefinitely. They eyed this Western land with proprietary design, eventually planning to settle it. They early recognized the value of this land to the west and regarded it as land that could be sold after the war. As settlers flocked to Kentucky country, Virginia began selling its western lands, much of it before the war eventually ended.

Congress debated the rights of the states claiming Western land, drawing a line between those colonies that had the king's charter to Western lands and those that did not. But claiming Western land and fighting for it were different propositions. In retrospect, as this book will show, it was mostly Virginians who crossed over the mountains and fought to secure the "pleasant levels" of Kentucky.

CHAPTER 1

1775

The Fourteenth Colony

THE YEAR 1775 IS MOST OFTEN REMEMBERED AS THE START OF THE AMER-
ican Revolution. Even before the year began, some colonists in New England were actively in revolt against the Crown. Late in 1774, the Provincial
Congress, sitting in Concord, appropriated £15,625 to purchase guns and
ammunition for use by the minutemen in a vain attempt to counterbal-
ance the military power of the opposing British forces. Gen. Thomas
Gage, in charge of the king's army, was virtually besieged in Boston, and
commerce at this important colonial port was at a standstill. Colonial delegates had sent King George III a Declaration of Rights stating their griev-
ances, but this petition availed nothing. Neither the king nor the
Parliament paid the slightest heed to their complaining subjects. Because
differences between the Americans and the home government were irrec-
oncilable, armed conflict seemed inevitable.

Since 1753, a period of twenty-two years, advances on the Western
frontier had been restricted by the policy of the royal government. Settlers
were forbidden by the superintendents of Indian affairs to move onto land
that had not been cleared of Indian title. In Kentucky, the limits of the Indian treaty line were somewhat vague, but the majority of informed people
believed that only the land east of the Kentucky River was open for settlement. To complicate matters, John Murray Dunmore, governor of Virginia, had approved two land grants for his friends John Connolly and
Charles Warrenstaff. Located at the Falls of the Ohio, these tracts were sixty
miles beyond this boundary. Floyd and company, legal deputy surveyors of

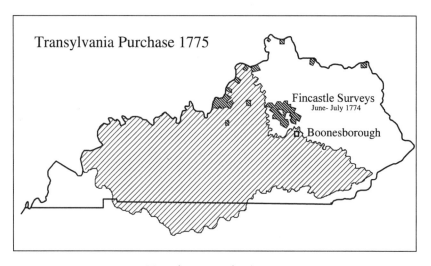

Transylvania purchase, 1775.

Fincastle County, likewise had surveyed thousands of acres beyond the Kentucky River. James Harrod's abandoned camp had also been established west of the Kentucky River, but none of these encroachments had been approved by the secretary of state for the colonies. Neither the British Parliament nor the Crown had confirmed the right for Virginia to expand westward beyond the Kanawha River.

Neither Lord Dunmore, the royal governor of Virginia, nor James Harrod, an uneducated frontiersman, paid the slightest attention to the royal restrictions. The spring of 1775 brought another development that was completely without any government authority or precedent. A group of private individuals, organized as the Transylvania Company, purchased a large section of Kentucky from the Cherokee nation. Under the leadership of Col. Richard Henderson, a former judge from North Carolina, these men acquired all the land south of the Ohio between the Kentucky and Cumberland Rivers for the sum of 2,000 pounds sterling.[1]

Henderson met with the Cherokee at Sycamore Shoals on the Watauga River in what is now east Tennessee. William Farrar, an employee of Henderson, drove cattle to the treaty, which were fed to the Indians along with great quantities of corn, flour, and rum. Sam Wilson, who witnessed the exchange, said that the Indians were sober, but that "Dragging Canoe told them it was the bloody Ground, and would be dark, and difficult to settle."[2]

James Robinson, another witness, kept a day-by-day account, estimating that there were 1,200 Indians at the treaty and that the chiefs told Henderson that they owned that land (Kentucky) and offered to sell Henderson the part located north of the Kentucky River. Henderson, believing that the Cherokee had already sold this territory to Virginia, refused this offer. At this, "Dragging Canoe got angry and withdrew himself from the Conference. And the other Indians immediately followed him and broke up the Conference for the day." Infuriated, he declared that there were bad people among both his nation and the whites, and that there was a dark cloud over Kentucky. He went on to say that his countrymen would not hurt the new settlers, but he was afraid that the northern Indians would.[3] On the third day the Indians complained that their payment was too small. Finally, on the fourth day, even Dragging Canoe agreed to give up Kentucky, along with an additional strip of land needed for a trail from the Holston River to Kentucky. The parties then reconvened and agreed to the purchase. In exchange for this vast territory, Henderson distributed trade goods valued at £2,000 to all the Indians present. Afterwards Henderson gave additional goods to the Indians, "to the value of Two thousand weight of Leather" for a path to their Kentucky purchase.[4] Most seemed satisfied by the exchange.

Henderson later described his purchase as being "on the back of Virginia." In retrospect one may question the rights of the Cherokee to this tract because it had served as a common hunting ground for six or seven different tribes. Nevertheless, Henderson considered a deed from the Cherokee sufficient to set his plan in motion, a plan to establish a fourteenth colony. Even before negotiations were concluded, Daniel Boone left with a detachment to blaze a trail to the new capital of Transylvania.

Boone and his companions assembled at the Long Island on the Holston River (now Kingsport, Tennessee) and set out for Kentucky on March 10, 1775.[5] These self-styled adventurers included Daniel's brother Squire and Michael Stoner, the scout who had accompanied him to Kentucky in 1774. Others in the party were Richard Callaway, James Bridges, William Bush, James Coburn, John Hart, William Hicks, Thomas Johnson, Capt. Thomas Twitty, Felix Walker, and several Negroes. The men followed the ancient Indian trail that led through Moccasin Gap, then over Wallen's Ridge and Powell Mountain. Two years before, Boone had traveled this same trail in an attempt to settle in Kentucky, but the party had been driven back after the Shawnee killed several of the group, including his son James and Henry Russell, the son of William Russell.

For the first part of the trip Boone and his companions had no need to cut a new road because one had existed along this route since ancient times. This was the famous Athiamiowee, or Warrior's Path, the only practical route over the Cumberland Mountain and through the water gap of Pine Mountain. By 1775 the path was well known, having been discovered by Dr. Thomas Walker in 1750 and used extensively by hunters since 1760. Squire Boone had been over the trail at least four times and Daniel three. Harrod's men had used it for their Kentucky exodus in 1774, as had the survivors of Hancock Taylor's surveying party.[6] Earlier in the spring of 1775 the McAfee brothers had traveled to Kentucky by this route. Although Daniel Boone is traditionally credited with blazing the way through the wilderness, many others had previously used a similar, if not identical route.

In the spring two brothers, Joseph and Bryce Martin, had moved west down this same road to settle a station that they had begun several years before. In a rolling valley on the south side of Cumberland Mountain near a place called White Rocks, they had erected some cabins.[7] Their settlement was only fifteen miles east of Cumberland Gap. As far as Martin's Station, the road was passable for wagons, but farther west only packhorses could be used. Although Boone and his men may have been surprised to find Martin's Station occupied, they certainly knew that other white men had preceded them to Kentucky.

The narrative of Felix Walker indicates that many of Boone's road cutters were well-to-do citizens out sight-seeing. They traveled with slaves and even brought a Negro woman to cook their meals. To them it was a gay adventure with a promise of profit. The rich Kentucky land was there to be claimed, and a gentleman had the same rights to it as an ignorant backwoodsman. Whether elected or appointed, Daniel Boone led the group, having been promised payment in land by Colonel Henderson for his services. Michael Stoner was paid as a hunter but was required to furnish his own supplies and gunpowder.

The trailblazers followed the ancient Indian path over the Cumberland Gap and reached Cumberland River at the point where it flowed through a water gap in Pine Mountain. This gap in Pine Mountain was a geological oddity that provided the easiest way to traverse the twin mountain range. Here the pathway crossed the icy river, and the men were forced to follow it. For nine miles they traveled in a northerly direction along the banks of the river. Where it turned westward, the men turned north with the old trail and soon reached Flat Licks. This was a place used so frequently by

Daniel Boone and companions looking at new land.

the Long Hunters that a nearby stream had acquired the name Stinking Creek from the stench of animal entrails strewn along its banks.

At this point Boone departed from the Warrior's Path and followed a parallel hunters' trail that led to the waters of the Rockcastle River. He then traveled up the Far Fork directly toward the heart of the Bluegrass country.[8] Only the latter part of the trace was exclusive to Daniel Boone; the Indians had used the southern part for centuries. Though the route he selected was suitable, considering the terrain, it was not extensively used until the coming of the railroads and modern highways.

Two weeks after leaving Long Island on the Holston, Boone's men reached the cane land where they discovered "the pleasing and rapturous appearance of the plains of Kentucky."[9] Their journey was nearly over, and several members of the company visited a small salt lick, intending to kill

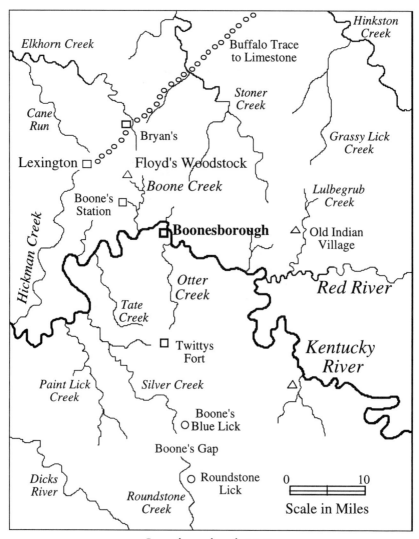

Boonesborough and vicinity.

some buffalo. Much to their disappointment, they found the lick devoid of game, a sign, according to Boone, that Indians might be nearby. Not long afterward, his intuition was confirmed.[10]

On March 24 Daniel Boone and his companions camped on Taylor's Fork of Silver Creek, not far from the grave of Hancock Taylor. Located on the headwaters of the creek near a spring, it was a pleasant setting, well situated for the next day's journey to the Kentucky River, only twelve miles away. Their journey was nearly over. The gentlemen pitched their tents, and campfires were built to cook the food and to warm their weary bones. The horses, hobbled and belled, had been put out to feed on the lush spring grasses. A feeling of optimism prevailed, so no guards were posted. In a country recently bought from the Cherokee and off limits to the Shawnee, they felt that no guards were necessary.

The attack came just before sunrise. Muskets were fired from the darkness beyond the camp, and several balls penetrated the tent where Capt. Thomas Twitty, Felix Walker, and Negro Sam were sleeping. Sam immediately rushed outside, received a mortal wound, and fell into the smoldering campfire. Walker, though badly wounded, managed to escape with some of the others into the woods. Half asleep, Squire Boone, mistakenly grabbed his jacket instead of his powder horn as he made his hasty retreat into the woods. Capt. Daniel Boone silently began to collect the men around him, and together they cautiously returned to camp. They found that the Indians had departed and that Captain Twitty had been shot through both knees. Unable to walk, he told them that when the Indians had come into the tent to scalp him, his bulldog had driven them off. In leaving, one of the warriors struck it with his tomahawk, killing it instantly.

When the sun came up, the company appraised their predicament. One man had been killed and three wounded. Several more had fled into the woods and were still missing. Some of the horses could not be found, but fortunately the Indians had not taken any valuable supplies, particularly the powder and lead. There was the possibility that the Indians would return, but Boone's companions could neither continue nor retreat without abandoning the wounded. As a practical alternative, they remained at camp and built a temporary fort for protection. They quickly cut down some trees and constructed a couple of cabins situated so that the men in one could cover an attack on the other; the cabins also sheltered the wounded men. Between the cabins they constructed a little pen where they could keep their horses at night. Two or three days later, Capt. Thomas Twitty died and was buried next to Sam and his faithful dog. On a nearby tree the survivors carved TT to serve as his grave marker. Originally called the Little Fort, this place became known subsequently as Twitty's Fort.

Soon after the attack on Boone's camp, one of the company found the son of Samuel Tate wandering about in the woods. The frightened lad explained that the day before, on March 27, Indians had also attacked his party. Daniel and Squire Boone traveled about seven miles west of the Little

Fort to investigate. They found the scalped bodies of two men, Thomas McDowell and Jeremiah McPeters. Samuel Tate and his brother had escaped by running down the icy stream that still bears their name.

Realizing that their situation was critical, Boone dispatched a scout to warn the men at Harrodsburg of the possibility of an attack. He also recommended that they join him for mutual protection. On the first of April, Boone managed to send a message to Colonel Henderson, then in route to Kentucky, requesting that the Transylvania settlers hasten to the Kentucky River. "My advise [*sic*] to you, sir, is to come or send [aid] as soon as possible. Your company is desired greatly, for the people are very uneasy, but are willing to stay and venture their lives with you, and now is the time to frustrate their [the Indians'] intentions and keep the country, whilst we are in it. If we give way to them now, it will ever be the case."[11]

Boone added that he was starting for Otter Creek where he intended to erect a fort. Carrying the wounded Walker in a sling between two horses, the company followed a buffalo path northward to the Kentucky River.

Meanwhile, Henderson and the other prospective settlers had reached Martin's Station where loads were transferred from wagons to packhorses. Waiting for stragglers until April 7, they set out for Cumberland Gap in a snowstorm. They had not gone far when John Luttrell, who was at the head of the column, received word of the attack on Boone's camp. Soon after, Boone's letter arrived, and by evening everyone had heard the bad news. Nathaniel Hart, one of the stockholders in the Transylvania Company, decided that it would be best if he turned back and situated himself in Powell Valley to "make corn for the Cantuckey people."[12]

Despite their fears, Richard Henderson and about fifty others continued toward Kentucky. The next day they made the difficult climb over Cumberland Gap. Along each mile of the wet, slippery trail they encountered small groups of men traveling in the opposite direction, returning from Kentucky "on account of the late Murders by the Indians." The story quickly became exaggerated, and additional attacks were said to have occurred on the Ohio River. Henderson attempted to persuade those returning to turn around and join his company, but his efforts were fruitless. Instead, some of his own company joined the retreat. Those remaining plodded to the Cumberland River ford, reaching it on April 9. Here Nathaniel Hart and his men, who had finally summoned enough courage to proceed, overtook them.

The following day Henderson dispatched Capt. William Cooke to ride ahead to tell Boone that the settlers were on their way. Originally, two men had promised to accompany Cooke on this mission, but at the last minute they both found reasons not to go. After being supplied with a Dutch oven, a blanket, and the promise of 2,000 acres of choice Kentucky land, Cooke said he would make the trip alone. At the same time, William Calk and two others climbed to the top of the nearby Pine Mountain and discovered that Indians had been hiding there, spying on their camp.

The next morning Henderson and his followers resumed their journey, but their progress was hampered by rainy weather and flooded creeks. Despite delays, food was no problem because they slaughtered some of the cattle they were driving along the trail. On April 12 they met another company returning home, this one led by Thomas Madison. Two of Calk's companions, Phillip Drake and Abraham Hanks, turned around and went back with Madison's party. On the sixteenth Henderson met seventeen more men retreating from the Bluegrass, but several, including Samuel and Robert McAfee, were persuaded to join Henderson and the Transylvania group on their trip to the Kentucky River. James McAfee said good-bye to his brothers and joined those who were headed for home.

For ten days Henderson traversed the "Wilderness" on Boone's newly blazed path. By the eighteenth his party reached the canebrakes in what is now Madison County. Here they met Michael Stoner and three others sent by Boone to guide the party to the Kentucky River about twenty miles away.

While Boone and his followers were awaiting Henderson, he and his men occupied their time constructing a small fort on the banks of the Kentucky River about a mile below Otter Creek.[13] Boone later said that a man had died at Boonesborough prior to the arrival of Henderson, but no account of this tragedy has survived. Boone's fort consisted of six or seven cabins connected by walls on two sides, and the steep slope of the riverbank on the third. This little stockade was within three days of being completed when Henderson arrived on April 20, but no further work was ever done on it. It is likely that construction of the fort ceased when Col. Thomas Slaughter and his company unexpectedly arrived at Boonesborough. Greater numbers gave the men a greater sense of security.

The Slaughter company, consisting of about fifty men, had set out from the upper Ohio and had come down the river as far as the Big Sandy. There they unloaded their boats. Guided by John Harmon, they traveled by horseback overland, unexpectedly reaching the Kentucky River only a few miles from Boonesborough.[14] Slaughter's company reported that they were headed for Harrodsburg, none of them having heard of the Transylvania purchase of Kentucky land. These men stayed at Boonesborough for several days, but when the threat of further Indian attacks diminished they proceeded on their way. The arrival of this large body of reinforcements likely convinced the small party of Indians that they could no longer harass the intruders who had invaded their hunting ground. Later reports indicated that the Indians who had killed the white men were Pics.[15]

Reaching Boonesborough, Col. Richard Henderson discovered that Boone's men had already explored the countryside, and many had selected homesites along the nearby creeks and bluffs where they were busily erecting cabins. Unfortunately, this was not the way the colonel had planned to begin his new colony. To get his plan under way, he immediately began laying out streets and lots for a new town. By April 23 this task was completed, and he assembled all the men. They drew town lots at random, after which they traded sites with each other until everyone was satisfied. But many men, including Nathaniel Hart, even after receiving a town lot, decided that they preferred their outlying cabins beyond the new town limits.

Henderson discovered another problem that needed immediate attention. If they were attacked, Boone's little fort was too small to protect all the settlers. He sought advice from his partners Luttrell and Hart but soon learned that they were not interested in any new fortifications. Henderson then realized that he must continue on his own, so he laid out the plan of a fort on the town commons and began the construction of the magazine. The new location was about 50 yards west of the Kentucky River and about 300 yards southeast of Boone's original fort. A small branch or creek separated the two structures. On the bank of the little creek, not far from the river, the men found both freshwater and sulfur springs. Fortunately, there was no great urgency to finish the first fort or to work on the second. Henderson was also able to acquire the town lot opposite the proposed fort, a lot on which there was a giant elm tree. The tree later served as a meeting place for all town activities and was famous years later for its longevity and its associations with the site.

About the same time that Henderson was surveying lots at Boonesborough, the Fincastle surveyor John Floyd crossed the mountains at Cumberland Gap on his way to Kentucky. Earlier in the spring Floyd had traveled to Williamsburg and personally delivered a letter from Col. William Preston to Governor Dunmore, who had instructed the surveyor to lay out tracts in Kentucky for sale to Virginians. Preston told the governor that he would "cheerfully wait for my Fees until money can be raised out of the Sales."[16] Floyd and the other Fincastle deputies, James Douglas and Isaac

Portrait of John Floyd.
<small>THE FILSON HISTORICAL SOCIETY,
LOUISVILLE, KENTUCKY</small>

Hite, were probably instructed to make such surveys as well as to continue their job of marking off tracts for French and Indian War veterans.

In Powell's Valley, John Floyd collected several other groups under the commands of Maj. David Robinson, Joseph Drake, and Thomas Madison. These men had started for Kentucky before Henderson, and some had almost reached the Bluegrass. When they heard of the murders, they had turned back. Now, encouraged by the presence of the twenty-five-year-old surveyor, they were ready to resume their journey. Members of this combined party included John Todd, James and William Robinson, William and Samuel Meridith Jr., Patrick Jordan, Thomas Carland, David McGee, John Dickerson, Thomas Carpenter, Jacob Boofman, Matthew Jouett, William Oldham, James Knox, and Benjamin Logan. John May, a good friend of John Todd, decided against going to Kentucky and returned home, but he sent his slave along with Todd to make improvements for him.[17] Another member of the party was Alexander Spotswood Dandridge, the grandson and heir of Alexander Spotswood, a former governor of Virginia and also the nephew of Martha Washington. Floyd made military surveys for both Bartholomew and Alexander Dandridge the year before.

The men under John Floyd followed in Boone's footsteps until they reached Hazel Patch near the Rockcastle River. There they detoured westward on an old hunter's path called Scagg's Trace. James Knox was a Long Hunter who knew Kentucky geography and had probably piloted Harrod's company over this same path on their retreat the year before. Floyd's company soon reached the headwaters of Dicks River and passed the Crab Orchard. On May 1, about twenty-five miles south of Harrodsburg, they reached a large spring where they decided to stop and make a permanent camp. They called it St. Asaph in honor of a canonized Welsh monk. Within a day John Floyd and Joseph Drake left their companions and headed to Boonesborough to confer with Henderson. James Knox shortly departed for the Falls of the Ohio in order to make improvements on his 1774 preemption claim. Several other men accompanied Knox as far as Harrodsburg.

Kentucky was rapidly being overrun with settlers, mostly Virginians, who intended to stake claims on any vacant tract that they found to their liking. Some made a point of visiting Boonesborough to discuss terms for taking up Transylvania land south of the Kentucky River, but others seemed satisfied to travel around the countryside in small bands, building cabins in isolated locations. Henderson, always mindful of his proprietary interests, fully understood that this situation could quickly get out of hand, but he lacked the means to prevent unauthorized men from settling on the land he had purchased from the Cherokee. He sent word to the other settlements for newcomers to "settle somewhere in a compact body for mutual Defense," but very few paid any attention.

On the south and west sides of the Kentucky River at St. Asaph, there were originally about thirty men, and perhaps fifty others had reached Harrodsburg with James Harrod. Another fifty were with Colonel Slaughter. By June neither place had any significant number of permanent residents, both being in the order of camps rather than towns. That summer Boonesborough was the only place with over a dozen occupied cabins. Interestingly, James Harrod did not live at Harrodsburg but at another station he built called Boiling Springs.

Colonel Henderson was particularly apprehensive when John Floyd arrived in Kentucky because Floyd was employed as a deputy surveyor under Col. William Preston, a very influential person in Fincastle County. Preston had not only vigorously objected to the Transylvania purchase, but he had done everything (from Henderson's viewpoint) in his power to stop the project, including misrepresenting the Transylvania position to the governors of

Virginia and North Carolina. Floyd by his "honest, open countenance" nearly convinced Henderson that he had nothing to fear from his presence in the area. After all, Floyd could make official surveys north of the Kentucky River without interfering with the Transylvania claim.

For his part, John Floyd was prepared to work on both sides of the river. He thought that he could still earn money north of the river by running surveys for men with government warrants and perhaps also obtain a position as surveyor in Transylvania. Floyd's philosophy of joining and working with diverse political factions was afterwards adopted by others, a practice embodied in what later became the state motto, "United we stand, divided we fall."

The gentlemen in Floyd's company, as well as others who had visited Boonesborough, appear to have been impressed with Henderson's deed from the Cherokee and offered to deal with Henderson on his terms. Col. William Christian, one of the most prominent citizens in Virginia, told Floyd that it was Patrick Henry's opinion that the Transylvania purchase "would stand good" and advised Floyd to deal with him. Christian held the same opinion. Initially, the company's terms seemed fair to all; anyone could purchase land on credit. The cost of land was only one-fifth of a shilling per acre (or £1 per 100 acres). The deed for the land would be awarded when the buyer furnished a promissory note or his bond.

Like Floyd, Col. Thomas Slaughter, in hope of profit, decided to work closely with the Transylvania company. Although it was not widely known, Richard Henderson offered Colonel Slaughter 100,000 acres if he could settle a certain number of families on company land within a limited time, probably one year. This contract was made in writing, and soon after, Slaughter led a party down the Cumberland River to explore and select a site for this venture.

There can be little doubt that Henderson and his partners were greatly concerned about the settlers who had come to Kentucky on the "invitation" of Captain Harrod. Henderson wrote that

> these Men got possession [of our land] some time before we got there, and I could not certainly learn on what terms or pretense they meant to hold land, and was doubtful that so large a body of Lawless people from habit & Education would give us great trouble & require the utmost exertion of our abilities to manage them and not without considerable anxiety and some fear. [Another concern was that Harrod's men] had not contented themselves

with the choice of one tract of land apiece, but had made it their entire business to ride through the Country marking every piece of land they thought proper, built cabins, or rather pig pens to make their claims notorious . . . without actually putting more than a total of three acres under cultivation.[18]

To resolve these problems, Richard Henderson decided to call a convention of the Kentucky settlers in hope that a republican form of government would end the "lawless conditions" that then existed. John Floyd supported the idea. By coincidence, James Harrod and George Slaughter arrived at Boonesborough on May 7 and agreed to the plan. Each of the four settlements south of the Kentucky River selected four delegates to meet in Boonesborough on May 23. They purposed to establish laws for the new colony of Transylvania. Deputy surveyor John Floyd, John Todd, Alexander Spotswood Dandridge, and Samuel Wood represented St. Asaph. Harrodsburg sent Thomas Slaughter, John Lithe, Valentine Harmon, and James Douglas, another Fincastle deputy surveyor. Boiling Springs furnished James Harrod, Nathan Hammond, Azariah Davis, and Isaac Hite, a third Fincastle deputy surveyor. Because Boonesborough was the largest of the settlements, it was allowed six delegates: Daniel Boone, Squire Boone, William Cooke, Samuel Henderson, William Moore, and Richard Callaway. The conference, which lasted six days, ended in harmony. The delegates recognized the Transylvania Company as "Sovereigns of the Country as well as Lords of the Soil" and agreed to enter all land claims with the proprietors.[19] His anxieties at least temporarily relieved, Henderson was well pleased. Henderson had established Transylvania, the fourteenth colony.

Unfortunately for Henderson, the golden age of the new colony was short lived. Dozens, then hundreds of adventurers continued to arrive in Kentucky. At the same time, many who had arrived only a few weeks earlier began to return home. The main attraction was land, and many, having spent a month or so traveling to Kentucky and blazing a few trees, cutting down some brush, or starting the construction of a cabin, were satisfied that they had a bona fide claim in the new country. Those claiming land in Transylvania needed only to select a site and register their claim in the company's land book. After the claim was made, there was little reason to remain, except perhaps to explore the country to find land better than that of the first claim. Some of the man who arrived at Boonesborough during May 1775 included parties led by Capt. Marquis Calmes, Benjamin Berry, Lawrence Thompson, Samuel Coombs, and John Bowman.

The latter was accompanied by Joseph and Abraham Bowman, his brothers, and James Francis Moore, the cousin of James Harrod.

John Bowman was soon to become the ranking militia officer in Kentucky, and one of Virginia's most active land speculators. He was the son of George Bowman of Frederick County, Virginia, and his mother was the daughter of Joist Hite, the grandfather of Isaac Hite. In the spring of 1775, after leaving Boonesborough, John Bowman selected a site on Harrods Run where he blazed some trees and planted a crop to establish a land claim. Joseph Bowman, later to serve in Illinois under Clark, built a cabin at a nearby spring. Abraham Bowman traveled even farther to make a claim. Possibly encouraged by his cousin, Isaac Hite, he planted corn sixty-five miles west of John and Joseph, on Goose Creek near Hite's preemption, and thereby established his own claim for land.

Although the zeal in Transylvania slackened after the Boonesborough convention, activities on the other side of the river were just beginning. Assisted by the Fincastle County surveyor James Douglas, Nathaniel Gist and his brothers surveyed land on the headwaters of Stoner's Creek and began making improvements. On June 6 Floyd made military surveys on Boone's Creek for Benjamin Logan, Thomas Madison, David Robinson, and other members of his company. Although Floyd had made a military survey for him in 1774, John Howard began to make improvements on another tract of land that he liked better. This tract was situated on a stream later called Howard's Creek. That summer he hired several men to clear the land and start constructing farm buildings. During the summer James Douglas joined Isaac Hite and others then at Harrodsburg to explore the various branches of the Licking River. This company included David Williams, Isaac White, Evangelist Hardin, Edward Williams, John Shep, Roger Patton, and Patrick Jordan. The latter claimed to have been the chainman for James Douglas during the summer. On this trip some of the best land was preempted through claimants who invested the time to make the required improvements.

John Floyd, assisted by his chainmen Jacob Boofman, William Gillispie, Robert Boggs, and Jonathan Martin, surveyed a number of tracts in the vicinity of Lexington, basing the claims on military warrants. Floyd made a preemption survey for himself on the headwaters of Boone's Creek, where he built a cabin and raised some corn. This tract he called Woodstock. Nearby, his friend John Todd began another "plantation" called Mansfield, and northwest of Mansfield, Todd selected a tract for John May; on both sites he and the slave owed by May cleared some land and

Kentucky River cliffs.

planted corn. Northeast of Boonesborough, Floyd's chainman, Jacob Boofman, discovered a spring that he claimed for himself. As it turned out, it
was located on a tract that Daniel Boone had selected for James Hickman.
Boone requested that Floyd run the survey for Hickman, but when Floyd
discovered the conflict, he informed Boone that he wanted Boofman to
have the land and would survey Hickman another tract "on land as good as
that."[20]

During the summer many leaders in Virginia were aware that their
new government had no firm policy regarding distribution of public land.
It was well known that many veterans of the French and Indian War were
having surveys made based on their military warrants and that many private citizens were preempting Western land on the basis of "settlement"
claims. Many believed that starting a cabin, clearing land, or planting a
crop would be ample evidence of their intentions to move onto the property. For this reason the Virginia Assembly formed a committee to look
into the matter. They decided that Dunmore's plan to divide and survey
unoccupied land for public sale should be abandoned but made no provisions to issue grants or dismiss the claims of those who already had legal
surveys.[21] A legal survey could only be made by the deputy county surveyor. Thus the land question was left in legal limbo.

Many of the newcomers to Kentucky, especially those who resided on
the headwaters of the Potomac River or on the Monongahela, reached their
destination either by passing through Pittsburgh or by using a shorter overland route to Wheeling or Grave Creek, then going down the Ohio River.
Some settlers did not even bother to go to Kentucky at all but decided to
take up land closer to their old homes. They settled in the area now encompassed by West Virginia and western Pennsylvania. People seeking to
preempt land soon populated the areas around Wheeling, Pittsburgh, and
old Fort Redstone. Some who planned to migrate to Kentucky decided to
make the trip in two stages. During the first year they planted crops on the
upper Ohio, the second year in Kentucky. Thus, by 1776, most of those
who desired to preempt Kentucky land had come all the way.

John Smith, James Harrod's companion in 1773, returned to Kentucky
with Charles Lecompt, William Steward, William McConnell, and the
Corn brothers, Deal, Solomon, and William. They stopped at the Big Bone
Lick then headed southward and made improvements on the waters of the
Elkhorn. Lecompt established a claim at a large buffalo stamping ground,
one of the few that retained that name after the buffalo had vanished.
Camped at a spring, William McConnell and some of his companions

heard news of the battle of Lexington in faraway Massachusetts. They commemorated the event by naming the place Lexington. Several years later a fort nearby was called by the same name, and finally the name was used for a town. Francis McConnell found a place nearby that he liked better and made an improvement by the big pond on the 1774 military survey of Mary Frazier, heir of George Frazier. Others who made improvements along Elkhorn Creek were David Perry, Hugh Shannon, Francis McConnell, Garrett Jordan, John Maxwell, William Lain, John Lee, Joseph and William Lindsay, John Alexander, and William McClelland.

Thomas Glenn, who had come to Kentucky with the surveyors in 1774, returned with his brother David and later joined forces with Edward Holeman, Patrick Irvin, Cyrus McCracken, Joseph Blackford, Andrew Miller, and Bill Rue to establish preemption claims along Glenn's Creek south of the present-day Frankfort. These men found a number of good springs, including one that they called the Versailles Spring. Glenn's Creek is named in honor of Thomas Glenn. Soon after returning home, Glenn was put in jail and charged with the murder of his indentured servant Peter Eglington. The case was heard, and Glenn was found innocent of murder, but guilty of "beating his Servant Ill" and fined £1,000.[22]

William Bryan (the uncle of Rebecca Boone, wife of Daniel Boone) with four of his brothers and twenty-five of his neighbors also made the trip to Kentucky in 1775. These men, all from the Yadkin River area of North Carolina, scouted around and were attracted to property on North Elkhorn that Floyd had previously surveyed for Col. William Preston. If any members of the party noticed the surveyor's blazes, they ignored them. They made the usual improvements by blazing some trees and planting some corn.[23]

Another group came down the Ohio and up the Kentucky River to Drennons Lick, then explored the country to the southwest. John Porter, Robert Foreman, Thomas Baird, and Robert Elliot happened upon the headwaters of a creek that they named Clear Creek, and the next branch they named Fox Run. This same creek also went by the name of Brashears Creek. Marsham Brashear also had built a cabin near the mouth of this creek near Salt River. This part of the country—in what is now Shelby County—was dominated by a large hill, a conspicuous landmark soon to be named Jeptha's Mountain by Squire Boone.

Land hunters who explored the waters of the Licking River soon discovered a number of large buffalo trails, two of which led all the way from Limestone Creek on the Ohio River (now Maysville) to Lexington. The principal trail crossed the Licking River at the Lower Blue Licks, thereby providing those coming down the Ohio River with the shortest and best route to either Harrodsburg or Boonesborough. Simon Kenton is said to have found his way into Kentucky by using these trails. They were certainly known by John Martin, Alexander Pollock, John Miller, John Hingston, and John Haggin, all of whom made improvements near the path. Another group, only known as Wells and company, quickly staked off a number of claims on the waters of the lower Licking River and then returned home.[24]

On June 4, 1775, two canoes, carrying James Nourse, Benjamin Johnson, Nicholas Cresswell, George Rice, Edmund and Reuben Taylor, and their three servants, docked at Harrod's Landing on the Kentucky River. The Taylors were cousins of Hancock Taylor, the Fincastle deputy surveyor who was killed on the Kentucky River by Indians in 1774. For eleven days the men camped at the nearly deserted town of Harrodsburg, then the Taylors moved to join their other cousins, Hancock, Henry, John, Richard, and Willis Lee, who were then starting a settlement generally called Leestown, on the Kentucky River near Bensons Creek. This station later served as the base of operation for the surveyors working for the Ohio Company, who, of course, also made surveys and improvements for themselves.

In many ways Leestown was an ideal site, being at the hub of several large buffalo trails leading towards Harrodsburg, Versailles Springs, LeCompt's Stamping Ground, Drennons Lick, Lexington, and eventually Boonesborough. Leestown was immediately north of a large meadow that Hancock Taylor had surveyed for James McAfee in 1773 and another survey that he had made for his father Sgt. Zachary Taylor on a 200-acre military warrant.[25] This Leestown site was eventually incorporated within the city limits of Frankfort, which in time became the capital of Kentucky.

On June 14, James Harrod visited Harrodsburg where James Nourse and Benjamin Johnson promptly solicited him to act as a land locator. After purchasing some horses, the newcomers met Harrod at Boiling Springs and from there traveled to Boonesborough by way of Knob Lick and Twitty's Fort. Both Nourse and Johnson possessed military warrants issued by Governor Dunmore, but Henderson insisted that they could not be used to claim land in Transylvania because any land in the new colony would have to be purchased from the company. Harrod, Nourse, and Johnson then crossed the river into Fincastle County, Virginia, and continued northward to the waters of the Licking, where they made several surveys. Because none of these men were official deputy surveyors, their trip was a waste of time, their unauthorized surveys illegal. Their guide, James

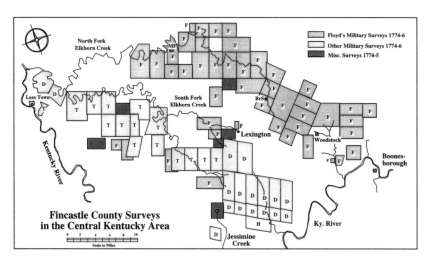

Fincastle County surveys in the central Kentucky area.

Harrod, was not at all familiar with the area and was uncertain whether he was on the waters of Eagle Creek or the Licking.

On their way back to Boonesborough, the men stopped at the camp where Nathaniel Gist and his brothers were still making improvements. On June 27, James Nourse considered his mission completed. By way of Boone's Trace, he returned home in company with North Alexander, David Wilson, and Jonathan Jennings.

Another man who arrived in Kentucky in 1775 was George Rogers Clark. On May 4 he secured a passage at Wheeling in the canoe of James Nourse and Nicholas Cresswell. The men traveled down the Ohio together, then up the Kentucky River, but Clark joined another company headed by Michael Cresap near Drennons Lick. When Cresap headed back up the river, Clark moved to Leestown. By mid-July he had joined another company headed by Maj. John Crittenden, who had also come down the Ohio from Wheeling. This party included William and Andrew Linn, Thomas Clark, and Thomas Brazer. They were later joined enroute by Thornton Farrow, Luke Cannon, William Bennett, and a man named Guy, who appears to have been a servant. Together they visited Boonesborough, then went northwest to make improvements at Somerset and Grassy Lick Creeks. Above the lick, Farrow, Clark, and Crittenden built cabins, and Clark surveyed 15,360 acres. On July 20 Clark passed through Boonesborough, again enroute to Leestown.[26]

Like Nourse, the majority of land seekers returned after they had staked off their claims. Michael Cresap, for example, stayed in central Kentucky for only two or three weeks, probably the average time required to find and improve a tract of land. Nicholas Cresswell, an Englishman who never had any intention of claiming Kentucky land, stayed at Harrod's Landing only a few days and then joined a returning party comprised of Henry Tillings, Thomas O'Brian, John Clifton, Joseph Brashear, and several others. He was surprised to find that he and Tillings were the only ones who had pants, the remainder being clothed in "breechclouts, leggins and hunting shirts, which [had] never been washed, only by the rain, since they were made."[27]

During July, Henderson reported that numerous groups were leaving. Among the leaders were Marquis Calmes, Benjamin Berry, John Luttrell, and John and Valentine Harmon. Luttrell, one of the Transylvania proprietors, took off in search of his slave, who had taken his best riding horse and headed for home in Carolina. Samuel Henderson, Joel Walker, and the Harmon brothers accompanied Luttrell. By the middle of summer it appeared that Kentucky was destined to be the permanent home for only a few die-hard frontiersman. A determined attack by any of the surrounding Indian tribes at this time would certainly have depopulated the entire country. Although the Cherokee attacked several men in Powell's Valley, the Indians did not disturb the settlers in Kentucky.

The battle of Bunker Hill occurred on June 17, and shortly thereafter George Washington took command of the American forces in Boston. At the time both the British and Americans sent delegates to the Indian nations, urging them to remain neutral in the "family quarrel" of the white men.[28] Having recently sold Kentucky, the Cherokee chiefs could not complain of these new Western settlements. For the Shawnee, the memory of their recent defeat at Point Pleasant convinced them that an attack on the Virginians would not be in their best interest. Henry Hamilton, the British governor at Detroit, wrote, "The Virginians are haughty Violent and bloody, the savages have a high opinion of them as Warriors, but are jealous of their encroachments, and very suspicious of their faith in treaties."[29] The Illinois, Miami, and Huron in the North and the Creek, Choctaw, and Chickasaw in the South were all reluctant to act without the approval of the tribes that were closer to the new settlements. For this reason all the tribes avoided central Kentucky at the time of the initial settlements.

There was an incident, however, that put the frontier settlers on their guard. In June, while returning from Kentucky, William Cooke came upon several other men who were also traveling back to their homes. When they reached Powell's Valley, a party of Indians attacked their camp. One man, Peter Shoemaker, was hit in the neck with several balls and collapsed. Everyone, including the Indians, decided he was beyond recovery. As the Indians came rushing into the camp, Shoemaker suddenly grabbed his gun and shot one of the attackers. He then seized another man's gun and shot a second Indian. The remaining Indians were so confused by this sudden and belligerent recovery that they fled. The men treated Shoemaker's wounds, the bleeding stopped, and after a few days of discomfort, he recovered.[30]

During the latter part of August, Daniel Boone led a second party west. This caravan included women and children. In addition to members of his own family, he was accompanied by the families of Hugh McGary, Thomas Denton, and Richard Hogan, the latter intending to live in Harrodsburg. About twenty single men also accompanied the group. The company started north on Boone's Trace, packing all their possessions that could be carried on horses and driving their livestock along the trail. One of Boone's children even brought a cat.

On reaching Hazel Patch, Boone left his newly blazed trail and followed Scagg's Trace to the headwaters of Dicks River for the convenience of families going to Harrodsburg. They separated near the present town of Broadhead, with Boone's group intercepting his trace again on Roundstone Creek. The other party, under the direction of Hugh McGary, soon lost its way, but was lucky enough to meet with Silas Harlin, who guided them to Harrodsburg.[31]

The cabins erected at Harrodsburg in 1774 stood on low ground along the side of a little creek. When McGary's party arrived, "they selected an eminence about 300 yards further west, on account of a spring which issued from the foot of a rocky bluff on the north side. There McGary, Denton, Harrod and three others erected their cabins."[32] On this site they built their fort. By the time the Poage party arrived in February 1776, only Hugh Wilson and his family still occupied any of the old town cabins. Within two weeks, in September 1775, a second party, which included the family of Richard Callaway, reached Kentucky and settled in Boonesborough. The arrival of women and children gave the settlements an atmosphere of permanence.

When moving long distances, the early pioneers could not transport many possessions. They loaded their packhorses with only the most essential items, herding their cattle and hogs along the trails. The estates of deceased settlers give an indication of the items carried over the trails to Kentucky. For example, the Abraham Vanmeter family owned a rifle, frying pan, pitchfork, a length of chain, fire tongs, a lamp, a tea kettle, dishes, a trap, a hand mill, iron wedges, a large bell, an auger, a hammer, a set of plow irons, a whip saw, a spinning wheel, several pots, a large ten-gallon kettle, and one grindstone.[33]

Staunch patriots, most Virginians opposed the existing "royal government." In March, when its leaders called for a convention at Richmond, the delegates provided for the organization of the state militia. In May, the Virginia Convention, as ruling body of the colony, met and passed a resolution of sympathy for the minutemen in Massachusetts. The governor, Lord Dunmore, objected. Dunmore then ordered the garrisons at Fort Dunmore (Pittsburgh), Fort Fincastle (Wheeling), and Fort Blair (Point Pleasant) to disband and the stockades to be evacuated. Many objected because these military outposts along the Ohio River posed a threat to hostile Indians. Capt. William Russell, in charge of Fort Blair, procrastinated until the middle of June, then moved the stores and state-owned cattle back to the Holston. Not long after, the governor himself abandoned the governor's mansion in Williamsburg and took refuge on a British warship, the *Fowey*, at Yorktown.

John Randolph, the very influential Virginian who served as the king's attorney, turned Tory and fled with the governor. His son, Edmund Randolph, decided that the best way to clear his tarnished family name was to serve under Washington. Thomas Jefferson, Richard Henry Lee, and Patrick Henry jointly signed a letter of recommendation, and he was appointed as Washington's aide-de-camp. When John Randolph left for England, he had in his possession the land grant for the DeWarrensdorff tract at the Falls of the Ohio. This lost document caused quite a bit of trouble in later years when the city of Louisville was established.

Seeking a means to thwart those disloyal to the Crown, Governor Dunmore decided to punish the planters who opposed him by freeing their slaves and indentured servants. Throughout the summer he sent numerous sloops from his fleet to lure Negroes from the Tidewater plantations. Using the slaves and indentured servants whom he was able to muster, plus a few loyalists, he eventually assembled 350 men to oppose the rebels.

In November Dunmore's little army had its mettle tested at Kemp's Landing in a skirmish against some militia from Princess Anne County. About two-thirds of the Americans took to their heels after the first volley, but a company of gentlemen volunteers fought bravely until driven off by superior numbers. Soon after this skirmish Governor Dunmore issued a proclamation declaring martial law and summoning all able-bodied men to arm. Those who disobeyed his orders were to be treated as traitors. At the same time he formally emancipated any Negroes or indentured servants working for rebels. Quickly responding to this threat, the Virginia Convention ordered that any Negroes caught fleeing would be returned to their masters, but any captured under arms would be sent to the West Indies and sold.

Not everyone in power, however, was a "red hot liberty man." In Augusta County, John Connolly and John Croghan headed a Scotch-Irish faction that controlled the county. The group included some militia officers such as Capt. Alexander McKee and Lt. Simon Girty. As late as September 23, 1775, county officials still required the "usual oaths" to his Majesty's person.[34]

But even the Tory stronghold of Augusta County had dissenters. During the session of county court that met on September 20, 1775, George Wilson was accused of having "violently seized and carried away Maj. John Connolly from this place, and also advising others not to aid the Officers of Justice when called upon to apprehend the afors'd disturbers of the peace." George Wilson was called to court but did not appear. Three days later, John Gabriel Jones attended this court and insulted George Croghan and the other commissioners "in a very gross manner." He was suspended from the practice of law and fined £200. Still in control, Croghan decided to cash in on some of his former influence with the British governor by registering a deed for a large tract of land given him by the Iroquois. Some of the settlers objected, saying the deed was over two years old and that the usual three witnesses to the signing of the deed were not present. But their objection was overruled, and the deed was proven to the satisfaction of this Tory county court.

In the fall John Connolly traveled to Yorktown and met with Governor Dunmore. Connolly proposed to go to Detroit where he would organize and supply an army of Tories and Indians. With this army he would move along Lake Erie, then turn south and capture Fort Pitt. By promising land grants to the Virginians settled on frontier, Connolly hoped to win their support to the British cause. Even if they resisted, he thought his army could take Fort Pitt and Fort Fincastle (at Wheeling) and then march over the mountains to join forces with an army the governor was raising at Alexandria. Impressed with this ambitious plan, Dunmore urged Connolly to start for Detroit. Unfortunately for Connolly, Benedict Arnold's capture of Montreal had blocked the easy journey by sea, forcing him to travel by land. En route, patriots arrested Connolly and two companions on November 20, 1775, and imprisoned them near Hagerstown, Maryland.

By this time Governor Dunmore had organized 300 Negroes into his "Ethiopian Regiment" and occupied Norfolk. His army was estimated at 3,000 men, including loyalists and white indentured servants who had fled from their masters, but only about 400 were actually qualified to be soldiers, because most of them had not the slightest idea how to use a gun. Nevertheless, this force posed a threat to the new Virginia government.

With the coming of winter, the new settlers in Kentucky had much to occupy them. Harvesting crops planted in the spring was one of the most important tasks. Because there was no place to store the grain, they constructed log cribs at the edges of the cleared fields. John Floyd reported that he finished his house at Woodstock and spent a month killing and butchering meat to see him through the winter. Most of the single men who had been living in the outlying cabins scattered over the countryside moved to the more permanent towns such as Boonesborough, Harrodsburg, and Leestown. By winter only a few isolated cabins on the Licking or Elkhorn remained occupied. Even those who lived in the little village of Saint Asaph had long since returned home or moved to Boonesborough or Harrodsburg for the winter.

In the late fall William Whitley returned, bringing his wife and two children. The eldest child was tied on the horse behind his mother, who carried the youngest on her lap. At times along the trail the horse would fall, and Esther Whitley and the children would be pitched off together, for being tied together "where one went all must go."[35] On the thirty-three-day trip to Kentucky, Whitley was accompanied by his brother-in-law George Clark, who also brought his wife and children. The two couples stopped at what is now called Walnut Flat Creek, and constructed some cabins, as they were "then in the habit of settling out to our selves."[36]

But even when the cold December wind made traveling uncomfortable, some could not resist exploring and preempting choice land. Isaac Hite gathered some of his friends and headed for the Falls of the Ohio. This group, consisting of Abraham Hite Sr., John Bowman, Peter Casey, Ebenezer Soverain, Moses Thompson, Nathaniel Randolph, and Peter Higgins, made numerous land claims along Goose Creek before reaching their destination.

Before the year was out, Colonel Henderson left Kentucky and returned to the East to mend his political fences. He left John Floyd in charge of the land office at Boonesborough. Henderson and Floyd made an agreement that the Transylvania Company would respect Floyd's claim to his surveys at the Falls made in 1774. In return, Floyd would use his influence to persuade Col. William Preston to acknowledge Henderson's purchase. Henderson probably visited Preston prior to returning to Kentucky. On December 1 Floyd wrote Preston that "[h]e says you would have removed every prejudice he ever had against you, but that it was done long ago."[37] In the same letter Floyd reported that prospective settlers had entered 560,000 acres of land in Transylvania. Unfortunately, few of these tracts were then occupied. Floyd, who coveted the position of Transylvania surveyor, was relieved when his antagonistic rival Arthur Campbell arrived at Boonesborough and failed to get the appointment. All during the summer Campbell had been sending anonymous letters criticizing Preston and Floyd to influential men on the frontier. He signed his missives with the colorful pen name Philo Ohio.

An incident that occurred just before Christmas Eve ruined Campbell's hope of becoming a respected leader in Kentucky. A letter by John Williams explains why:

> On Saturday about noon, being the 23rd, Col. Campbell, with a couple of lads, Saunders and McQuinney, went across the river. On the opposite bank they parted. Campbell went up the river about two hundred yards and took up a bottom. The two lads, without a gun, went straight up the hill. About ten minutes after they parted a gun and a cry of distress was heard, and the alarm given that the Indians had shot Col. Campbell. We made to his assistance. He came running to the landing with one shoe off, and said he was fired on by a couple of Indians. A party of men was immediately dispatched under the command of Col. Boone, who went out, but could make no other discovery than two Moccasin tracks, whether Indians or not could not be determined. We had at that time over the river, hunting, etc., ten or a dozen, in different parties, part or all of whom we expected to be killed, if what Col. Campbell said was true; but that by many was doubted. Night came on; several of the hunters returned, but had neither seen nor heard of the Indians nor yet of the two lads. We continued in this state of suspense until Wednesday, when a party of men sent out to make search for them found McQuinney killed

and scalped in a corn field, at about three miles distance from town on the north side of the river. Saunders could not be found and has not been heard of.[38]

Most of the settlers thought that Campbell had been careless to let the boys wander off, and even worse, that he acted in a cowardly way by deserting them and running from the Indians. In truth, this incident reminded the Virginians that not all Indians approved of settlements on their hunting ground.

CHAPTER 2

1776
The War Starts in the West

THE YEAR 1776 BEGAN FAVORABLY FOR THE AMERICANS. GENERAL WASH-
ington's army had bottled up the British in Boston, and the remaining
891,350 square miles in the thirteen united colonies were almost completely free of the king's authority.[1] In spite of the fact that an American
attack on Quebec had failed on New Year's Eve—leaving Gen. Richard
Mongomery dead and Col. Daniel Morgan a prisoner—most patriots
were optimistic and expected the war to be over within a year.

Governor Dunmore occupied Norfolk, but all signs pointed to a stay
of short duration. Before the first of the year, Col. William Woodford collected 500 Virginians and advanced as far as "Great Bridge," a long causeway through swampy ground—the only practical land approach to the
city. Instead of attacking the British at the causeway, the Virginians tricked
Dunmore into believing there were only 300 militia opposing his army.
Dunmore ordered his 120 British regulars to attack the American position.
The American riflemen killed or captured a considerable number of them,
forcing the survivors to retreat. Colonel Woodford then sent part of his
men on a flanking attack through the swamp. This drove Dunmore's
Ethiopian Regiment and the remainder of the British Regulars into their
fortifications on the causeway. The British withdrew from these positions
a few days later and took refuge in Norfolk.

Col. Robert Howe, commanding 500 men from North Carolina, reinforced the Virginians after the battle. Within a few days Dunmore realized that he was beaten and abandoned the town. He and his troops

prepared to board ships in the harbor, and many of the residents joined him. When the ships were full, the remaining loyalists tried to escape through the swamps. While the victorious Americans were debating what to do with Norfolk, whether to fortify or abandon it, four British ships opened fire with their cannons. The warehouses closest to the harbor caught fire, and the flames spread to nearby residences. By January 2, much of the town lay in ashes.

In Kentucky, Col. Richard Henderson busied himself with the affairs of the Transylvania Company, organizing a group to begin surveying the valuable land at the Falls of the Ohio. Because no specific details of this trip have survived, we know only that Henderson had his men build a cabin to serve as a land office. It also seems probable that some of the choice tracts around the Falls were acquired through the Transylvania Company by persons who had land already surveyed in 1774 and then registered in Fincastle County, men such as Edmund Taylor and John Floyd. John Williams later reported that "one of the great complaints was that the proprietors, and a few gentlemen, has [sic] engrossed all the lands at and near the Falls of Ohio, which circumstance I found roused the attention of a number of people of note."[2] There were already thirty surveys at the Falls entered legally in Fincastle County, including several thousand acres each for Henry Harrison, William Byrd, James Taylor, Alexander Dandridge, John Ashby, and Hugh Mercer.

Daniel Boone also went to the Falls that spring, but finding activities somewhat dull, he left the company. Taking only a single companion, he began hunting in the area. First he followed Goose Creek to its headwaters, then moved to the waters of Floyd's Fork. Near the place called Seaton Spring, he made an improvement for his friend Robert Pogue on land that was to be the subject of a lawsuit many years later. Others, including Joseph Daugherty, made improvements around the Falls, hoping they could acquire some of this potentially valuable land.

On March 17, Gen. William Howe evacuated Boston, and American troops moved into the city. Another spring migration to Kentucky began at about the same time. From southern Virginia and the upper Ohio small parties of settlers and adventurers began to arrive at the new towns. Some who had made improvements the year before returned to protect their claims. To conform to an old custom, many planted corn.

Samuel Wells and company returned to their improvements south of Limestone and built a few more cabins; then most of the company, with the exception of their leader, disappeared from Kentucky history. Samuel returned home and was soon after charged with wife beating.[3] One company, consisting of William Markland, John Lyons, James Kelly, William Braden, Thomas and Harry Dickerson, and John and Rezin Virgin, stopped at Cabin Creek where they found Simon Kenton, who agreed to serve as their guide. He told them that better land could be found farther west. The men then paddled a few miles farther down the Ohio and landed at Limestone (now Maysville). While Markland and Lyons stayed with the boats, Kenton escorted the others inland where they managed to establish settlement claims. Possibly they encountered John Hinkston, who by then was living in a cabin he had constructed on the south fork of the Licking. Daniel Gillaspy and Joseph Tomlinson made improvements nearby but soon returned to Virginia. John McFall was another person attracted to this area.

Farther south, at Floyd's "Royal Spring" on the Elkhorn, John McClelland was building a station and planting corn. Charles White was one of the men in this company. When John Floyd learned that the little station was located on his military survey, he angrily decided to evict the squatters. When he saw McClelland's poor wife and children, however, he realized what a hardship it would impose on them to be driven from their new home. Instead, he agreed to sell the land to McClelland for 300 pounds on credit.

Early in the spring, Benjamin Logan returned to Kentucky with his family and began work on his house at the old St. Asaph camp. With the Logans came Benjamin Pettit, who with his family settled about ten miles southwest on the headwaters of the Hanging Fork of Dick's River. The two families assisted each other in building cabins and planting crops. A few miles to the east William Whitley and his brother-in-law George Clark started work on permanent cabins.

Early in the spring John Floyd made a quick trip to the Eastern settlements to deliver the land surveys made under his authority as a deputy surveyor of Fincastle County. On his return he was threatened by "acquaintances" of Col. Arthur Campbell, who had returned home shortly after his disgrace at Boonesborough. As Floyd later wrote:

> We are all well, & are six in number. Mr. Todd overtook us last night. Captain Jonathan Martin is also along; he came without any persuasion. . . . The gentlemen marched with the Col° as far as the Seven Mile ford & was with him a night. Several of his acquaintances stayed on the road, and some threatened to flog me,

but had not the courage to make the attack. Pray continue to it that the Gen[tlema]n may not sit in the Convention.[4]

Campbell simply may have been jealous of Floyd, who at the time was prospering as a paid surveyor in the new country. But this incident could have been the result of a larger conflict of interests still present in Virginia. When the break between the patriots and the loyalists began in 1775, Henry Lee and Patrick Henry stood out against the entrenched interests and leadership of the ruling families and individuals—the Randolphs, Blairs, Benjamin Harrison, and Carter Braxton. At the outbreak of the Revolution, Virginia's leaders met to organize a defense of the colony. Under Henry's strenuous leadership they passed by a majority of one vote a resolution for arming the colony.[5] Later, George Morgan, John Campbell, and their associates with Western land interests maintained a policy of inaction on the frontier and went so far as to suggest to Governor Henry that the Virginia settlements in Kentucky should be abandoned. It seems probable that Preston and Floyd had opinions regarding the surveying of land in Fincastle County, which were objectionable to Arthur Campbell since this Scotsman also sent anonymous letters to influential people of Virginia and North Carolina criticizing the Fincastle surveyor and his assistant.

In spite of these aggressive "gentlemen," Floyd, Todd, Martin, and their companions continued to drive their cattle along the crude trail and returned to Boonesborough by May 14. Here Floyd learned that the Harrodsburg men had made a second revolt and that "Jack Jones is at the head of the banditti."[6] He also reported that there were then twenty-eight Tories settled on the Elkhorn and that civil war was about to break out among the settlers. A few days later he wrote to Colonel Preston:

> The Devil to pay here about land—pray try to get something by the Convention with regards to settling these lands, or there'll be bloodshed soon. An Election of delegates, I am told, is to be at Harrodsburg, 1st of June to send to [the] Convention in Vi[rgini]a. They solicit people on the No[rth] side [of] the Kentucky to come & vote, imagining (I suppose) by the people on that side joining them to be all represented as inhabitants of the extreme western parts of Fincastle, in the same manner as West Augusta.[7]
>
> Hundreds of wretches come down the Ohio & build pens or cabins, return to sell them; the people come down & settle on the

lands they purchase; these same places are claimed by someone else, & then quarrels ensue. In short they now begin to pay no kind of regard to the officers [*sic*] land more than any other. Many have come down here, & not stayed more than 3 weeks, and returned home with 20 cabins apiece, & so on. They make very free with my character, swearing I am engrossing the country and have no warants [*sic*] for the land, & if I have, they will drive me and the officers to hell.[8]

As a surveyor, Floyd had much to lose by land anarchy in the new country. He had spent two years surveying thousands of acres of land on military warrants for which he had expected to receive substantial fees. In 1774 the Fincastle surveyors had charged 2/1/8 for each 1,000-acre survey, but this was not all profit since they were required to pay chainmen and markers to assist them.[9] Floyd realized that if Henderson's claim was invalidated, his efforts to collect that portion of his fees would also be in vain. Likewise, the officers were slow in paying, many apparently feeling that they would settle with the surveyor after they received their bona fide grants from the Commonwealth.

His friend John Todd also criticized the group of "outlyers" from the Monongahela, as indicated by one of his letters:

I'm afraid to lose sight of my house lest some invader should take possession. But why do I preach politicks [*sic*]? Tis a country failing, and not one Mac from Conocheague but would make a fool of Waller himself in talking landed politicks. I'm worried to death almost by this learned ignoramus set; and what is worse, there are but two lawyers here, and they can't agree.[10]

The two lawyers he was referring to were himself and John Gabriel Jones. Although Todd had no military warrant, he had managed to make several land claims on the basis of actual settlement and had entered them in the books at the Fincastle County surveyor's office.

Most of the "Macs" (the Scotch-Irish faction consisting of the McConnells, McCrackens, McClellands, and their associates) acted on the assumption that the surveys that had been made for Virginia veterans of the French and Indian War on the warrants signed by Governor Dunmore would be null and void because the governor would soon return to England. Their idea of a proper and legitimate land claim was to pile up a few logs so that the next fellow who happened along would think a cabin was under construction. Many of these "Macs" thought that surveys were unnecessary since according to their custom, the boundary of their land would be half the distance to the next cabin.[11]

The Harrodsburg revolt, as Floyd termed the movement, was credited to George Rogers Clark and John Gabriel (Jack) Jones. Jones was the nephew of Gabriel Jones, an influential Virginia gentleman who had been the law partner of Thomas Jefferson and the father-in-law of John Harvie of Albemarle, who later became head of Virginia's land office. George Rogers Clark was from Caroline County, and his family had been good friends of Thomas Marshall, Abraham Hite, Thomas Bullitt, and James Madison. Clark had not been a leader in the anti-Transylvania movement but nevertheless was elected a delegate. Clark later stated that he found the people had a variety of opinions about Henderson's claims.

> Many thought it good, others doubted whether or not Virginia could, with propriety have any pretension to the country. This is what I wanted to know. I immediately fixed my plan,—that of assembling the people, get them to elect deputies, and send them to the Assembly of Virginia, and treat with them respecting the country. If valuable conditions was [sic] procured, to declare ourselves citizens of the state—otherwise establish an independent government, and, by giving away a great part of the lands and disposing of the remainder otherwise, we could not only gain numbers of inhabitants, but in good measure protect them.[12]

The few settlers in Fincastle County at this time were not overly anxious about their Indian neighbors. There had been incidents, but only one, the death of Willis Lee, occurred in the far western part of the county that spring. Lee had first come to Kentucky in 1773 with his cousin Hancock Taylor, accompanying Taylor and the other surveyors on their second expedition to Kentucky in 1774. But in April 1776 a band of Indians attacked and burned several cabins at Leestown. Willis Lee was shot in the chest and another man wounded. The surviving defenders realized that Lee's wound was mortal and abandoned their post for Boonesborough. Before leaving, they attempted to make the victim as comfortable as possible. A short time later Daniel Campbell and Robert Edminston arrived and found Lee dead, "a pail of water sitting by his head, his hands lying on this breast, and the blood coming up through his fingers."[13]

Another incident occurred in June when the twin sons of Andrew Mc-Connell and an indentured servant, herding some cows to the milking shed, were attacked by a party of Mingo Indians. The indentured servant was instantly killed and one of the boys captured. The other twin, though well hidden from the Indians, could not bear to see his brother taken and gave himself up. When the boys reached the Shawnee towns with their captors, they were recognized by Joseph Nicholson, who knew their father. He purchased the lads for a rifle, and they were returned to Pittsburgh under the care of Col. George Morgan. Morgan thereupon sent them to their uncle William McConnell, then in Westmoreland County. The boys were in captivity about sixty days. Tragically, their father was among those killed six years later at the battle of Blue Licks.

Otherwise, the "Kentucky levels" were peaceful. A spy who had been at Detroit reported that the town was guarded by only a corporal and twelve privates. The British "Citidal" was manned by a corporal and four privates, and the militia at Detroit consisted of Frenchmen who wished to remain neutral.[14]

Most of the leaders on the Virginia frontier were young men. In the summer of 1776 George Rogers Clark was only twenty-three years old. Isaac Shelby was twenty-five, John Todd and John Floyd twenty-six, and William Whitley twenty-seven. Of the first pioneers to visit Kentucky as hunters and explorers, Squire Boone was only thirty-one and James Harrod about the same age. Benjamin Logan was thirty-three. At forty-one, Daniel Boone was the old man of the group.

Back in Williamsburg the political leadership held a convention to decide the question of independence and to set up a new government to replace the regal government that had been ruling the colony for over 150 years. The new state constitution required "the legislative, executive, and judiciary departments shall be separate and distinct, so that neither exercise the Powers properly belonging to the other." The legislature was composed of a House of Delegates and a Senate, who annually selected a new governor.[15]

Among the items changed was the old policy that every Virginian must be a member of the Episcopal church. In the future, citizens "should enjoy the fullest toleration in the exercise of religion." The fact that Virginia communities were small and isolated accomplished easily what in England had required decades of theological controversy. Without intending to do so, Virginians had purified the English church of its hierarchy and its excessive reliance on Catholic ritual. The Episcopal Church in America was not even provided with a bishop. These traits were the very defects to which Massachusetts Puritans so strenuously objected. Over the years the Church of England in Virginia had gradually become the most tolerant sect in the colonies. Standing for moderation in all things, the established Church of Virginia became the bulwark of decency in the community.

Virginians had founded their community not as religious refugees united by a common fanaticism but as admirers of the English way of life. Their desire to increase their population and their lack of interest in theology created a general laxity in enforcing laws against dissenters. Virginians were not passionate about religious dogma for the simple reason that they often knew nothing about it. From time to time, of course, they had to restrain religious troublemakers who menaced the peace or security of the colony. Virginians forbade the coming of Puritans in 1640 and the assembly of Quakers in 1662.

By 1744, Virginia's tolerance toward religion was embodied in law: the act of that year, while still requiring all to attend church regularly, permitted any Virginian to satisfy the law by attending the church of his choice. The Virginia government, however, generally refused to grant these dissenting sects any legal status. When the militant, sometimes called "New Light," Presbyterians invaded Virginia in the 1740s, the Reverend Patrick Henry, uncle of the famous Patrick, and Anglican minister of the parish of St. Paul's in Hanover, still vigorously objected to them. In 1770, Virginia authorities were still imprisoning undisciplined Baptist preachers, and only one Presbyterian church existed in Virginia in 1775. The authorities looked on these restrictions as emergency measures that expressed no general spirit of persecution. In 1776 Thomas Jefferson estimated the number of "dissenters" to the Episcopal Church at 55,000, or about 14 percent of the population. Most of these were Baptists, not Presbyterians, as some historians would now have us believe.

One resolution submitted to the Virginia legislature was not passed; this was Thomas Jefferson's proposal that all slaves born after a certain date be freed and returned to Africa. For the rest of his life Jefferson was much displeased by the failure of the legislature to pass this bill. As late as 1821, he wrote that "the day is not distant when it [the government] must bear and adopt it, or worse will follow. Nothing is more certainly written in the book of fate than that these people are to be free."[16]

About the same time, Col. Richard Henderson and John Williams reached Williamsburg and presented a letter to the convention pertaining to the Transylvania purchase, setting forth the moderate and easy terms they intended to use in selling the land. But the members were not all that impressed with Henderson's claim. A few days later the delegates resolved that settlers on the Western frontier should hold their lands without payment to any private person or company unless approved by the legislature. Not only that, they resolved that the first persons who settled on vacant Western land should have a preemption right to that tract. Furthermore, no one was to purchase land from any Indian nation under any pretense whatever. The Virginia Convention then in effect issued a manifesto that until the disputed title to the Transylvania land was determined, no person was to take possession of any tract that was entered or surveyed by this company, except the person in whose name the land was entered. They also prohibited settlement on land southwest of the Green River.

In June a large number of settlers assembled at Harrodsburg and drafted a petition to the Convention of Virginia requesting that Kentucky, including that portion claimed by the Transylvania Company, be recognized as part of Virginia. They also requested that two elected delegates, Capts. John Gabriel Jones and George Rogers Clark, be received by the Virginia Assembly. After a long and difficult journey over the Appalachians, the two men discovered that the assembly would not meet again until October. Jones then returned to the Holston to join a force being recruited to fight the Cherokee. Clark took the opportunity to call on Gov. Patrick Henry. The governor favored recognizing the Western settlers as citizens of Virginia. Patrick Henry, it should be noted, was then holding, by virtue of military warrants, 7,000 acres of Kentucky land on Elkhorn Creek that had been surveyed for him by John Floyd in 1774.

Even with the governor's support, the Virginia legislature failed to take timely action on the matter. Arthur Campbell, the county lieutenant who had been passed over for the position of Transylvania surveyor, managed to block recognition for several months, and the Western settlers, as before, were left to run their own affairs. Campbell is often portrayed as a liberal who sided with the poor settlers against political domination by the rich landowners. Yet a closer look indicates that his motives were always political and selfish.

While the Kentuckians were seeking Virginia's protection, more important things were happening in the East. On June 20, 1776, George Washington was selected by the Continental Congress to take command of the "Army of the United Colonies." Five days later, General Howe, intending to end the colonial uprising, sailed into New York Bay and began unloading German mercenaries and British troops.

Both sides realized that the time for peaceful compromise had passed. On July 4, Congress issued the Declaration of Independence. This document was to have a profound effect on all the colonies, including the western part of Virginia, since the American Congress had finally declared their independence from their mother country, England. As the document stated, "We hold these truths to be sacred and undeniable, that all men are created equal and independent, that from that equal creation they derive rights inherent and inalienable, among which are the preservation of life and liberty and the pursuit of happiness." To people on the frontier, the pursuit of happiness was wishful thinking.

In August, a committee presented Congress with a preliminary draft for the Articles of Confederation, which gave Congress power to determine boundary disputes between states. This provision, together with an article to confirm the Indiana and Vandalia land claims, was rejected. A new committee was formed, proposing that Congress have no power to alter boundaries or restrict states' rights, but in case of dispute, to form courts to decide such issues. In effect, Virginia was the largest claimant of land, its charter extending from the Atlantic Ocean to the "South Sea." Obviously it ran to the Mississippi River and included all land north of 36.5 degrees latitude. North Carolina and Georgia also extended to the Mississippi, with Georgia being the second largest claimant. Connecticut sided with Virginia. Its delegates believed that "[a] man's right does not cease to be a right because it is large."[17]

But the controversy was only theoretical. The only Western land controlled—if "controlled" is the proper word—by the Americans at the time was Kentucky. The thirteen colonies were urged to sign the Articles of Confederation as soon as possible, but they mostly procrastinated. In 1776, many colonies had large Tory populations, and many citizens still hoped to settle the differences with England peaceably. On the first vote for independence taken on July 1, Pennsylvania and South Carolina opposed separation from England, Delaware's vote was split, and New York abstained. There were so many Tories in New York that many high-ranking American officers began to wonder whether the colony was worth defending.

There was also a great deal of animosity between the Northern and Southern troops in General Washington's army. The New England Yankees suspected and distrusted the Southern soldiers. The Southerners reciprocated with dislike and even contempt for their comrades from the North. The better uniformed and equipped Continentals from Pennsylvania,

Delaware, and Maryland especially looked down upon the homespun rustics of New England. One Pennsylvania officer complained that the regiment from Marblehead, Massachusetts, contained "a number of negroes, which to persons unaccustomed to such associations, had a disagreeable, degrading effect."[18] Many Pennsylvania Germans did not approve of slavery because they did not want to be associated with black people.[19]

In the West, British agents had already begun wooing the Western tribes to their cause. Resentful of American encroachment on the frontier, the Indians began to make alliances with the king's representatives. Initially, the agents of both governments preached neutrality in the "difference between the white people" and suggested that the best interests of the tribes would be served by keeping peace. Despite increasing pressure for war from their neighbors, the Shawnee, still licking their wounds from the defeat of 1774, officially remained neutral until 1776. Likewise, the older Cherokee chiefs were able to keep their warriors in check despite agitation from Dragging Canoe and his followers. But when the British policy changed in 1776, a delegation of Northern Indians, consisting of Shawnee, Delaware, and Mohawk, visited the Cherokee country preaching war. Painted black and bringing belts of black wampum, the Ohio tribesmen reported that the Americans had designs against all the Indians and urged the Cherokee to join the common resistance. The latter accepted the symbolic wampum and promised action.

It is interesting to speculate what might have happened if the Americans had handled their affairs with Canada differently. In the summer of 1775 Washington had authorized Gen. Phillip Schuyler to advance on Montreal. Schuyler mustered nearly 2,000 militia, whereas the British were holding several major Canadian cities and forts with fewer than 700 regulars. But Schuyler was incapable of making a rapid advance, and it was not until August 27, 1775, that his second in command, Gen. Richard Montgomery, moved the troops forward. After a slow and lengthy ragtag campaign, he succeeded in capturing Montreal on November 11. In the meantime Benedict Arnold led a small force through the north woods of Maine and arrived at Quebec on November 9. With him he had only 500 men, a force insufficient to invest the largest city in Canada. In December, Montgomery and his army sailed up the St. Lawrence to reinforce Arnold, but the Americans failed to take the city. In a night attack General Montgomery was killed and 426 Americans captured. The Americans continued to harass Quebec for several more months, but the outcome had been decided in December with their failure to take the city.

In retrospect, if the Americans had concentrated on holding Montreal and the head of the Richelieu River, the entire course of the Revolutionary War might have been changed. Washington had no navy, so there was little hope that the Americans could keep Quebec even if they had won the city. As a practical matter, a garrison at Quebec would have to be supplied by sea. Montreal, located farther up river, could have been protected by forts on the St. Lawrence and easily supplied by small boats from upper New York by way of Lake Champlain. The occupation of Montreal would have served to cut off the small British outposts at Niagara and Detroit, ultimately ending any permanent alliances between the British and the Northern Indians. If ever the Americans at Montreal were seriously outnumbered, they had the option to retreat and hold out at Fort Oswegatchie or at Fort Ontario at Oswego. But by withdrawing from Montreal, the Americans abandoned the only practical route to the Northwest Territory. The British soon took control of the St. Lawrence River. They were then able to supply their Indian allies by boating goods down to the Great Lakes.

The Cherokee began their organized raids on the Virginia settlements in July with raiding parties that struck isolated outposts all along the frontier. On the twentieth, Chief Dragging Canoe, leading a large war party, crossed above the Cherokee ford of the Holston and attacked the outpost at "Island Flats" on Long Island. Most of the settlers received warning early enough that they were able to take shelter in the fort, but several women, bathing in the river, were bypassed by the Indians. To protect these stranded damsels, the militia decided to leave the fort to attack the Indians. There were about 170 men on each side, and the contest took place in the woods. The Indians quickly lost thirteen killed under fire from the militia's accurate rifles. One of the many wounded was Dragging Canoe, who called off the attack.[20]

On the same day, the Cherokee also laid siege to Fort Caswell in North Carolina, a post commanded by John Sevier. Well supplied with food and ammunition, the defenders were able to hold out for two weeks until the Indians, finally discouraged, packed up and left.

Farther north, in Monongahela and Ohio Counties, leaders attempted to strengthen their defensive posture by stationing militia at some of the most important private forts. They placed scouts at strategic places along the trails over which Indian war parties traveled. To replace Fort Blair at Point Pleasant, burned by Indians, Matthew Arbuckle from Botetourt County mobilized a company of bachelors and built Fort Randolph, a strong stockade with blockhouses and cabins. He and his men remained at

Virginia's western counties, 1776.

the fort to become its garrison. Another fort was built at Lewisburg, and militia were assigned to Arbuckle's old fort on Muddy Creek, on Indian Creek, and at Donnally's Fort. In addition, "spies" were stationed along the Ohio River, at the head of the Gauley River, and at the mouth of the Greenbrier. Despite these precautions, small bands of Indians, many of them Mingo, managed to elude the scouts and attack isolated settlements from deep in the Monongahela valley to Pittsburgh. On August 2, Capt. John Stuart wrote to Col. William Fleming requesting reinforcements because a "large number of Indians [have been] discovered makeing [*sic*] for our frontiers."[21] When traders informed Col. William Preston that the Cherokee intended to attack the lead mines at Chiswell, he ordered a militia company to be stationed there for protection. The major source of musket and rifle balls for the military, the mine was afterward protected by a stockade. The lead mines were supervised by Col. James Callaway of Bedford County.[22]

Isolated settlers also were killed in Kentucky County, causing panic among many of the inhabitants. One such person was James McDaniel, who was making salt at Drennons Lick.[23] He, his wife, Ann, and his year-old son had been living on Gilbert's Creek in a little settlement established by Ann's father, Samuel Coburn. People such as these, scattered throughout the countryside building cabins and making improvements, hurriedly re-

treated to the more established towns such as Boonesborough and Harrodsburg. Widow McDaniel and her father moved to Harrodsburg, but in
doing so lost forty horses, forty head of cattle, and most of their other possessions. Many fearful settlers entirely left the country. Huston's Station at
the present site of Paris was the first Kentucky station to break up. The people took refuge at McClelland's. Abandoned soon after were Hinkson's on
Licking, Lee's Town on the Kentucky River, and Harrod's Boiling Spring
Station near the Salt River.

   Floyd attempted to recruit some of the displaced settlers for the defense of Boonesborough, but most were determined to go home. William
Whitley and his companions decided to abandon their houses and ten
acres of corn. When they reached Logan's Station, Logan asked them to
make a stand with him. They refused, causing the people around Whitley's
and Logan's to move north to Harrodsburg.[24] Bryan's Station had been settled in the spring, and two groups of "half-faced cabins" were built some
distance apart but facing each other for protection. A good fence was built
around the settlement to protect the corn and to hold the horses. By mid-
summer, however, it had been practically abandoned. All but two of the
station's defenders had returned to North Carolina to bring out their families. When they heard that the Indians were going to war, they and their
families simply stayed at home.

   After the others had been abandoned, only three stations remained.
These were McClelland's, Harrodsburg, and Boonesborough. Defenders at
these places began surrounding cabin groups with palisades. At Boonesborough the defenders commenced, erecting a new fort just above the Lick
Branch on the banks of the Kentucky about 300 yards above old Fort
Boone. They located the new fort on the town commons where Colonel
Henderson in April 1775 had cleared a spot and built a magazine. There
John Gass found Henderson and his particular friends living in a few cabins when he first arrived at Boonesborough in the winter of 1776. Until
this emergency, not one of the Kentucky stations was fortified or even partially protected by walls.[25]

   By fall the Kentuckians needed ammunition and fresh meat. The small
amount of powder produced in the Atlantic states was needed there. The
Chiswell lead mines were worked vigorously to supply lead for the American armies. The Transylvania Company had furnished much of the ammunition during the first year, and Maj. Arthur Campbell of Holston had sent
Daniel Boone a limited supply of powder and lead. On September 7,
1776, Boone reported that he had distributed to the people "the powder at

six shillings per pound, and the lead at ten pence, except one pound of powder and two pounds of lead, which had been delivered to the Scoutes [*sic*]."26

On July 21, 1776, John Floyd wrote his assessment of the threat facing the vulnerable new settlements in Kentucky:

> The situation of our country is much altered [as] the Indians seem determined to break up our settlement. . . . They have, I am satisfied, killed several [and] many are missing who, some time ago, went out about their business who we can hear nothing of. Fresh sign of Indians is seen almost every day. I think I mentioned to you before of some damage they had done at Leesburg. The seventh of this month they killed one James Cooper on Licking Creek, the fourteenth they killed a man whose name I do not know at your salt spring on Licking Creek. . . . We are about finishing a large fort and intend to try to keep possession of this place as long as possible. They are, I understand, doing the same at Harrodsburg, and also on Elkhorn at the Royal Springs [McClelland's Station]. A settlement, known by the name of Hinkston, is broke up; nineteen of which are now here on their way in, [John Hinkston] himself among the rest, who all seem deaf to anything we can say to dissuade them. Then at least [some] of our own people, I understand, are going to join them which will leave us with less than 30 men at this fort. I think more than 300 men have left the country since I came out, and not one has arrived except a few cabbiners [*sic*] down the Ohio.27

In the same letter Floyd also reported what is still the most famous kidnapping in Kentucky history. He began by describing what the Indians had done on July 14:

> [They] took out of a canoe within site [*sic*] of this place [Boonesborough], Miss Betsy Callaway, her sister Frances, and [Jemima] a daughter of Daniel Boone's; the last are about 13 or 14 years old, and the other grown—The affair happened late in the afternoon; they left the canoe on the opposite side of the river from us which prevented our getting over for some [time] to pursue them. We could not, that night, follow, more than five miles before dark. Next morning by daylight we were on the tracks, but

found they had totally prevented our following them by walking some distance apart through the thickest cane they could find. We observed their course, and on which side we had left their signs and traveled upward of thirty miles. We then imagined they would be less cautious in traveling, and made a turn in order to cross their trace and had gone but a few miles till we found their tracks in a buffalo path, pursued and overtook them in going two miles, just as they were kindling a fire to cook. Our study had been more to get the prisoners without giving the Indians time to murder them after they discovered us, then [sic] to kill them.

We discovered each other nearly at the same time. Four of us over fired and all rushed on them, which prevented their carrying anything away except one shot gun without any ammunition. Boone and myself had each a pretty fair shot just as they began to move off. I am well convinced I shot one through, and the one he shot dropt his gun, mine had none. The place was very thick with cane, and being so much elated on recovering the three poor heartbroken girls, prevented our making any further search; we sent them off almost naked, some without their moccasins, and not one of them [with] so much as a knife or tomahawk.

After the girls came to themselves enough to speak, they told us there were only five Indians, four Shawnees and one Cherokee, [and they] could all speak good English. They said they should take them to the Shawnee Towns, and the war club we got was like those I have seen from that nation. . . . They also told them the Cherokees had killed and drove all the people from Watago and thereabouts, and that fourteen Cherokees were then on the Kentucky [River] waiting to do mischief.[28]

Fortunately for the white settlers, the Indians disappeared from Kentucky after the kidnapping. The two warriors who had been shot both died, one prior to reaching the Ohio. Chief Cornstalk, not having approved of the affair, sent his apologies to the Americans but then traveled to Detroit to confer with the British.[29]

In hindsight, it would appear that the Kentucky settlers should have expected trouble from the Indians during the summer months. To the south, American militia forces began preparing for war against the Cherokee. Harrod and Logan knew of this because they had gone to the Holston on horseback for powder and lead, leading a packhorse. They returned in twenty days with some powder and lead they had acquired from Col. William Christian at the Long Island of the Holston, where he was preparing for his Cherokee campaign.[30] Before July had ended, Col. Andrew Williamson of South Carolina had raised 600 militia, a battalion of Continentals, and twenty Catawba scouts, a total of 1,120 men. He soon launched an attack on the Cherokee lower towns, burning villages and destroying crops. The army assembled under Colonel Christian of Virginia attacked from the north, while a third army from North Carolina under Gen. Griffith Rutherford reinforced Williamson. These forces completely overwhelmed the Cherokee, ending their effectiveness as a cohesive fighting force for several years. Only Dragging Canoe and his most loyal followers remained hostile. Refusing the terms offered by the Americans, they retreated farther into the interior to what is now Chattanooga.

By August 1776, Kentuckians no longer feared invasion from the Southern tribes. The defeat of the Cherokee was also influential in keeping the Northern Indians at home for a while. Because there were no more reports of Indians around Boonesborough, the Bluegrass enjoyed a peaceful respite.

The first wedding in Kentucky took place at Boonesborough on August 6 when Betsy Callaway married Samuel Henderson, one of her rescuers. Under Transylvania authority, Daniel Boone officiated as magistrate. Betsy (Elizabeth) wore a plain Irish linen dress, and the groom borrowed Nathan Reid's hunting shirt because his own was so worn. Watermelons were probably the only delicacy served at the wedding feast. Col. Richard Callaway consented to the match but required a bond of Henderson that the marriage be "again solemnized, by authority less doubtful, at the earliest opportunity."[31] This pledge was said to have been fulfilled at a later date. People relaxed, and some of the settlers returned to their cabin claims beyond the protection of the fort.

On September 8, 1776, Capt. John Floyd, hoping to find a position as surveyor in one of the proposed new counties on the frontier, left Boonesborough for the capital at Williamsburg. He was accompanied by Capt. David Gass, Nathan Reid, John McMillen, and others. While acting as the advance scout for the party, McMillen was ambushed and killed in Big Moccasin Gap near the North Fork of Holston.[32]

In October the Virginia legislature decided to look at the method of distributing public land. It had been nearly three years since Governor Dunmore and the council had decreed that settlers could hold the land that they had improved and could "have fifty Acres at least, and also for

every three Acres of Cleared Land, fifty Acres more and so in proportion."[33] The legislature altered this by declaring that settlers on "waste and
ungranted lands situated on western waters who had settled prior to 24
June 1776, were entitled to 400 acres to include their settlement." However, the legislature failed to provide any method for the government to
register such land, other than what had been done in the past. Nevertheless, a few of the men who had been in Kentucky traveled to Col. William
Preston's office in Smithfield, and Colonel Preston entered their settlement
claims. Doubting their legality, Colonel Preston wrote a disclaimer after
the entry, which stated that they had produced "memorandums of entries
of land on Western Waters and demanded that they be entered in my book
which hath been complied with, provided the same be legal, but should it
appear otherwise, there is no advantage to be taken of the surveyor."[34]

In autumn the Northern Indians were invited to a peace treaty at Pittsburgh. Cornstalk, who represented the Shawnee, and White Eyes, who
represented the Delaware, were devoted to peace but could do little with
their tribesmen.[35] Most frontiersmen did not immediately realize that so
many Shawnee warriors had decided to renew their 1774 policy, that is, to
"Rob the Pennsylvanians and kill the Long Knives" (Virginians). War parties killed some isolated settlers in Ohio County, destroying any houses or
cornfields that they found deserted.

Robert Patterson, David Perry, and several others left for Pennsylvania
in October. Traveling up the Ohio, they were ambushed by Indians after
passing Point Pleasant. Col. Dorsey Penticost later made a report of this incident:

> On the 11th, seven men on their return from Caintuck were
> fired on in their camp nearly opposite the mouth of Hockhock-
> ing; one was killed on the spot and scalped; one shot through with
> two bullets, of which he died the next day; two of the men had an
> arm broken each, one slightly wounded, the other two not hurt.
> When the men awaked, the Indians were amongst them with their
> tomahawks and war clubs; a scuffle ensued, but the Indians being
> prepared & having the advantage the men were obliged to run,
> one was cut with a tomahawk by the side of this back bone to the
> hollow of this body, another cut under the shoulder to the ribs.
> After plundering the camp, they crossed the river. One of the well
> men ran back to Fort Randolph, the other (Edward Mitchell) to a
> neighbor of mine, sent the person who was slightly wounded up

to Grave Creek, & hid the wounded in an obscure place & sustained them nine days upon paw paws. The Captain of the militia stationed at Grave Creek, with 33 men of his own company, joined with an Ensign & 12 men of the Regulars at Wheeling, went down, & four days ago came up with the wounded, who are likely to do well.[36]

Patterson and Perry were two of those wounded.

Frontier defense was complicated by a shortage of arms and ammunition. In July 1776, Capt. George Gibson and Lt. William Linn of the Virginia militia, with fifteen men, traveled from Fort Pitt down the Ohio and Mississippi Rivers to New Orleans to purchase gunpowder. Spanish officials permitted them to buy 12,000 pounds but insisted that the transaction be conducted in such a manner as to preserve the illusion of Spanish neutrality. Both France and Spain at this time wanted revenge for Britain's earlier conquests but were afraid to make any commitments that would cause Britain to declare war on them. For this reason, Gibson was required to remain in New Orleans while Linn took charge of the powder. He recruited additional boatmen and started upriver with his valuable cargo, manned by a party of fifty-three men.

In December, George Rogers Clark and John Gabriel Jones obtained several kegs of powder from the Virginia legislature for the Kentucky militia. They carried the valuable cargo to Pittsburgh where they acquired a boat and gathered "seven hands." About the time they reached the Scioto, 356 miles below Pittsburgh, they were discovered by the Shawnee, who followed in pursuit. Two months before, it had been reported that four "companies" of Indians had gone to war, one to invade Greenbrier, one to raid along the Monongahela, and another to attack Kentucky.[37] Clark's men had stumbled into the last party but had the advantage of distance when the Indians finally launched all their canoes. The white men soon learned that their heavily loaded bateau was slower. Both parties exerting themselves to the utmost, the pursuit continued for nearly forty miles. Just above the present Manchester, Ohio, there were several large islands in the Ohio. By steering his boat behind the first and dodging around the second, Clark was out of sight long enough to pull ashore on the second island and hide the powder. As Clark said later, "We hid our stores in four or five different places, at a considerable distance apart; and, running a few miles lower in our vessel, set it adrift and took by Land for Harrods Town." The

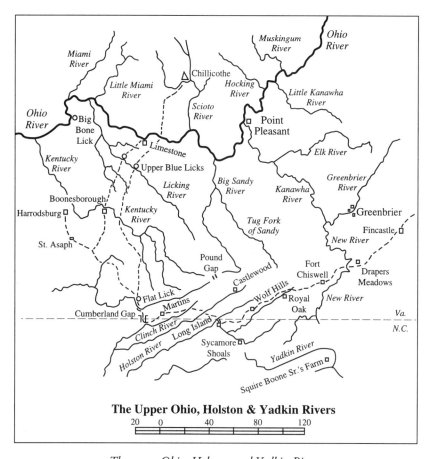

The Upper Ohio, Holston & Yadkin Rivers

The upper Ohio, Holston, and Yadkin Rivers.

Americans went ashore in the vicinity of Cabin or Limestone Creek, to continue their retreat across country with the Indians not far behind.

They passed by the Blue Licks, about twenty-four miles from their landing place, and Clark reported the tragedy that followed:

> [T]he third day from our leaving the River got to Hinkstons Cabbin [*sic*] on the West Fork of Licking Creek.[38] While we ware [*sic*] resting ourselves, four men came to us that had been Exploreing [*sic*] Land in that quarter and informed of the situation of affairs in Kentucky; that very little damage had yet been done, that

Jno Todd was with a party some whare [sic] in that part of the
Cuntrey [sic]; that if we could find him we should be strong
Enough to Return to the River; but this was uncertain. As several
of our party was much fatigued, we agreed that my self and two
others should proced [sic] to Harrods Town for the proposed
party; that Mr Jones and the Rest should Remain in that neighborhood untill [sic] our Return. In a short time after I had set out,
Col Todd arrived at the same place and after some consultation
concluded that they ware able to go to the River and bring on the
amunition & other stores and accordingly set out with Ten men
and between the Blue Lick and the River on 25 Dec'r met the Indians on our Trail and got totally routed. Mr Jones was killed and
three others got killed and taken prisoners.[39]

Chief Pluggy and his warriors were the attackers. They had not quit
Kentucky after the first encounter. Following the deaths of John Gabriel
Jones and others, John Todd and his men retreated to the nearest settlement, McClelland's Fort at Royal Springs, about thirty miles away at the
present site of Georgetown. It is very likely that the Kentuckians had
horses and that the Indians were on foot, an advantage that gave the white
men time to prepare for the next attack.

On December 29, the Indians, said to number fifty warriors, attacked
this small fort situated near this well-known spring. The appearance of this
place more closely resembled a creek flowing from a cave than a normal
spring. The water afterward did form a creek, which emptied into the
nearby Elkhorn.

During this battle Chief Pluggy was killed. Inside the fort John Mc-
Clelland and Charles White were mortally wounded; Robert Todd and Edward Worthington also received gunshot wounds but recovered. Although
the Indians came out slightly ahead during this encounter, the loss of their
leader persuaded the others to retreat. They were wise enough to know that
they were at a disadvantage during the siege, as mounted white reinforcements could ride up and attack their flank or rear. Though the Virginians
outnumbered the Indians then in Kentucky, everyone was aware that a
unified effort on the part of the Northern tribes could change things almost overnight.

And they did. The Shawnee temporarily retreated, but throughout
1777, the year of the "Bloody Sevens," Kentucky raged with war.

CHAPTER 3

1777
The War Continues

THE SETTLERS AT MCCLELLAND'S FORT WAITED INSIDE THE WALLS FOR several days, cautiously hoping the Indians had gone. About the same time, George Rogers Clark and his guide Simon Kenton had reached Harrodsburg and recruited what they believed to be sufficient militiamen to retrieve the kegs containing 500 pounds of powder. The force consisted of Simon Kenton, James Harrod, Silas Harlin, Isaac Hite, Benjamin Linn, Samuel Moore, Leonard Helm, Jacob Sodowsky, Andrew Francis, William McConnell, and about twenty-five others. They left Harrodsburg on the second of January, but the records do not reveal whether they proceeded to McClelland's Station before they recovered the powder. According to Simon Kenton, "at the Blue Lick the Company separated—some went the upper road [and] the rest went the road leading to the head of Lawrences creek & the road was then well known to the Company by that name."[1]

Within a short time and without incident, the men reclaimed the powder and returned to McClelland's Station. On January 6 John McClelland died of his wounds, and about three weeks later, on January 30, George Rogers Clark escorted the widows, the orphans, and the remaining able-bodied militiamen from McClelland's Station to Harrodsburg "because of threatened Indian attack and to strengthen the remaining posts."

At this low ebb, Boonesborough and Harrodsburg were the only remaining Western outposts in Virginia. Benjamin Logan and his friends had temporarily abandoned their little settlement at St. Asaph and moved to Harrodsburg, but whenever they were able, Logan and his neighbors resumed work on a little fort that they hoped to occupy in the spring. The distance between Harrodsburg and St. Asaph was over twenty miles (about a five-hour walk), but Logan and his companions were determined to live near their preemptions.

In the East, after a successful campaign in New Jersey, General Washington's troops wintered in Morristown. Their British opponents were satisfied to wait in New York until spring before continuing their campaign. Gen. William Howe diverted himself in feasting, gaming, and banqueting as well as in dalliances with his mistress, Mrs. Joshua Loring.[2]

In March 1777, the council of Virginia voted to send an expedition into the Indian country and destroy Pluggy's town, but George Morgan, whom Congress had appointed Indian agent for the Middle Department, feared that such a campaign might escalate into a general Indian war. He convinced Congress that for the present it would be best to restrain Virginia. As a result, the proposed campaign was called off.[3] On June 1, 1777, Congress appointed Brig. Gen. Edward Hand to lead the defense of the upper Ohio. But before Hand arrived at Fort Pitt, the British government had instructed Henry Hamilton, its lieutenant governor and commandant at Detroit, to hold a grand council of all the Indians north of the Ohio. His purpose was to induce them to abandon their neutrality and declare war on the Americans. In retrospect, it is doubtful that this council was necessary since many of the Northern Indians were already on the warpath.

The Virginia frontier was protected by a number of isolated outposts, many of which were too small to withstand a prolonged siege. The fort at Pittsburgh was the key to the northern frontier. Farther down the Ohio were small outposts at Wheeling, Grave Creek, and Point Pleasant, the last fort on the river. The fort at Long Island was the main outpost on Virginia's southern frontier. Two hundred and sixty miles southwest of Point Pleasant lay Virginia's most exposed frontier outpost, Harrodsburg.

In Kentucky, Benjamin Logan and some of his friends left Harrodsburg in February to occupy the little fort they had constructed at St. Asaph. This fort was about 150 feet long by 90 feet wide. It had blockhouses at three corners and a cabin at the fourth. There were three cabins along the north side, occupied by the families of Benjamin Logan, George Clark, and Benjamin Pettit. Three more cabins lined the south wall, occupied by the families of William Whitley, William Manifee, and James Mason. Nine single men occupied another cabin and the blockhouses. Among them were James Craig, Azariah Davis, Burr Harrison, William Hudson, John King, William May, John Martin, and a free mulatto named

Daniel Hawkins.[4] Two of the wives, Jane Manifee and Esther Whitley, were very proficient with rifles and could outshoot most of the men. Thus one might say that Logan's Fort contained "seventeen guns." The fort was built on a little hill about fifty yards west of the St. Asaph spring. A ditch covered with puncheons and dirt ran from the fort to the spring, so that water could be obtained safely during a siege. After McClelland's Station was abandoned in January, Kentucky County had been reduced to two settlements, Boonesborough and Harrodsburg. Logan's Fort increased the number to three again.

On January 31, 1777, Fincastle County, Virginia, ceased to exist. In its place were now three new frontier counties, Montgomery, Washington, and Kentucky. The northern part of Augusta was divided into Ohio, Monongalia, and Yohogania Counties, the latter overlapping Washington and Westmoreland Counties, Pennsylvania. David Rogers was appointed the county lieutenant of Ohio, John Campbell county lieutenant of Yohogania, and Zackquill Morgan county lieutenant of Monongalia. William Fleming, still recovering from his wounds received at the battle of Point Pleasant, continued as the county lieutenant of the unaltered Botetourt County.

The newly appointed officers for Kentucky County were David Robinson, county lieutenant; Benjamin Logan, sheriff; and George May (the brother of John and William May), surveyor. Justices of the peace included George Rogers Clark, Isaac Hite, and Robert Todd. The militia commissions for the new county arrived on March 5, naming John Bowman colonel; George Rogers Clark major; and Daniel Boone, James Harrod, Benjamin Logan, and John Todd captains.

The following day, March 6, 1777, James Ray, William Coomes, and Thomas Shores made a sortie to Shawnee Springs, about four miles northeast of Harrodsburg, to clear land for Ray's stepfather, Hugh McGary. After working several hours, Ray and Shores left their chopping to visit a nearby camp where James Ray's brother, William, along with William Coomes, was making sugar. Here a party of about seventy Indians under the command of Black Fish rushed the sap drinkers, killing and scalping William Ray and capturing Thomas Shores. James Ray escaped "by his uncommon fleetness," and Coomes managed to slip away undetected. Black Fish later said that a boy at Harrodsburg outran all his warriors. When Ray reached the fort, he reported seeing forty-seven Indians. He had run about four miles, chased most of the way by Indians. Coomes hid in a treetop and watched the "Indians [*sic*] wild orgies over the dead body of Wm. Ray and around their captive." Shores, the captive, eventually joined the British at Detroit and never returned to the United States.[5]

After James Ray sounded the alarm, the officers called their men in from the fields for a muster. The militia lined up in time to witness a violent argument between their captain, James Harrod, and Hugh McGary, the stepfather of William Ray. McGary wanted to lead the company out to the sugar camp to rescue William Ray, Thomas Shores, and William Coomes, thinking that they might all still be alive. Keeping a cool head, Captain Harrod refused and ordered the men to stay and protect the fort. A heated argument followed during which McGary raised his gun and threatened to shoot his captain unless he changed his mind. After this threat and some pleading on the part of Mrs. McGary, Harrod reconsidered. Toward evening a party of mounted men from Harrodsburg under McGary and Harrod reached the sugar camp, where they rescued William Coomes and buried William Ray.

Having discovered that Indians were in the neighborhood, the settlers at Harrodsburg finally made a serious effort to complete their fortifications—and not a day too soon. Some of the men worked all night repairing the walls and putting up sections of the stockade.[6] The next morning, March 7, the Indians attacked again. John Cowan, one of the defenders, provides an account of the attack:

> The Indians attempted to cut off from the fort a small party of our men—a few shots exchanged. The loss on our side, some cattle killed and horses taken, and four men wounded. Their loss, one killed and scalped and several supposed wounded.[7] This attack was a little after sunrise, and a few minutes after, Thomas Wilson and his family escaped into the fort from one of the cabins built in 1774. Afterwards, the Indians burnt the cabins.[8]
>
> On the 7th inst. a small party of Indians killed and scalped Hugh Wilson near the fort, and escaped.[9]

One of the wounded, Archibald McNeal, died twelve days later. Two others, Hugh McGary and John Gass, were among those who recovered.[10] Despite the danger, the men at Harrodsburg found it necessary to leave the fort for supplies. As Clark noted in his diary, "8 [March] Brought in corn from the diff't cribs until the 18th day."[11]

Boonesborough did not escape the attention of the Indians. As previously noted, Boone and his men had started work on a new fort immediately after the rescue of the Boone and Callaway girls in 1776. The fort was not completed and occupied until winter, 1776–77. On March 7, 1777, the same day as the attack on Harrodsburg, a party of Indians, probably a detachment from Black Fish's band, appeared before Boonesborough and killed a Negro at work in the field. John Cowan later reported that he received "accounts of one man killed and another wounded."[12] Hearing this news, the people living in cabins scattered along the Kentucky River and up Otter Creek took refuge at Boonesborough. Boone was "diligent in instructing and directing his men, constantly keeping sentinels at the fort, and scouts ranging the country."[13] The messengers who delivered this news were Simon Kenton and William Myer, who appeared at Harrodsburg on March 18.

At the time of these attacks, the total population in Kentucky numbered about 250. The number of men able to defend Boonesborough on April 15 was said to be "twenty-two guns." The May population of Harrodsburg was 81 militiamen with 4 others not fit for service, 24 women, 70 children, 12 slaves, and 7 children of slaves, a total of 198.[14] Levi Todd reported only 102 men and boys able to bear arms.[15] The various Indian nations could obviously collect much greater numbers of warriors, but they had rarely been regimented or organized in a manner that favored mobilization of large armies.

Virginia law required that all free males, aged eighteen to fifty, serve in the militia, with certain exemptions such as land office registrars and clerks, millers, gunsmiths, iron and lead workers, seminary professors, keepers of public gold, tobacco inspectors, judges, congressmen, and the attorneys general. The governor exercised his authority to appoint militia officers. In Kentucky County at this time, the ranking officer was Maj. George Rogers Clark. The leaders attempted to form rifle companies consisting of thirty to fifty men, but in the frontier counties this was not always possible. The pay records show quite a few militia companies with fewer than twenty-five men in the ranks. Militiamen were required to furnish their own arms, their own clothing, and often their own food. In some cases the militia served on foot, but frequently the entire force was mounted, each man riding his own horse. When activated, the militia was a collection of civilians on temporary military duty.

The logistics of Indian warfare favored small bands of warriors that could strike the enemy quickly. They carried little food and subsisted on what could be killed and eaten during the campaign. They had only the ammunition that they could carry, and when it was gone they would head

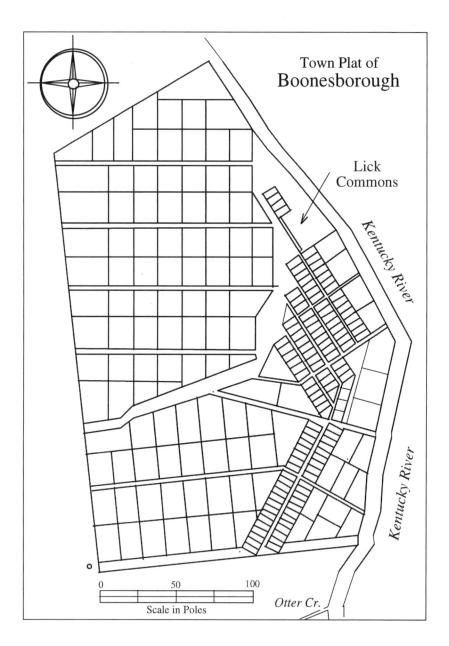

Town plat of Boonesborough.

for home. The so-called civilized armies, such as the one led earlier by General Braddock, needed roads on which their supply wagons could travel. On the frontier, the lack of a large, well-supplied force could be to their disadvantage, because the Virginians could take refuge in their forts when the main Indian force approached their vicinity. When the warriors split up into small groups to hunt or when they left to try their luck at attacking another settlement, the whites at the first settlement had an opportunity to recover and bring in supplies. But when the frontier settlements were on the defensive, the Indians had the advantage of surprise.

There are not any accurate inventories of the weapons carried by either the frontier militia or their Indian opponents. The little information we have would indicate that neither side had any standard type of weapon but that white men were frequently armed with rifles, while many of the Indians carried smoothbore trade muskets. The rifle had the advantage of being more accurate and killing men at a greater distance. Originally, this advantage was offset by a slow rate of fire. Men trained to use the standard British "Brown Bess" musket could average four shots per minute, but its .75-caliber balls would often miss a man standing only sixty yards away.

A backwoods invention made the rifle more suitable for combat and eventually established its superiority over the musket. Some unknown genius discovered that a greased patch placed over the bullet lessened the time needed to reload, and also became a gas check to utilize the full force of the exploding powder. An experienced rifleman using such a patch could fire about three rounds per minute and usually shoot the balls inside an inch target at fifty yards. If anyone wanted to fire faster with a rifle, he could load subsequent rounds using buckshot or an undersized ball. It was discovered in battle that at 100 yards only about 40 percent of the musket balls hit a man-sized target, whereas the rifle accounted for 50 percent accuracy at 300 yards.

American patch-loading also resulted in economy of ammunition. Because of the increased gas pressure, it was found that a .50-caliber, half-ounce ball was effective, while British smoothbores were made for a .75-caliber one-ounce ball. In other words, shot for shot, the rifle would kill more men at a greater distance using only half the powder and lead. Whenever the Virginians were protected by a fort, a slow rate of fire was not so important as accuracy. The men on both sides of these walls looked for concealment, and close shots were rare. But out in the open men could wait until the enemy was near, fire, and then charge, expecting to finish the battle with the bayonet or, more often on the frontier, with a knife or tomahawk. Some men found it comforting to carry a pistol into combat, and a few found the combat effectiveness of a double-barrel rifle to be ample compensation for its extra weight.

On March 9, only two days after the Indian attack on Harrodsburg, "Ebenezer Corn & Co arr[ive]d from Capt. Linn on the Mississippi."[16] That same day a messenger was sent back to the Holston settlements, no doubt requesting aid. Quite likely, another reason to communicate with the authorities back East was that Corn and his companions brought important news concerning the progress of the boat carrying the valuable load of gunpowder up the river to Pittsburgh. Three days later, Ebenezer Corn followed the messenger to the Holston.

On the twenty-eighth, about thirty or forty Indians again attacked the stragglers around Harrodsburg. This time they "killed and scalped Garrett Pendergrass, [captured and] killed Peter Flinn."[17] On April 3, an alarm was given at daylight, but no fighting took place. On the sixth, Michael Stoner made his way into the fort and reported casualties from Indian attacks as far away as Rye Cove on the Clinch River. On April 9, more warriors were reported in the vicinity of Harrodsburg.

In spite of their troubles, on April 19 the defenders at Harrodsburg self-consciously continued their civic routines, holding both an election and performing a wedding. The Kentucky settlers elected John Todd (perhaps favored because of his wounds or his profession as an attorney) and Richard Callaway as the first county representatives to the Virginia burgesses. On election day, James Barry married Widow Wilson, whose husband, Hugh Wilson, had been killed on March 7. The widow's mourning was not long. It should not be thought, however, that her remarriage was evidence of indifference about the loss of her first husband. In this pioneer community, men outnumbered available women over three to one. Naturally, a widow with small children had a very real need for a husband's protection and support. A man's sympathy for her helpless condition often won reciprocal affection. In any event, early remarriages were common.

On April 24, the Boonesborough defenders, numbering only twenty-two riflemen, fought off an attack despite a successful maneuver by the Indians to draw the garrison out of the fort. In the ensuing free-for-all, Daniel Boone, Isaac Hite, John Todd, and Michael Stoner were wounded. Daniel Goodman was cut off, tomahawked, and scalped before Simon Kenton, from the fort gate, managed to kill the offending Indian. On this occasion Kenton is said to have managed to save the life of Boone by carrying him

Simon Kenton rescues Daniel Boone. OUR PIONEER HEROES AND THEIR DARING DEEDS, D. M. KELLEY.
H. W. KELLEY PUBLISHER, 1854

into the fort.[18] Kenton then traveled to Harrodsburg to report this attack, arriving there on the thirtieth.

Even with 40 to 100 Indians at Boonesborough, Harrodsburg was not safe, as evidenced by John Cowan's report of activities on the twenty-fifth.

> Fresh signs of Indians seen at 2 o'clock. They were heard imitating owls, turkeys, &c. At 4 [o'clock a] sentry spied one and shot at three at 10 o'clock. [April] 28th—Indians seen within 200 yards of the fort—party went out, but nothing done. [April] 29th. The Indians attacked the fort and killed Ensign [Francis] McConnell.[19]

This was the same man who had made an improvement on Mary Frazier's military survey near the big pond, a few miles west of the Lexington spring.

The Indian offensive extended to the upper Ohio. On April 6 a man was killed on Raccoon Creek, twenty-five miles from Pittsburgh, another at Wheeling. Farther south, at the old plantation of Shadrach Muchmore, a couple and their four children were "burned to cinders."[20]

Early in May, Gen. John Burgoyne arrived at Quebec to lead a British force down Lake Champlain and the Hudson River to separate the New England colonies from the Middle and Southern colonies. His army contained 3,724 British infantry, 3,016 German mercenary troops, 247 artillerymen, plus Canadians and Indians. With a little aid from Gen. William Howe in New York, Burgoyne thought he could easily accomplish his goal. Howe, however, was making other plans, namely to capture the American capital, Philadelphia. This initiative forced Burgoyne to proceed on his own.

At the same time, Lt. William Linn, accompanied by fifty-three men, slowly made his way along the upper Ohio with the 9,000 pounds of gunpowder. As unlikely as it seems, he had managed to pass north of the besieged Kentucky forts without any problems. Early in the year Governor Henry became concerned about their safety. Col. Dorsey Penticost instructed Capt. William Harrod to send Lt. Nathan Hammond and En. Andrew Steel with a small party down the Ohio to find Linn and his men. If they did not find him by the time they reached Kentucky, they were authorized to go to Harrodsburg. How far Hammond and his men traveled is unknown, but this cargo was eventually unloaded at Fort Henry (Wheeling) in May.

Back in Kentucky County, Virginia, the situation was no better in May than it had been in March and April. Defenders at Fort Harrod observed scattered parties of Indians on May 1, 4, and 6. From a distance of 200 yards, they fired at them without hitting anyone. On May 12 Squire Boone and Jared Cowan slipped into the fort, having arrived from the old settlement.[21] Again on the sixteenth and eighteenth, Indians were both seen and heard. Also on the eighteenth, Hugh McGary and John Haggin were appointed messengers and sent to Fort Pitt. Five days later, the new legislators, John Todd and Richard Callaway, assembled a small party and left for Williamsburg. Apparently Todd's wounds had healed sufficiently for him to travel.

Benjamin Linn and James Francis Moore also left the Kentucky country at this time, setting out for the Mississippi. Major Clark assigned them the duty to act as spies in hopes of learning the enemy's strength in Illinois. He directed them to go as hunters who had come to dispose of some beaver skins. This was Clark's first step in preparing for an expedition to wrest the country north of the Ohio from the British. In view of the desperate straits of the pioneers at this time, it seems amazing that he should have considered so bold an offensive feasible.

About the third week in May, Black Fish assembled most of his warriors near Boonesborough. On the twenty-third, he attacked for the third time in three months. For three days, the Indians kept up a heavy barrage, wounding three of the twenty-one defenders. They unsuccessfully tried to set fire to the fort. Ingeniously, one of the men converted an old musket into a water gun, which was used to extinguish the flaming arrows whenever one lodged in a wall or roof. The men at St. Asaph knew what was taking place at Boonesborough, because one of their scouts, John Kennedy, had seen the battle from a distance. George Rogers Clark described the attack in writing:

> A large party of Indians attacked Boonsborough Forts [*sic*][,]
> kept a warm Fire until 11 Oclock at Night[,] began it the next
> Morning[,] & kept a Warm Fire until Midnight[,] attempting several Times to burn the Fort—3 of our men were wounded, not
> mortally[.] The Enemy suffered considerably.[22]

On Sunday, May 25, the warriors abandoned their siege of Boonesborough and moved on to St. Asaph, where they attacked on Tuesday morning, May 27.[23] The fifteen men at Logan's new little fort were prepared for them. This attack continued for several days without any casualties in the fort. On May 30, no Indians being seen, the defenders assumed that they had withdrawn. Several cows remained outside the walls. Since milk was needed, Ann Logan, Esther Whitley, and a Negro woman left the protection of the fort accompanied by a guard of four men. They had gone only a short distance when they discovered that they had walked into a trap. The Indians appeared from their hiding places and opened fire. William Hudson was shot in the head and killed, Burr Harrison badly wounded, and John Kennedy wounded by four musket balls. James Craig, the remaining guard, managed to escort the women and the wounded Kennedy to the fort. The firing continued for most of the morning.

From inside the fort, the defenders watched the Indians scalp Hudson. Fortunately, Harrison had fallen in a clearing closer to the fort walls, and the Indians were fearful of approaching his body during the day. Watching him closely, the men in the fort discerned that he was still alive but could not move. Benjamin Logan decided it was necessary to bring him into the fort before dark, and so at twilight he crawled outside the fort, pushing a large bag of wool in front of him as a shield. By this means he managed to reach Harrison unharmed. Logan then threw Harrison on his back and raced for the gate. The Indians were not alert, and he managed to reach the gate before the first shot was fired. It missed, and before the second Indian could fire, both men were safely inside.

After killing most of the settlers' livestock, the Indians finally departed on June 1. The size of the attacking force was estimated at fifty-two warriors. Reports indicated that one of the Indians had been shot in the leg. Burr Harrison died of his wound about two weeks later, but Kennedy recovered.

Though Black Fish moved his main force to Boonesborough and then to Logan's, he left a few men behind at Harrodsburg to harass the settlers there. On May 25 one man returning to the fort was suddenly confronted by an Indian. At a distance of only forty yards, the Indian raised his rifle and took aim. Fortunately, the gun snapped without firing, saving the man's life. The next day a party was organized to hunt down the Indian, a foray that resulted in Squire Boone being wounded.

Although a hundred Indians or so ranged about the neighborhood, the settlers at the different forts managed to stay in touch. John Cowan kept a record of the events:

> 27th [May] Alarms this morning. Express arrived from Logan's and informed us that Boone's Fort was attacked on Friday morning last and a brisk firing kept up until Sunday morning when they left the place. . . . June 2d, Indians seen at different places today. 4th—Express arrived from Logan's and says that the Indians attacked that place . . . 5th, Express returned from Boonesborough and says that Tuesday last they went within $1^1/_2$ miles of the fort, and found a large body of Indians there and thought not fit to attempt going in.[24]

Traveling between the forts was dangerous and required skilled woodsmen. Using the trails or buffalo roads, they traveled about twenty miles from Harrodsburg to Logan's, and from Logan's to Boonesborough about forty miles farther. This trail crossed Dick's (later Dix) River and Paint Lick and Silver Creeks, to the headwaters of Otter Creek, then down Otter Creek to the Kentucky River. Using another, shorter, less traveled route, one could go from Harrodsburg to Boonesborough by way of the Shawnee Springs, crossing the Kentucky River, Jessamine, Hickman, and Boone Creeks, and the Kentucky River again, a distance of forty miles. When Indians were about, these trails were too dangerous to travel. Avoiding trails and going through the woods lengthened the distances. Of course, some of the men making the trip, especially those referred to as the express, went on horseback.

On June 5 Capt. James Harrod and a companion set out for the Holston settlements. The following day they passed through St. Asaph and were joined by Benjamin Logan. The Kentuckians desperately needed supplies, especially powder. It is likely that Harrod intended to enlist aid from the militia on the Holston. In March, the Virginia council had authorized 100 men from Botetourt and Montgomery Counties to assist the Kentucky settlers or to escort them back to the Holston if the Indian force was too numerous. When John Todd reached Williamsburg in June, he presented a petition to the legislature on behalf of the inhabitants of Kentucky County, asking Virginia to recruit and send 150 men more, above the 100 men already ordered to be mobilized for their protection. The legislature agreed and authorized him to recruit these men, and if unable to get sufficient volunteers, to apply to the county lieutenants of adjacent counties for the additional men from their militia units.

Col. John Bowman, the absent ranking officer of the Kentucky County militia, was to be in command, and he was already organizing the men for the expedition. Logan returned alone by June 25, making the long and difficult trip of about 488 miles in nineteen days or less![25] News that reinforcements were on the way encouraged the other settlers, who were still suffering from the presence of the Indians.

On June 20 it was reported from Kentucky that "Daniel Lyon, who parted with Glenn and Lard on Green River to go to Logan's fort, had not come in yet. A part of a leather hunting-shirt was found. It was thought to be his. Indians seen today, and much sign."[26] On the twenty-second the Indians killed Barney Stagner, brutally cutting off his head. He had taken his horse out of the fort to graze and had frequently been warned not to venture so far from the walls. That same day the spies that had been sent to Kaskaskia returned and reported to Maj. George Rogers Clark on the number of British troops at that station.

On July 6, 1777, a buffalo bull walked up to the fort with the cattle and was immediately slaughtered, the meat probably being used two days later to feed the wedding guests attending the marriage of Lt. William Linn and his bride. According to George Rogers Clark, there was "great merriment" that day. On the eleventh, Capt. Harrod returned, reporting that Colonel Bowman and his companies were on the road and would soon reach Kentucky. During the next two days, the men reaped wheat, the first ever sown in Harrodsburg. It was raised to the west of the fort in a field of not more than four acres. On the sixteenth, Harrod took a company of men from the fort to meet the colonel and "inform him of the state of the fort."[27] On the twenty-sixth, Harrod returned again and reported that he had left Bowman at the road forks, presumably at Hazel Patch, and Bowman was headed by that road to Boonesborough. On the same day Hugh McGary and John Haggin returned from their trip to Pittsburgh and reported that there was no prospect of peace with the Indians.

While marching to the besieged Kentucky outposts, Bowman instructed some of his company to take the other road fork, the one leading to Logan's Station. As John Cowan reported, this proved to be a mistake:

> Express arrived from Logan's and says six young men, part of Col. Bowman's company who had left him, were attacked on Monday going to Logan's, that Andrew Gressom [Grayson] was killed and scalped, Jonas Mannifee [*sic*] and Sam'l Ingram wounded, but not mortally.[28]

These Indians had been hiding along the road leading east from Logan's Station, hoping to waylay some travelers. William Whitley and some of the others at the station had been out gathering corn nearby and heard the gunfire. After scalping Grayson, the Indians left on his body a British proclamation signed by Henry Hamilton, lieutenant governor of Quebec, then stationed at Detroit. The proclamation offered good treatment to all who deserted the American cause. Anyone willing to serve the British until the end of the "rebellion" was promised 200 acres of land. The Kentuckians soon had revenge, as they "Surrounded 10 or 12 Ind[ian]s near the Fort, killed 3 and wounded others. The plunder took was sold for upwards of £70."[29]

Clark reported that Colonel Bowman arrived at Boonesborough on August 1 and at Logan's Fort on the twenty-sixth, finally reaching Harrodsburg on September 2. The county lieutenant had brought two companies, about 100 men—one commanded by Capt. Henry Pawling and the other by Capt. John Duncan. Shortly after their arrival, Duncan resigned his commission and was replaced by Isaac Ruddle.[30] Court was held immediately after John Bowman's arrival, and those holding office or militia commissions were sworn in.

Although Indians still lingered about the fort, they kept a respectful distance and did no harm. A few days later, twenty-seven men left Harrodsburg for home. They may have been Harrodsburg defenders who decided that they were no longer needed since Col. John Bowman's militia was present. They may have been some of the newly arrived militiamen whose enlistment had expired. Their identity has never been determined. If those leaving were not militiamen, then the eighty-one men present for duty in Harrod's company in May numbered only sixty in early September.

On September 11, thirty-seven men left Harrodsburg and went to Joseph Bowman's preemption for corn. Afterwards, while shelling, they were fired on by Indians. In the skirmish that ensued, the settlers held the ground until reinforced. They found two Indians dead and much blood, but the score was about even. Eli Jared was killed and six others wounded—among them Daniel Bryan, who died that night. Fortunately, this was the last Indian raid in Kentucky for the year. Capt. William Bailey Smith and forty-eight militiamen reached Boonesborough on September 13. They were followed a few days later by 150 more soldiers. The deployment of these troops show that even during this early phase of the war, the Virginia government intended actively to support its most western counties against invasion by the British and allied Indians.

On the upper Ohio, the leaders had expected an attack from the Indians. During the summer eleven companies of militia marched at Fort Henry, but by the end of August no attack had occurred, so nine of the companies returned home, leaving only two companies under the command of Capt. Samuel Mason. There was also a supply company from the Beech Bottom fort, twelve miles north of Wheeling, under Capt. Joseph Ogle. Fewer than sixty men remained on duty at Fort Henry.

After nine of the eleven companies departed, the Indians chose to attack. During the night of August 31, 1777, about 200 Wyandotte and Mingo with a few Delaware and Shawnee crossed the Ohio, concealed themselves in a cornfield, and formed two long columns extending from Wheeling Creek to the Ohio River. About sunrise on September 1, Andrew Zane, John Boyd, Samuel Tomlinson, and a Negro left the fort to search for horses. Six Indians fired upon the party and killed Boyd. Zane escaped by leaping over a cliff, which tradition insists was seventy feet high. Tomlinson and the Negro ran back to sound the alarm that brought some defenders outside the walls.

Captain Mason, believing there to be only a few Indians in the vicinity, sallied out of the fort with fourteen men. They advanced well beyond the fort before being attacked and overwhelmed by the Indians. Unaware that they were outnumbered, Captain Ogle went to their aid with a second detachment of only twelve men. His force was also nearly annihilated. Of the twenty-six men who left the fort, only three, including Captains Mason and Ogle, escaped death. For three days the Indians besieged Fort Henry, whose garrison had been reduced to thirty-three men. Though the Indians did not succeed in taking the fort, they killed all the livestock in the vicinity and burned the crops.

Several weeks after the Indians lifted their siege of Fort Henry, forty-six men under Capts. William Foreman, William Linn, and Joseph Ogle left to reconnoiter southward along the Ohio. They expected to obtain canoes at the mouth of Grave Creek but found that all the inhabitants had fled and their little fort lay in ashes. The next morning they headed back to Fort Henry. Capt. William Linn insisted on taking his men across the rough, hilly land beyond the river bottom, but Capt. William Foreman, believing the Indians would be intimidated by his large force, marched his men along the easy route through the river bottom. At McMechen's Narrows, about midway between Moundsville and Wheeling, Indians ambushed the party, killing Foreman and twenty of his men and capturing another. His defeat occurred on September 27, 1777.

In nearby Augusta County the court was attempting to establish law and order on the upper Ohio in another way. The sheriff was ordered to employ workmen to build a "Ducking Stool at the Confluence of the Ohio with the Monongohale [sic]," and two men were fined for profane oaths or swearing, one five and the other ten shillings.[31] The court also established prices to be charged at taverns—a pint of whiskey cost two shillings; a quart of beer, one shilling; a hot breakfast, one shilling, six pence; a dinner, two shillings; lodging with clean sheets, six pence per night; and feeding a horse hay or fodder, two shillings per day. Public money was also provided to build chimneys in the new courthouse and jail. Citizens were encouraged to be inoculated for smallpox, and wives of "poor soldiers in Continental service" were paid two pounds per month while their husbands were away fighting the British.

Back in Philadelphia, Congress was still working on the Articles of Confederation. Virginia had opposed the amendments that Western land would be controlled by all the colonies and instead offered her own amendment that no state shall be deprived of territory for the benefit of the United States. Strengthened by this amendment, the Articles of Confederation were finally adopted by Congress on November 15, 1777. At the time, most of the land north of the Ohio and south of the Cumberland rivers was indisputably in possession of the British and their Indian allies, so most of the Eastern delegates did not think the Western land would ever be possessed by Virginia or the other states that claimed it.

In November, Chief Cornstalk, one of the few remaining friendly Shawnee, visited Fort Randolph under a flag of truce. He came as a point of honor to notify the commandant, Captain Arbuckle, that he could no longer keep his promise, given three years earlier after his defeat at Point Pleasant, that he would keep the peace. The formal treaty promised at that time had never been enacted and he felt he could not with honor endure the suffering visited on his people. Arbuckle had some of his soldiers escort Cornstalk, his son Elinipsico, and a lesser chief named Red Hawk to a secured room. While they were in custody, word came that two white hunters had been killed by Indians. A group of enraged troops broke into the room and fired their rifles point blank into the helpless men. Cornstalk—the Shawnee who had done the most to maintain the uneasy peace, his son, and Red Hawk were gratuitously killed by the soldiers to avenge the hunters' deaths.

Most settlers feared the prospect of Shawnee retaliation for Cornstalk's death. His murder shocked Gov. Patrick Henry, who attributed Cornstalk's untimely death to a Tory conspiracy. The assembly appointed a commission to investigate the alleged conspiracy, but turned up no real justification to exonerate the wrongdoers. Col. William Fleming, the county lieutenant of Botetourt County, sent a letter on behalf of the governor to the chiefs and warriors of the Shawnee Nation in an effort to mend the ruptured peace, urging them to:

> lay down the War hatchet, and not attempt to disturb our Frontiers until you shall hear the good word from our Governor, which he will send to you by the Commissioners. [He reminds them that] [w]e are grieved, that this Accident, we mean the Murder of the Cornstalk, his Son and two more of your people [*sic*] should have been committed by Virginians; as it was an Action unworthy of the Character [of] Warriors and brave Men. But as it was done by a few hot headed rash young Men [who were] enraged on seeing the Body of one of their Officers brought to this Fort, when he [was] murdered, as they believe, by some of your People, close by the Garrison; and as Action is disapproved of by all the great Men and good People of Virginia, as well as by the Governor and his Council, we expect you will the more readily overlook it, and not attempt to revenge it on the Innocent & Helpless; especially

when you considere [*sic*] how often your hot headed young Men, contrary to your Orders, and without your knowledge have murdered and robbed many of our people on the Frontier, in times of profound Peace, without the least Provocation. There [*sic*] Murders and Robberies were overlooked and not revenged; because our great Men believed your Chief and Warriors understand that they were not committed by the Consent of your Nation.[32]

After this first real taste of war on the frontier, many began to show their Tory sympathies. In Montgomery County, Colonel Preston complained that Captain Burke and most of his company had refused to take the oath of allegiance to Virginia. Along the Holston River, Col. Thomas Lynch's zealous method of dealing with Tories added the word "lynch" to our language. Nevertheless, Tory sentiment remained strong in the South, particularly among the Scotch and Scotch-Irish.

In Kentucky, food became a critical problem. Very little corn had been planted since planting time was late April or early May. A few "volunteer" crops were discovered where kernels accidentally lost during the fall harvest had sprouted and grown to maturity. Some settlers, bragging about the fertile soil, said that such a cornfield yielded seven or eight bushels an acre. Despite this shortage, there was still plenty of wild game available, including buffalo and deer. Salt licks provided a means of preserving the meat so long as the men were able to boil the salt water to get the salt.

There were several good natural salt licks in Kentucky, the most frequently used being Drennons Lick and Bullitts Lick. In 1775 Richard Henderson had employed Michael Stoner and several others to make salt at Drennons Lick. Bullitts Lick was frequently used by the residents of Harrodsburg, and Colonel Bowman had proposed to make this lick public property. Exactly how he proposed to override the rights of Col. William Christian, who had a preemptive military survey on the property, he never explained. There was another well-known salt spring, called the Lower Blue Licks on the Licking River, located on the well-worn road between Lexington and Limestone. At this place, Daniel Boone was to suffer his worst defeats.

CHAPTER 4

1778
Winning the West

ON THE FIRST DAY OF JANUARY 1778, DANIEL BOONE LEFT BOONESBOR-ough, leading a party of about thirty men northward to the Lower Blue Licks "to make salt for the different garrisons in the country."[1] This famous salt spring was located along the north bank of the Licking River on a large buffalo trail that extended from central Kentucky to the Ohio River. Exactly why it was decided to make salt at this particular lick has never been explained. As mentioned, there were two other major salt springs in Kentucky and numerous smaller ones, including one located only a few yards outside the gate at Fort Boonesborough. The Lower Blue Licks, forty-five miles from Boonesborough, was the closest of the major salt licks, but it was about sixty-five miles from Harrodsburg. At fifty miles, Bullitts Lick was closer to Harrodsburg, but it was over eighty-five miles from Boonesborough. If both forts needed salt, Drennons Lick would have been a good choice since it was about fifty-eight miles from Harrodsburg and only sixty-five miles from Boonesborough. When the settlers had needed salt two years before, Colonel Henderson had sent Michael Stoner and some others to Drennons Lick, the only lick accessible by boat. Nevertheless, on this occasion Boone and his companions selected the Lower Blue Lick, despite the fact that it was closest to the Shawnee villages and only ten miles from Athiamiowee, the well-traveled Indian war road.[2]

The salt-making operation proceeded smoothly for about a month. There were no incidents. While some of the men cut and hauled wood, others poured the brinish water into kettles and boiled it away to obtain the salt. Since it was winter, the fires kept the men warm, so the work was hard but not unpleasant. Very likely, the salt makers constructed cabins or sheds in which to sleep at night, and hunters were designated to provide fresh meat. Near the end of the month the first load of salt was packed up and taken to Boonesborough. Then came disaster.

After a hard snow, Daniel Boone traveled out five or six miles toward Mays Lick to hunt buffalo. The animals fed on cane in the winter, and the closest cane was in that area. After killing one buffalo, he loaded about 300 to 400 pounds of meat onto his horse and started back to the Blue Lick. He had not gone far when he was spotted by some Indians, who easily overtook him and his overloaded horse.[3] Boone later wrote an account of his capture:

> On the seventh day of February, as I was hunting, to procure meat for the company, I met with a party of one hundred and two Indians, and two Frenchmen, on their march against Boonsborough [sic], that place being particularly the object of the enemy. They pursued, and took me; and brought me on the eighth day to the Licks, where twenty-seven of my party were, three of them having previously returned home with the salt. I, knowing it was impossible for them to escape, capitulated with the enemy, and, at a distance in their view, gave notice to my men of their situation, with orders not to resist, but surrender themselves captives.[4]

The Shawnee marched Boone and the other captives northward and crossed the Ohio River. Ten days later, they arrived at Old Chillicothe, the Shawnee village on the Little Miami River. On March 10, ten of the captives, including Daniel Boone, were taken to Detroit, a three-day journey. Here, in Boone's words, they were "treated by Governor Hamilton, the British commander at that post, with great humanity."[5] The British proceeded to purchase all of these captives from the Indians, except for Daniel Boone, whom the Indians were reluctant to sell. Finding Boone could not be redeemed, the governor gave orders to the king's commissary to furnish Captain Boone with a horse, saddle, bridle, and blanket, and also with a quantity of Indian silver trinkets to use among the Indians as currency. The horse furnished was "a poney" [sic].[6] Boone himself later described his predicament:

During our travels, the Indians entertained me well; and their affection for me was so great, that they utterly refused to leave me there with the others, although the Governor offered them one hundred pounds Sterling for me, on purpose to give me a parole to go home. Several English gentlemen there, being sensible of my adverse fortune, and touched with human sympathy, generously offered a friendly supply for my wants, which I refused, with many thanks for their kindness; adding, that I never expected it would be in my power to recompense such unmerited generosity.[7]

Thus Boone returned with the Indians to Old Chillicothe, where he was adopted as a son by Chief Black Fish.

In February 1778, Gen. Edward Hand, upriver from the Kentucky country, decided to take the offensive. He set out from Pittsburgh with some 500 men, mostly Pennsylvanians, to capture a British powder magazine at the mouth of the Cuyahoga River. Finding the Beaver River flooded, he deviated from his original intent and ended the expedition by raiding two Delaware towns. The expedition bore little fruit. Three Indians were killed—a man, a woman, and a boy—and two squaws were captured. Thereafter, this botched expedition was contemptuously referred to as the "Squaw Campaign."

On March 28, Capt. Alexander McKee, Lt. Simon Girty, and two others, together with their servants, left Pittsburgh to join the British. McKee had been on parole to General Hand since September 1777 but was not imprisoned. Upon reaching Detroit, McKee's rank of captain was honored, and he was appointed a deputy Indian agent. Girty's defection was more of a shock than McKee's. Fluent in Indian languages, he had been frontier guide for the governor during Dunmore's War and was a friend of Simon Kenton, having once saved the frontiersman's life.

While McKee and Girty were traveling north, several veterans of Eastern Revolutionary battles decided to visit Kentucky. This group consisted of Maj. George Bedinger, Col. William Morgan and his son Ralph, Thomas Swearingen and his brother Benonni, John Taylor, John Strode, James Duncan, John Constant, Sam Dusee, and two Negro slaves owned by Swearingen. They left Berkley County, Virginia, on March 1 and proceeded overland by way of the Cumberland Gap and Boone's Trace. By this time the Indians had returned to Kentucky and were again harassing the inhabitants of Boonesborough. On April 6, a man identified as Captain Stearns left the fort at Boonesborough with a party of ten or twelve men, heading south on Boone's Trace for the Eastern settlements. About twenty or thirty Indians followed this group, while ten stayed behind to watch the fort.

Major Bedinger and party were on their way in and luckily missed the path being used by the Indians to follow Stearnes. They wandered in a thick cane patch for about half a mile before getting back to the trail. Once back on the trail, they saw signs of Indians and pushed on toward Boonesborough. At dark when they were within six miles of the fort, someone proposed that they go off the trace and sleep without fires. Col. William Morgan, who had been with Braddock, said that they needn't trouble so much since they wouldn't die till their time came. So they built a huge fire, ate, and slept. Next morning they discovered signs of an Indian party. Evidently the Indians, seeing the fire, mistook their carelessness for stratagem and avoided them. The next morning they reached Boonesborough, where they were warmly welcomed by the inhabitants.

Stearnes's party had been attacked by Indians that evening, and most of them were massacred. Jacob Stearnes, the captain's son, arrived with the news about two hours after Bedinger's party arrived. At the time there were only fifteen or twenty people in the fort, then commanded by Capt. John Holder. Next to Holder in influence at this time were Capt. David Gass and Capts. James and Samuel Estill.

George Bedinger and his companions quickly fell into the routine of the fort. The men of Boonesborough were divided into hunting squads of four or five, and his group consisted of himself, the Swearingen brothers, Ralph Morgan, and John Marveson. They would generally leave the fort at night, hunt buffalo, and return again at night with the meat. Bedinger also planted corn at William Bush's settlement on Howard Creek and, as was customary, blazed some trees to define a land claim on Muddy Creek.

Early in 1778, Indians also killed one of the Harrodsburg men. Nathan Hammond, who had first visited Kentucky as one of Captain Bullitt's party in 1773 and who was a delegate to the Boonesborough convention from Boiling Springs in 1775, was killed near his preemption claim. The nearby creek was afterward called Hammon Creek. He had served as drummer in the Harrodsburg militia company. In 1777 he had served as a lieutenant in the militia at Graves Creek under William Harrod. On April 28, in Yohogania County, Daniel Brooks was appointed as administrator of his estate.[8]

The first of the captured salt boilers to escape the Indians and reach the settlement was Andrew Johnson. He had convinced Indians that he was a fool, afraid of guns, and afraid to leave camp by himself. The Indians made sport of him and because he was small named him Pe-Cu-La, the Little Duck. In fact, he was a skilled woodsman waiting for an opportunity to escape.[9] Reaching Boonesborough, he guided a small party consisting of William Whitley, John Haggin, and others to the Indian country near Chillicothe, where they attacked some Indians at a sugar camp and stole seven horses. They routed the Indians, perhaps killing two and wounding two, and then returned safely to Boonesborough.[10]

Black Fish asked Boone who could have performed this bold act. More to annoy the Indians than really believing it, Boone responded that the culprit was Pe-Cu-La. Black Fish discounted the idea because Pe-Cu-La was a fool and could never have reached Kentucky. Boone corrected him, saying he was no fool but a fine woodsman. "Then why did you not tell me so before?" inquired Black Fish. "Because," said Boone, "you never asked me."[11] On returning to Boonesborough, he learned that Johnson had in fact organized and piloted the expedition against the sugar camps:

> It gave the Indians much concern, as unimportant as it was, it being the very first enterprise of the Kentuckians against their towns; & was the first proof to them that the captivity of the large party of salt boilers was in a fair way to result as disastrously to the Indians as advantageously to the whites.[12]

While many of the Kentucky inhabitants were being held prisoner at the Indian village, George Rogers Clark managed to recruit men for his projected invasion of Illinois. In May he left Pittsburgh with about 150 of the 350 men authorized for the campaign. He had sent Maj. William Bailey Smith to recruit 200 troops on the Holston, but the results were disappointing. In that area only part of a single proposed company, fifty men under Capt. Thomas Dillard, had been raised. Some living on the frontier were so opposed to sending men to Kentucky that on the march Clark's soldiers were threatened with prison if they did not return to defend their own communities. Coming down the Ohio, Clark did not have to worry about this problem because there were no white settlements on the river below Point Pleasant.

Not long after Clark sailed down the Ohio, on May 16, 300 Wyandot and Mingo arrived at Fort Randolph and demanded its surrender. When the temporary commander, Capt. William McKee (not a close relation to Alexander McKee) refused, the Indians proceeded to kill nearly all of the

150 cattle grazing outside the walls of the fort. As evening came on, the Indians changed their tactics, pretending that they really wanted peace. McKee then sent an Indian woman—Nonhelema, also known as Katy—outside to read the Indians a proclamation from Governor Henry stating that Virginia desired peace with the Indians. The Indians replied that they approved of the governor's message and promised to withdraw across the Ohio.

The Americans in the fort soon became aware that instead of returning home, the Indians were going up the Kanawha, presumably to attack the Greenbrier settlements. On May 18 McKee sent two men to warn the Greenbrier residents, but the Indians were on both sides of the Kanawha, so they returned to Fort Randolph. When Captain McKee called for volunteers to make the trip, John Pryor and Philip Hammon stepped forward. Pryor and Hammon were good friends who had served together in Lewis's division at the battle of Point Pleasant. Disguised as warriors, they overtook the Indian force at Meadow River, only twenty miles from Fort Donnally. They succeeded in passing the Indians without being detected and about sunset reached that little outpost on the Greenbrier frontier. The alarm was immediately sounded, settlers hastily herded into the fort, and water barrels filled in anticipation of an attack.

The Indians struck about dawn. The defenders, numbering some twenty-five men and about sixty women and children, put up a vigorous fight. About three o'clock in the afternoon Matthew Arbuckle and Samuel Lewis arrived with sixty-six men from Camp Union. Creeping up to the rear of the fort, the relief party opened a devastating fire upon the Indians, forcing them to scatter in all directions. The militia relief force then rushed into the fort. The Indians soon returned to the attack, but within a short time they lost seventeen men. This convinced the attackers that the fort could not be taken, whereupon they broke up into small parties and proceeded to raid isolated farms. The defenders of the fort lost only four men.

None of the fort's defenders gained more glory than Dick Pointer, a Negro slave belonging to Andrew Donnally. When Indians broke into the yard of the enclosure and attempted to ram the door of the house, Pointer placed large water barrels against the door. He then exerted his own strength against the Indians, keeping them out long enough for the other settlers to arm themselves.

On May 27, Col. George Rogers Clark, traveling with the current, reached the Falls of the Ohio, the present site of Louisville. He stopped and camped on an island above the falls, formerly called Dunmore's Island

The Falls of the Ohio. CAUFIELD AND SHOOK STUDIO COLLECTION

by early surveyors in honor of the colonial governor of Virginia. By the summer of 1778 Governor Dunmore had long since been in exile. Several families had accompanied the troops to Kentucky. When they planted a crop of corn adjacent to this garrison, thereafter the island was known as Corn Island. This frontier army post consisted of a single blockhouse. Originally, Clark opposed the idea of settlers traveling with his troops, but once they had reached the Falls he "now found them to be of Real Service, as they were of little expense and with the invalids would keep possession of this Little post until we should be able to Occupy the Main shore."[13]

While Clark was camped at the Falls, James Harrod married Ann Coburn McDaniel, the widow of James McDaniel, who had been killed in 1776. Ann and her young son had moved to Logan's Station soon after it was finished, as had her father. Not long after the ceremony, which was conducted by John Todd, a company of militia from St. Asaph were preparing to leave to join Clark. The Coburns and Ann joined the riflemen, making the trip to Harrodsburg without incident. Coburn soon returned for some possessions. When he was about to start back to Harrodsburg the next day, Benjamin Logan advised him to wait so he could be escorted with others. Ignoring this advice, Coburn and two companions left on their own. Reaching the mouth of Knob Lick Creek at Hanging Fork—only

*Gen. George Rogers Clark
in uniform. This portrait
was painted after his death.*
THE FILSON HISTORICAL SOCIETY,
LOUISVILLE, KENTUCKY

three miles from Logan's Station—they were ambushed. One of the men escaped and hurried back to the fort where Logan quickly called up his company of thirteen militia to pursue the Indians. They found Coburn and another man dead and scalped, the Indians gone. Logan then sent Alexander Montgomery and some others to Flat Lick where they hoped to waylay the enemy. After they waited a short while, nine Indians appeared. Montgomery's men fired on them, wounding several.

About the same time that Clark was establishing his "little post" on the Ohio, General Hamilton, the British commander of Canada, was at Detroit trying to organize an offensive against Kentucky with the hope of eventually driving the Americans out of the entire Ohio valley. No doubt Hamilton counted on Daniel Boone to play a part in this campaign. Boone is said to have slyly exhibited to Hamilton his old commission of captain from Lord Dunmore. For just such a purpose he carried this document. Showing it to the general, he promised to be friendly to the British cause. He also agreed to give up the people of Boonesborough so they could be conducted to Detroit as prisoners. It is said that Boone did this to ingratiate himself with Hamilton, who offered nearly four and a half times the usual reward for Boone.[14] Black Fish refused to accept Boone's ransom, both because of the adoption and because he wanted Boone to accompany him to Boonesborough to arrange a peaceful surrender.

Hamilton's own defenses in the West were relatively secure. Detroit, his main base, could be supplied by ships from Niagara and beyond. He had a detachment in Vincennes consisting of 250 militia, and there were three garrisons along the upper Mississippi in Illinois. Cahokia, the northernmost Mississippi post, opposite St. Louis, had a population of 300 whites and 80 Negroes. Fifty miles farther south was Prairie de Roche, a town of 200, and below that, on the north side of the Kaskaskia River was the town of Kaskaskia, with a population of over 900 people. All of the Mississippi posts had forts and militia garrisons. Most people regarded the notion that Clark could capture and hold this vast area with only 150 soldiers as preposterous.

The weakness in General Hamilton's strategy to control the West was the fact that most of the white people in the Mississippi and Wabash communities were French, and in the spring of 1778, France became America's ally in the war against Great Britain. To many of these French-speaking inhabitants of the Western territory, Clark and his men were considered liberators rather than conquerors.

As early as July 1777, the French foreign minister had proposed armed intervention against England and the formation of a Franco-Spanish-American alliance. Louis XVI gave approval , but King Charles III of Spain refused. Nevertheless, even without Spain, the French opened their ports to American privateers, and French officers, including the Marquis de Lafayette, joined the Americans. Finally, on February 6, 1778, treaties were signed that allied France with the United Colonies. Although Louisiana was now Spanish, the majority of its white citizens were French. In fact, it was the French-speaking people, including many who were friends and cousins, that inhabited both sides of the Mississippi River. Only a few Spanish lived on this river.

George Rogers Clark had established his outpost on Corn Island "to stop the desertions I knew would ensue" when the troops were told of their destination.[15] Soon after, he was joined by about sixty Kentuckians, among them presumably Capt. Thomas Dillard and his understrength company from the Holston country. Posting the troops on an island, however, proved to be an unworkable solution. Before the end of the month, some of the men from the Holston waded ashore and set off for Harrodsburg.[16] A number of the Kentucky settlers were also recruited for Clark's expedition.

Among those who joined and served under Capt. John Mongomery were Simon Kenton and William Whitley.

Col. George Rogers Clark held a unique position in Virginia. He was authorized to command a "regular" Virginia army. His force was not part of the Continental army commanded by Gen. George Washington, nor was it part of the county militia organization. Clark could not call up troops from the militia but could request them from any of the county lieutenants. His troops were recruited from the Virginia population, and like any regular army, they expected to be fed, clothed, and paid. They were also promised a bounty, or a bonus, if they enlisted. After the land law was passed, Clark received a land warrant for 560 acres to cover the bounty money he paid the troops.[17]

About the same time, Daniel Boone was also crossing the Ohio. He later said that he discovered that 450 Indians, "their choicest warriors, painted and armed in a fearful manner," had collected at Chillicothe, ready to march against Boonesborough. He said that he had decided to escape at the first opportunity. On June 16 he left the Indian encampment and arrived home on June 20 "after a journey of one hundred and sixty miles; during which, I had but one meal."[18]

There appears to have been little or no communication between Clark's Virginia troops at the Falls and the inhabitants of Boonesborough. On June 24, 1778, Col. George Rogers Clark mustered his little army and ran down the chute over the rapids in the Ohio. He had about 175 men without baggage "except such as would equip us in the Indian mode." The men were formed into four companies under John Montgomery, Joseph Bowman, Leonard Helm, and William Harrod. On the fourth day they reached the mouth of the Tennessee River and "landed on an Island to prepare Ourselves for a March by Land."[19] They had traveled 329 miles down the Ohio, or about 82 miles per day. Clark said they rowed day and night. Thus they averaged almost three and a half miles per hour, a reasonably good speed for such a long journey.

Unloading the boats, the little army started their 100-mile hike northward over the prairies. With provisions for only four days, they did not reach Kaskaskia until the sixth day—very hungry. Clark describes the capture of Kaskaskia in his own words:

> On the Evening of the 4th day of July we got within three miles of the Town, Kaskaskia, having a River of the same name to cross to the Town. After making ourselves ready for any thing that

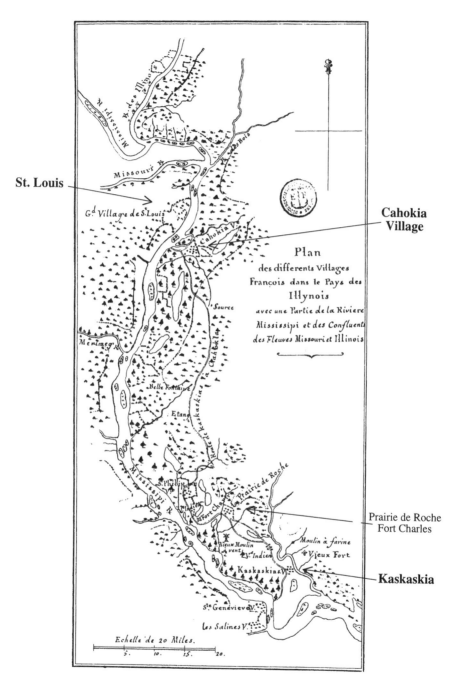

St. Louis

Cahokia Village

Prairie de Roche
Fort Charles

Kaskaskia

Map of the different French villages in the country of Illinois.

might happen, we marched after night to a Farm that was on the same side of the River about a mile above the Town, took the family Prisoners, & found plenty of Boats to Cross in; and in two hours transported ourselves to the other Shore with the Greatest silence.

I learned that they had some suspicion of being attack [*sic*] and had made some preparations, keeping out Spies, but they making no discoveries, had got off their Guard. I immediately divided my little Army into two Divisions; ordered one to surround the Town; with the other I broke into the Fort, secured the Governor, Mr. Roehbleve; in 15 minutes had every Street Secured; sent Runners through the Town ordering the People on the pane [*sic*] of Death to keep close to their houses, which they Observ'd, and before daylight had the whole disarmed.[20]

After taking Kaskaskia by force, Colonel Clark assembled all the male inhabitants and explained that he wanted them to be free. If they should choose to embrace the Americans' cause, they would enjoy all the privileges of government and have their property secured to them. Those who wished to side with the British were free to leave town. None did.

Clark then dispatched Captain Bowman and his company, augmented by a number of French volunteers to Cahokia. Arriving the next morning they were welcomed as liberators. At the same time, Simon Kenton and another man were sent to Vincennes as spies. They found it to be too well garrisoned for easy capture. When the British took over Vincennes in 1766, there were sixty families, and the fort was sadly deteriorated. The militia later made repairs and renamed it Fort Sackville. According to a census, there were 232 men, women, and children and 168 "strangers" or transits in the town. Because there was no currency at this outpost, peltry was the common medium of exchange. Recognizing that the Virginia troops were without food and greatly outnumbered by the French inhabitants along the Mississippi, Colonel Clark had to become a diplomat rather than a soldier. Instead of sending troops to Vincennes, he allowed a friendly priest and several other Frenchmen to convince the citizens to join the American cause. After learning of the capture of their friends in Illinois and the treatment they had received under Colonel Clark, the people in Vincennes acknowledged themselves to be citizens of Virginia and formed their own militia to govern the town.[21] The Virginia legislature decided that Illinois' population was sufficient for it to become a county, and appointed John Todd to be the first county lieutenant.

The Northwest Indians, consisting of the Wabash and Illinois nations, had not yet firmly allied themselves against the Americans, but they had been living peacefully with the French communities who were under the rule of the British. Impressed by Colonel Clark's easy victory, they soon made peace with the Americans.[22] Unfortunately, Clark's conquest did not influence the Shawnee and Huron, who continued to side with the British.

In Kentucky, the Indians continued to harass the settlers. In July several men were traveling toward Logan's Station when they were ambushed. William Poage was wounded and died several days later.[23] A day later, Indians fired on Benjamin Logan and some companions at the same location, wounding Hugh Leeper. When the men returned fire, the Indians disappeared. Some of Leeper's companions managed to carry him to the fort, although most of them were forced to spend the night in the woods.

While small war parties persisted in assaulting Logan's Station, the settlers at Boonesborough were awaiting a major attack by the Shawnee. Upon his return, Boone found his cabin deserted except for his cat. His wife, Rebecca, had taken the children and returned to North Carolina. He found that Boonesborough's defenses were still weak and incomplete. The news of the approach of a large body of Indians convinced the men that they needed to resume working, and they began to repair the palisades, one line of which was "almost wanting." They also strengthened gates and posterns, enlarged the upper end of the fort, and formed "double bastions." On the southeast and southwest corners, new bastions were built, the second-story walls being as high as a man's head. They lacked sufficient time, however, to finish the roof. The Henderson kitchen and the Phelps house, occupying the two river corners, also had projecting second stories.

These improvements were completed in ten days.[24] The old well inside the walls furnished only a scant supply of water, so the defenders started digging a new one. This fort "was 150 x 260 feet, the walls consisting of piles set like a corduroy road turned edgewise. At intervals along the barricade . . . were eight log cabins, the outer walls of which answered in place of the piles."[25] According to Moses Boone, there were also two free-standing cabins within the fort, one the residence of Colonel Callaway and the other Squire Boone's house and shop.

Around July 1, the defenders of Boonesborough sent a request to Logan's Station (St. Asaph) and Harrodsburg for reinforcements. About fifteen men came from Logan under Sgt. William Manifee, and a few from Harrodsburg; Boonesborough had at the time about forty-three men. The reduction of the garrison at Harrodsburg was partially offset by the return of some men who had been in Illinois. Their three-month enlistment having expired, these Kentuckians must have felt that the situation at home required their attention. Under the leadership of William Linn, they returned to the Falls of the Ohio, where they were discharged. Linn also carried orders for the Falls settlers to move from the island to the southern shore. A new fort soon was erected to protect those who had come to the Falls with Clark, and it eventually became the headquarters of his Illinois regiment.

William Hancock, another of the captured salt boilers, escaped and arrived at Boonesborough on July 17, 1778. On the same day, Hancock and Boone gave sworn depositions, which were sent back to Arthur Campbell on the Holston. The first reads as follows:

> The deposition of William Hancock, being first on the Holy Evangelists are as followeth to wit. This deponant [sic] saith that the 5th of this instant he was in company with Twelve Frenchmen in big Chillacotha [sic] Town, at which time there was a Grand Council held with the principal Indians, from different Nations. There was considerable presents made them by the French from Detroit two of which was a Captain and an Ensign and that the [sic] informed him, they were a coming at least 200 Men strong against this Garrison. This deponent saith that the Indians informed, they should come 400 strong and offer the English Flag to the Inhabitants and if the [sic] refuse the terms they intend to batter down our Fort with their Swivels, as the [sic] are to have four sent them from Detroit, which will be conveyed up the Mawma River and taken down the great Miami to the Ohio, and thence up the Kentucky to Boonesborough. This deponent [sic] further saith that the French and Indians are intended to be round the Fort and live on our Stocks till they starve us out further this deponent [sic] saith not.[26]

Hancock also reported that the Indians had postponed their attack for three weeks because of Boone's escape. News of the proposed invasion was sent to Williamsburg. When it arrived, the government authorized the county lieutenant of Washington County, Col. Arthur Campbell, to send a

*Portrait of Daniel Boone
by Chester Harding.*
THE FILSON HISTORICAL SOCIETY,
LOUISVILLE, KENTUCKY

supply of powder and lead to Kentucky, as well as a detachment of militia, not to exceed 150 men. The orders reached Campbell on July 31, and he proposed sending two companies of militia to the aid of the Kentucky settlers. Though this relief force was to assemble at Moccasin Gap on August 15, it never materialized.

In late August, Daniel Boone organized a small raiding party and started for one of the Shawnee towns on the north side of the Ohio. As an inducement for volunteers, Boone told the men he thought they might secure a sufficient number of Indian horses and furs to pay them well for their time and trouble while rendering an essential service to the country. Richard Callaway opposed the scheme, but Boone won over those who were reluctant.[27]

The exact purpose of this expedition has always puzzled historians. Why would Boone want to leave the fort just two weeks after Hancock had reported that the attack on Boonesborough would soon be under way? Most likely Boone felt that since the Indians were assembled in Chillicothe, he could make a quick raid on Paint Creek Town, which might be nearly deserted. Of the thirty men who originally joined Boone, eleven turned back when they reached the Blue Lick. They had hoped to find the Shawnee town deserted. Within four miles of Paint Creek Town, Kenton shot two Indians who were frolicking with a horse. He killed one and wounded the other, bringing a number of other Indians into the skirmish. About thirty warriors came out of the village to meet Boone and his nineteen companions. After a brief skirmish, Boone and all the party except Kenton and Montgomery hastily retreated. Kenton and Montgomery still wanted to try to steal some horses. Boone gave an account of the expedition:

> A smart fight ensued betwixt us for some time: At length the savages gave way, and fled. We had no loss on our side: The enemy had one killed, and two wounded. We took from them three horses, and all their baggage; and being informed, by two of our number that went to their town, that the Indians had entirely evacuated it, we proceeded no further, and returned with all possible expedition to assist our garrison against the other party. We passed by them on the sixth day, and on the seventh, we arrived safe at Boonsborough [*sic*]. On the eighth, the Indian army arrived, being four hundred and forty-four in number.[28]

On their way home, Boone and his party discovered the Indian army at the Lower Blue Licks. Making a circuit to avoid them, they reached Boonesborough September 6 after an absence of about a week. On the night-and-day march back, John Holder's feet gave out, and a man named Rollins stayed behind to assist him. Though many supposed this delay would put them in the Indians' hands, both managed to make it back the following night.[29]

The fort at Boonesborough has been described as being about 240 to 260 feet long, and 180 feet deep, with the northeasterly side "60 yards" from the river.[30] There is some confusion about directions because the fort and the town common were apparently laid out about 33 degrees west of north. The common was 35 poles (about 577 feet) square, with the main road crossing the common on the southwesterly side.[31] There were three buildings side by side inside but not attached to the fort walls, these being Colonel Callaway's house, Squire Boone's gun shop, and Squire Boone's house. The well was northwest of these houses, and there was a flagpole in front of Colonel Callaway's residence. The treaty was parleyed directly in front of the gate on the road just southeast of the lick about 60 yards from

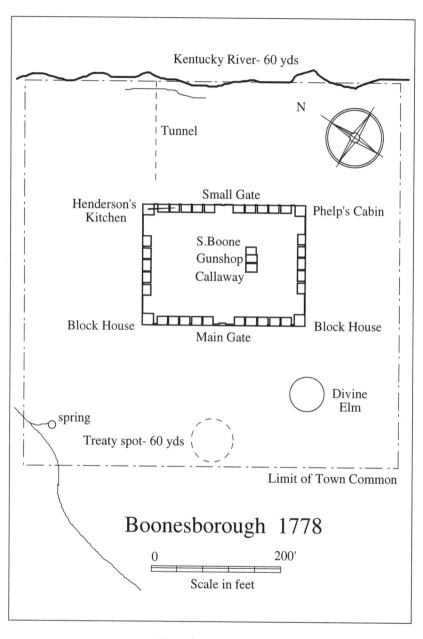

Kentucky River- 60 yds

N

Tunnel

Small Gate

Henderson's
Kitchen

Phelp's Cabin

S.Boone
Gunshop
Callaway

Block House

Block House

Main Gate

Divine
Elm

spring

Treaty spot- 60 yds

Limit of Town Common

Boonesborough 1778

0   200'

Scale in feet

Boonesborough, 1778.

the fort. Inside were blockhouses or "bastions" at every corner, but the ones on the southeast wall were so new that neither had a roof.[32]

Capt. Antoine Dagneaux DeQuindre led the attackers. He was accompanied by eleven other Frenchmen and a large number of Indians under various chiefs. Coming from the direction of Otter Creek, they marched along Boone's old trace as if on parade.[33] When they reached the front of the fort, Pompey, a former slave who lived with the Indians, came forward and asked for Boone, saying Black Fish wished to see him and that he had letters from Lieutenant Governor Hamilton. Boone and one or two others left the fort and met with Black Fish at a stump about sixty yards from the gate.

Much has been written about the lengthy conferences between the fort's leaders and the Indians. Offering generous terms, Black Fish apparently expected Daniel Boone to surrender the fort. John Bowman said that the Virginians believed the Indians were sincere in their offer of "Terms of Peace," particularly because the tribes in Illinois had made peace with Clark.[34] Boone is said to have informed the chief that he was no longer the leader of the fort, being outranked by Major Smith. Adopting the tactic of delay, he requested and received two days in which to consider the offer. On the second day, eight of the leading men emerged from the protective walls. They walked out to the little salt lick in front of the fort to confer with the Indians. John Bowman gave the following account:

> Black fish Made a long Speech, then gave the word go, Instantly a Signal Gun [was] fired and the Indians fastned [sic] on the Eight Men to take them off, the white People began to Dispute the Matter, tho unarm'd, and Broke Loose from the Indians, though thir [sic] being two and three Indians to one White man, and in Runing [sic] the above Distance [80 yards] upwa'ds of 200 Guns fired from Each Side and Every Man Escapted [sic] but Squire Boone, who was Badley wounded though not Mortol and got Safe to the fort.[35]

George Bedinger was told that "it was old John South that was wounded in the heel at breaking up of the conference."[36] Daniel Boone also received a minor wound after being struck with a tomahawk.

According to Boone, he and the others agreed to the conference based on the Indians' peaceful overtures:

[I]f nine of us would come out, and treat with them, they would immediately withdraw their forces from our walls, and return home peaceably. This sounded grateful in our ears; and we agreed to the proposal. . . . In this situation the articles were formally agreed to, and signed; and the Indians told us it was customary with them, on such occasions, for two Indians to shake hands with every white-man in the treaty, as an evidence of entire friendship. We agreed to this also.[37]

At this point, the scuffle began, and the Boonesborough men were very lucky to make it back to the fort. Outnumbered as they were, one would think the Indians would have caught a few or certainly shot down most of them as they sprinted toward the gate. Daniel Trabue, a witness, says there were 75 men in the fort and 1,000 Indians outside. His estimate regarding the size of the attacking force was obviously exaggerated. As mentioned, Boone said there were 440 Indians and 12 Frenchmen; Bowman said 330 Indians and 8 Frenchmen. In any event, the riflemen behind the walls must have provided a very effective barrage that sent the Indians scurrying for cover.

It is argued that Boone or Henderson could have chosen a safer place to build the fort. Had the Indians been equipped with modern firearms, this criticism would hold more validity. Under the best conditions, however, the closest point from which a person could shoot over the twelve-foot wall was about 240 yards away on the opposite side of the river. From the fort to the top of the hill on the western side is about 500 yards. Although the rifles at the time might carry that distance, few riflemen were skillful enough to kill a man at that range. Muskets, such as were carried by British soldiers and many of the Indians, were not effective beyond 100 yards. Indians shooting at the fort from the hillsides would also have had the problem of finding a clear place in which to sight through the thick upper branches of the trees in front of them. One must also remember that if they cut down trees on the hillside for a clear shot at the settlers in the fort, they would at the same time expose themselves to enemy fire from within its walls.

For this reason, most of the attackers apparently stayed on the west side of the Kentucky River and found firing positions at more modest distances. Surrounding trees and bushes that had not been cut down, including the "divine elm" that had been used for the first Boonesborough convention in

1775, afforded shooting screens for the Indians. Some Indians climbed into trees to get a better view of the fort. There was also an abrupt clay bank skirting the Lick Branch next to the fort, about six feet high, that afforded ample concealment for the Indians. It extended almost from the Indian encampment and circled around the fort to the north. The bank of the Kentucky River also furnished a place for shelter from the rifles of the fort's marksmen.[38]

Putting their characteristic caution aside, the Indians rushed the fort on the afternoon of Wednesday, September 9, 1778—to no avail. After some losses, they contented themselves with potting away at the fort from cover, being well supplied with ammunition. Once the firing began, it continued for nine days. Several unusual events occurred during this siege, including the use of a homemade cannon, an attempt to undermine the walls, and the successful effort to kill a particular enemy.

The cannon is said to have been made by Squire Boone by augering a hole in a gum log and wrapping the log with metal straps like those used for wagon wheel tires. Common sense would dictate that the bore was no more than three or four inches in diameter and the log no longer than about six or seven feet. One would further assume that this cannon was mounted on some type of wooden cradle. Daniel Boone is said to have opened a hole in the pickets large enough for a gun port.[39] One source claims the cannon was loaded with twenty or thirty one-ounce balls, but this may be a ballistic exaggeration. In any event, on one of the early days of the siege, the cannon was loaded with grapeshot and fired at a concentration of Indians, perhaps wounding one or two. The second time this weapon was fired the wooden barrel split, rendering it useless. With Squire Boone out of action with his wound, Richard Callaway had taken charge of the artillery.

In his quaint language Daniel Trabue gave an account of the incident:

> [T]he indeans had agreeable assembl'd several together at a Distance. Calleway loaded his Cannon and put in 20 or 30-ounce balls and fired at the Indeans. It made a large Report equal to a Cannon. The Indians [scattered] from that place much frighted and it was thought several killed or wounded. This Cannon was fired the second time and burstd. The last time it was fired was at a grope of Indeans at a Distance and it made them skamper perdidiously. Whether they was hit with the bullits or whether it was the big loul Report it was uncertain, but one thing is a fact they never

was seen in groupes right after that time. The indians some times would hollow aloud to our men and curse them and said, "Why Don't you shoot your big gun again?" Our men Did answer them, "Go many of you together and we will shoot it, but it is not worth while to shoot at one Indean when he is runing or [dodging].[40]

The attempt to undermine the fort began at the steep riverbank, where the Indians were not visible to the fort's defenders. The defenders, however, detected the mine after spotting the water discolored from soil dumped into it. The base of the mine was at the watermark, and presumably logs were cut and installed to support the roof. Boone stated that the settlers "immediately proceeded to disappoint their design, by cutting a trench across their subterranean passage. The enemy discovering our counter-mine, by the clay we threw out of the fort, desisted from that stratagem."[41] The map by Moses Boone shows the countermine running below the cabins on the eastern side of the fort.

Some might suppose that digging a sixty-yard-long tunnel would present no problem for several hundred Indians and their French Canadian allies, but the opposite is probably the case. The likelihood that anyone in this force was a skilled miner is remote. One would also suppose that the diggers had nothing more than a few basic tools, such as a few shovels and axes. Some reported that the Indians' only tool was a wood pole sharpened at the end. The sandy soil along the river would require that the tunnel roof be supported. A single cubic foot of earth weighs about 100 pounds, so removing the excavated soil would soon become a major problem. Every foot of excavation in a tunnel four feet wide by five feet high would require removing about a ton of earth and carrying it to the river. Thus to excavate a small tunnel sixty yards long would require moving about 360,000 pounds (180 tons) of material—no small job for the labor force available.

Nevertheless, the defenders estimated that the Indians dug about forty yards, or about two-thirds of the way from river to the fort, before their tunnel collapsed. Since rain fell almost every night during the siege, the weather was not ideal, and the sodden earth must have aggravated the difficulties for the diggers.

The fate of the former slave, Pompey, is the other tale most often told about the siege of Boonesborough. Future historians may not even include this incident since the story most certainly has what are now called "racial overtones." Pompey was a bilingual translator for the Shawnee, probably in his late twenties to midthirties. As a captive, Daniel Boone knew him.

Boone could understand the Shawnee tongue enough to engage in an ordinary conversation, and Black Fish and several other Shawnee could understand English, but Pompey could speak the Indian language better than any of the Americans. He was very likely a slave captured from a Virginia plantation during the French and Indian War. Probably captured when young, he was raised as an Indian. He was not very well liked by the white Americans because he acted "with much pomposity."[42]

Before the attack began, he rode up to the fort on "an old pony and wanted to swap it for a gun." After the siege began, Pompey climbed a tree and sniped at the Virginians in the fort. There are different versions of the particulars of his death. Some say he was shot out of a tree and others at the mouth of the tunnel. Although his death has been attributed to five different marksmen, the most likely candidate is William Hancock, who had only recently escaped from Chillicothe. Several thought it was Daniel Boone. Others believe it more likely that William Collins fired the fatal shot. Whoever pulled the trigger, Pompey was killed on the third day of the siege.[43]

Another black man, a servant of Col. Richard Henderson by the name of London, was also killed during the siege.[44] According to tradition, he had tunneled underneath one of the cabin walls and was sniping at the Indians from a foxhole outside the fort. After dark, one of the Indians saw the muzzle blast from his rifle, aimed at the spot, and killed him. After the siege, Nathaniel Henderson sent a petition to the state assembly asking for compensation for the death of the servant. He reasoned that as the "negro was ordered by the commanding officer to take a gun, and place himself in a dangerous post, & to keep watch and fire on the Indians, which he accordingly did and was killed. That if the said negro had been suffered to remain within his cabin, he could not have been hurt."[45]

Another casualty was David Bundrin, a Dutchman who was standing near a gun port partially blocked with a stone. A bullet struck the stone, causing a piece to split off and enter the front of his skull. Rendered speechless, he lived several hours, holding his head in his hands and moaning. Not seeming to realize the gravity of the wound, his wife kept telling him it was God's blessing that the bullet didn't hit him in the eye.[46] Jemima Boone Callaway was struck in the back by a spent ball, but she was scarcely hurt at all.[47] Possibly this was one of the shots fired from the distant hills or from an Indian in one of the trees.

Before the attack the cattle were brought into the fort. For added protection, the women and children took shelter in one of the houses built in the fort yard, probably the Callaway house. When the attack began and the Indians began shooting and yelling, the dogs began barking, and the cattle started running around these centrally located buildings, causing great concern to the women and children within the houses. After several days with little or no provender to feed them, it was necessary to butcher them for food. Those few killed by Indians firing from the trees were butchered after dark. Toward the end of the siege, the cattle became gaunt from lack of water and food, conditions that did not affect the appetites of the defenders.

On September 20, 1778, the settlers at Boonesborough awoke to find that there were no Indians in the vicinity. To the relief of all, the siege had been lifted. No one was more relieved than Daniel Boone, who was determined to return to his wife in North Carolina. But before he could leave, Colonel Callaway formally accused him of conspiring with the enemy. To settle the question, a court-martial was convened to try Boonesborough's namesake. The evidence adduced in Boone's defense, however, was overwhelming. Instead of being demoted, he was soon after advanced in rank from captain to major.

During the siege of Boonesborough, which lasted from September 9 until the twentieth, Benjamin Logan was preparing for the worst at Logan's Station. The inhabitants had dug a ditch between the fort and the spring, covering it "so that water could be got in a pinch."[48] This fort was also well supplied, but Logan decided to drive in some cattle in the event that they were besieged for a protracted period. While he was herding the cattle, nine or ten Indians hiding in a cane patch fired on him. Though wounded in two or three places—one of the balls broke his right arm—Logan managed to stay on his horse. He made his escape, supporting his useless arm by holding his thumb with his teeth. Once in the fort, he was treated by Benjamin Pettit, who applied the bark of a slippery elm tree to heal the bullet wounds.

Traveling from Boonesborough, William Patton reached Logan's Station near the end of the siege. He reported that he had been outside Boonesborough when the Indians arrived there, hiding in the hills in hope of getting inside. On the night before he reached Logan's, the Indians had made a final attack on Boonesborough's palisades with torches. From the screams and hollering Patton believed with certainty that the fort had fallen. The settlers at Logan's Station had no reason not to believe him.

For his defense Logan had only twenty-four men, but he decided to send one of them, John Martin, back to the Holston settlements for aid. While the attackers at Boonesborough placed it under siege, the Indians at

Logan's Station had managed only to steal a horse and kill some cattle. They organized no general attack. A likely reason is that the entire enemy force around St. Asaph consisted of the nine or ten Indians who had wounded Benjamin Logan.

Two or three days after the siege of Boonesborough ended, Kenton and Montgomery arrived at Logan's Station. While returning from north of the Ohio with a couple of stolen horses, they had noticed a wide trail made by Indians heading toward Boonesborough. For this reason, they avoided it and went on to Logan's. Arriving, they heard Patton's report that Boonesborough had fallen to the Indians. This news piqued Kenton and Montgomery's curiosity. They remounted their horses and headed for Boonesborough.[49] After the scouts had left, the defenders observed men in the distance and at first thought them to be Indians. Daniel Trabue heard a woman say, "Lord, have mercy on us. Yonder they come." As the party came closer, those in the fort recognized Manifee and the other men who had been sent to reinforce Boonesborough. A few days later, Capt. Thomas Dillard arrived with a small company from Virginia, making Kentucky County even more secure.

There are no historical records to tell us what occurred at Harrodsburg at the time of the Boonesborough siege. We do know that Col. John Bowman, commander of the Kentucky militia and commander of the area's largest body of fighting men, was living there at the time. In the middle of September there were about 75 men fit for service at Boonesborough, 23 at Logan's, 25 at the Falls, and 140 at Harrodsburg. Presumably the men at Harrodsburg, like those at Logan's Fort, had prepared for the worst and stayed behind their walls to wait for the anticipated Indian attack.

In October, Simon Kenton, George Clark, and Alexander Montgomery ventured back into Indian country to steal more horses. James Trabue had expected to join this party but was dissuaded by his brother, who considered the expedition too dangerous. His advice proved to be correct. On this trip the horse thieves were overtaken by the Indians. Montgomery was killed and Kenton captured. Only Clark escaped. Kenton, after being forced to run the gauntlet, received aid from his former comrade Simon Girty, eventually escaping and returning to Kentucky.

On June 23, 1778, Congress was still deliberating on the Articles of Confederation, which had been referred to the state legislatures for approval. The thirteen states were asked to report on their decision for approval, at which time Maryland again offered an amendment to restrict the rights of colonies to keep land beyond the Appalachians. The other states voted down this proposal. Rhode Island offered a similar amendment, stating that Congress should control all land that had previously been vested in the Crown of Great Britain. Had this proposal been adopted, it would have created a bureaucratic and legal snarl, but fortunately this amendment also failed. Thereafter, New York ratified the articles with the provision that final ratification was not to be adopted until all the colonies had done likewise. The articles were approved by all except Delaware, New Jersey, Georgia, and Maryland, so for a time it seemed that there would be only nine United States instead of thirteen. Following another appeal by Congress, Georgia and New Jersey ratified the Articles, and in the following year Delaware followed suit. Final adoption was postponed until 1781, when Maryland ratified them.

As far back as 1776, several commissioners, including John May, William Russell, Thomas Madison, Hugh Innes, and Arthur Campbell, had been appointed by the Virginia legislature to conduct a hearing into the land claim of "Richard Henderson and Company."[50] Depositions were taken of various individuals, including Charles and James Robinson, who had witnessed the original treaty with the Cherokee. Finally, in November 1778, surveyors such as John Floyd and James Douglas were called to testify. After hearing their testimony, which included the information that Gov. Patrick Henry, in partnership with William Byrd and William Christian, had also attempted to purchase land from the Cherokee, the legislature declared the Transylvania claim null and void. Their decision surprised no one, since one of the first acts of the legislature had been to prohibit any and all private purchases of land from the Indians.

To compensate the proprietors for their expenses, Virginia granted the company a large tract of land on the Ohio at the mouth of the Green River. The legislature also decided that Henderson's original treaty voided the Indians' rights in that area, so there would be no problem in selling the land to settlers and others who wished to purchase property in Kentucky. Virginia leaders then began creating a system to transfer this vast public domain into private ownership. They also hoped that the money collected from the sale of land would help retire their large war debt.

At this session several of the land companies petitioned to have their surveys carried into grants, but to no avail. The representatives, however, were informed that soldiers were anxious about the state selling off all the land before the war ended, and so the legislature reserved all of the territory between the Green, Cumberland, and Ohio Rivers for their benefit.

On the Western frontier, Gen. Lachlan McIntosh succeeded General Hand on June 18. Congress authorized him to command the 8th Pennsylvania, the part of the 13th Virginia then in the East, and two new regiments yet to be raised. The Board of War instructed him to attack Detroit with 3,000 regulars, reinforced by 2,500 Virginia militia. Virginia leaders opposed the plan, many feeling that General Clark would be better able to capture Detroit. Thus Congress cancelled the expedition and instead voted to assemble 1,500 regulars and militia at Fort Pitt for the purpose of destroying the Indian towns. When General McIntosh proved slow in starting the expedition, Governor Henry responded to pleas of frontier leaders and authorized a punitive force of 600 men to invade the Indian country. The Virginia council cancelled this plan, however, deciding that to equip even this small force was impractical.

In October, McIntosh's army finally began its advance. It marched down the Ohio to the mouth of Beaver Creek, where the troops built a large fort known at Fort McIntosh. In November, General McIntosh, accompanied by 1,200 men, pressed on to the Tuscarawas River in the land of the Delaware and built Fort Laurens. Fort McIntosh was located on the north side of the Ohio River about twenty miles below Pittsburgh, Fort Laurens about fifty miles west of the Ohio River on the headwaters of the Tuscarawas River, south of the present town of Canton, Ohio. The latter fort penetrated well into what had always been regarded as Indian territory.

Dangerously exposed and costly to maintain, the fort from the beginning had dubious value. Probably its only value to this campaign was for a short time to distract the Indians' attention from Kentucky. It certainly did not distract the British commander of Detroit from launching an offensive.

Lt. Gov. Henry Hamilton learned of McIntosh's campaign from Capt. Henry Bird, who told him he had nothing to fear from this brief invasion. Hamilton realized that if Great Britain was to win the war in the West, a major offensive would be necessary. He hoped to recapture the outposts recently occupied by George Rogers Clark and perhaps even to establish a British fort at the mouth of the Ohio. But his first task was less ambitious. He decided that he must recapture Vincennes. Afterwards, he could move against either the fort at the Falls of the Ohio or Kaskaskia.

Detroit is about 360 miles from Vincennes. An army could reach it by traveling on Lake Erie to the Maumee River, up the Maumee to the nine-mile-long Wabash portage near present-day Fort Wayne, Indiana, and then down the Wabash River to Vincennes. To reinforce the 60 English regulars under his command, Hamilton was able to enlist 115 French militia and

Western forts and villages.

about 60 Indians. He soon acquired sufficient small boats and canoes for the expedition and started south. Navigating the rivers, he stopped at numerous Indian towns where he hoped to gain allies for a major campaign against Virginia. In fact, more Indians did join him, and eventually his force numbered over 600 men. The weather became his main obstacle. When he began the trip, there had been a drought, which made it difficult for even small boats to move along the shallow rivers. After making the portage, Colonel Hamilton paid tribute to a colony of beavers whose dam had raised the waters of the Petite River (a Wabash tributary) enough to allow passage of his bateaux. In late fall the weather changed dramatically; a succession of hard rain and snowstorms produced floods.

Finally, as Hamilton's army approached Vincennes, somewhat reduced by desertions among the Indians, it managed to surprise and capture a patrol sent out by Capt. Leonard Helm, the American commander. Only then did he discover that the man who had led the Virginians to victory in Illinois was George Rogers Clark. After receiving this intelligence, he dispatched some of his French officers and a party of Indians to capture Clark, thinking that the Americans would be lax in posting a guard in the middle of winter.

Vincennes proved an easy mark. On December 17, 1778, the British troops marched into town and aimed a cannon at the front gate. Under a flag of truce Hamilton sent an officer to demand the fort's surrender. Inside, Capt. Leonard Helm had only three soldiers under his command. Though outnumbered almost 100 to 1, Helm brazenly asked Hamilton what terms he was offering. Hamilton and Helm soon came to an understanding, and the British marched in and hoisted the Union Jack. Fort Sackville did not impress Governor Hamilton. It had miserable pickets for a wall, no well, and its defenses consisted of two iron 3-pounders (a cannon having nearly a three-inch bore) with two swivel guns in reserve. The Indians who had accompanied Hamilton, finding that the Virginians had collected a large number of horses, promptly claimed them as trophies of war and rode off.

After taking control of Vincennes, Lieutenant Governor Hamilton decided that, given the lateness in the year and the bad weather, he must discontinue his campaign against the outpost held by the Virginians. He allowed the remaining Indians to choose between going home or raiding the settlements in Kentucky, whichever suited them. Most of the French militia from Detroit marched back, leaving only a total of eighty regulars and militia to defend the fort. Hamilton had hoped to keep Clark ignorant of his movements, but Francis Virgo, a Spanish trader from St. Louis, passed through Vincennes and later informed George Rogers Clark of the situation.

At year's end, the Virginians learned not only that the British had regained control of the Wabash country but also that they obviously intended in the spring to mount an all-out attack against Illinois and Kentucky.

CHAPTER 5

1779
The Counterattacks

ONE OF THE MOST AMAZING MILITARY CAMPAIGNS IN THE REVOLUTIONARY War occurred early in 1779. On January 29 of that year the merchant Francis Virgo arrived at Kaskaskia from Vincennes. General Clark learned from him that the British lieutenant governor, Henry Hamilton, had sent all his troops home except for about eighty soldiers. Because the harsh winter had flooded creeks and rivers, Clark decided that the weather would work to his benefit for "the badness of the Roads &c as an advantage to us, as they would be more off their Guard on all Quarter."[1]

Considering his options to retake Vincennes, Clark conceived a two-pronged attack. The larger force was to approach Vincennes by land, and a smaller force under Lt. John Rogers with his company of forty-six men was to attack by water.[2] The latter was installed in a "large boat prepared and rigged, mounting two four pounders [and] six large swevels [sic]."[3] This boat, carrying extra ammunition for the campaign, set out on February 4 with orders to anchor in the Wabash River about ten leagues, or 3.3 miles, below Vincennes. Here it was to await the remainder of the army led by Clark.

In a cold rain, Clark's men marched out on February 5. The "army" consisted of two companies of about 130 men, one group under Capt. Richard McCarty and the other under Francis Charlaville.[4] Sixty of these troops were French inhabitants of Illinois, the remainder veterans of Clark's old regiment. By the evening of the seventh, they had traveled thirty miles and camped in a square for defense. Floodwaters that covered the flat country forced his men to wade. As the rain continued, these little ponds deepened and appeared more frequently. Because the small creeks were flooded, crossings at the fords were made only by raft. During the fifth day of the march the troops managed to kill some buffalo, which provided them with some much-needed fresh meat. But the rain and flooding continued. When they crossed the Little Wabash, probably west of present Olney, Illinois, the marchers were still forty miles from Vincennes.

On February 13, Maj. Joseph Bowman reported that the troops had reached the place where the Big and Little Wabash Rivers flowed within three miles of each other. They discovered, however, that the flooding had merged them into a broiling expanse of water. They camped on high ground, a newly formed island, and proceeded to build a dug-out canoe.[5] Clark said he was then only five or six miles from Vincennes and could see the hills on the opposite side of the river near the town.

After traveling over 100 miles the first week and almost in sight of their goal, his army was unable to make a quick march to Vincennes because of the flooding. Another canoe was constructed, and some men were sent downriver to find the missing bateau commanded by Captain Rogers. It was nowhere to be found. The terrain south of Vincennes is very low, not only where the Embarrass River joins the Wabash but as far down south as the mouth of the White River. Eventually, Clark's men discovered another canoe. When it was added to the two small boats, the troops were able to ferry and wade to the town. While traveling the considerable distance from Kaskaskia had taken only seven days, traveling the last twenty or thirty miles had taken ten days.

As might be expected, the arrival of Colonel Clark took the British completely by surprise. Clark later wrote a report describing his initial contact with the enemy:

> [W]e lay still to about sun down when we began our march all in order with colors flying and drums brased [sic]. After wading to the edge of the town in water breast high, we mounted the rising ground the town is built on. About 8 o'clock Lt. [John] Bayly [sic] with 14 regulars was detached to fire on the fort, while we took possession of the town, and ordered to stay till he was relieved by another party which was soon done. [We] reconnoitred about to find out a place to throw up an entrenchmen[t] [and] found one and set Capt Bomans to work. [The barricade] soon crossed the Main street about 120 yards from the fort gate.[6]

Clark's men attempted to intercept a party of twenty-five British soldiers who were scouting outside the fort, but most of them managed to sneak back inside under the cover of darkness. On the following day, Clark demanded the fort's surrender. While negotiations were going on, a party of Indians returned to Vincennes, thinking the town was still under the control of the British. Clark's report describes what happened to them:

> There came a party of Indians down the hills behind the town, who had been sent by Govr Hamilton to get some scalps and prisoners from the falls of Ohio. Our men having got news of it pursued them, killed two on the spot, wounded three, took 6 prisoners, brought them into the town; two of them proving to be white men that they took prisoner, we released them and brought the Indians to the Main Street before the fort gate, there tomahawked them and threw them into the river.[7]

Hamilton's soldiers, watching from behind their gun ports, witnessed the execution. Utterly demoralized by these summary executions, the British troops promptly surrendered after being assured that they could march home with "their arms and accoutrements." Only Governor Hamilton and men of rank were detained as prisoners. The American flag was raised, marking a key event in the British experience in North America. From that time on, the British never held land on the Mississippi or its tributaries. On February 26—the day after the formal surrender—the bateau under Lieutenant Rogers finally arrived at Vincennes.

While at Vincennes, Clark learned that the British had supplies intended for Governor Hamilton coming down the Maumee River. He needed these supplies, so he promoted Helm to captain and sent him north with part of the troops in armed boats. They managed to surprise and capture the supply boats; forty prisoners were seized along with six tons of British supplies, including liquor and much-needed clothing. For a short time, the Virginians at Vincennes had warm uniforms and were drinking brandy!

Disposing of Lt. Gov. Henry Hamilton, his prize prisoner, was Clark's next task. He decided to send him back to Williamsburg. This assignment was the duty of Capt. John Williams, who with twenty-three guards escorted twenty-seven prisoners to the Falls, departing on March 7. Forced to walk a part of the way, Hamilton was greatly displeased with his treatment. At the Falls Capt. John Rogers took over the escort. The prisoners

Clark at Vincennes.

eventually reached Williamsburg, where Gov. Thomas Jefferson ordered Hamilton put in irons and placed in a jail cell.

In some respects, capturing Vincennes proved easier than holding it. Clark found himself in charge of an army he could not feed and a loyal French militia he could not supply. Another burden was the "friendly" Indians who had lost faith in the British and decided to become American allies. They expected the same favors previously furnished, especially food, rum, war paint, and ammunition. Suffering its own shortages, Virginia was unable to supply Clark with any of these presents. In fact, Clark found it necessary to rely upon several wealthy French inhabitants to feed his troops.

Nevertheless, in the spring of 1779 Colonel Clark decided to lead an expedition against Detroit. The British were badly in need of reinforcements, and the commander complained that little hope of any assistance were to be had from either the Canadians or Indians, and that all the

*British Lt. Governor
Henry Hamilton.
Hamilton was captured
by George Rogers Clark.*
THE FILSON HISTORICAL SOCIETY,
LOUISVILLE, KENTUCKY

Canadians were rebels. Because the Americans failed to organize a campaign, the opportunity was lost.

George Rogers Clark departed from Vincennes by boat on March 20, leaving Lt. Richard Brashear in command of Fort Patrick Henry, as the stockade was then called. He had two companies numbering a total of forty men, one under Lt. John Bailey, the other under Lt. Abraham Chaplin. Capt. Leonard Helm stayed on as the overall commander of Vincennes.

At about the same time, the British suffered an unanticipated setback in another quarter. On March 21, 1779, the British Indian agent John Stuart died in Pensacola. Stuart had been agent to the Cherokee and Creek tribes for many years, and his death left a large void in the British leadership in the South. Nevertheless, his successors urged the Southern Indians to take the war to the Americans. They were encouraged by a small band of Northern Indians who had come south under Hamilton's orders to organize an uprising of all the tribes. They hoped to drive the Virginia settlers east of the Appalachian Mountains.

In early April several hundred Chickamauga Cherokee and their Tory leaders set off on a campaign against Savannah. When this news reached

Richmond, Patrick Henry ordered an expedition against the Cherokee towns, appointing Col. Evan Shelby as the leader. Shelby, whose brother Isaac was to become Kentucky's first governor, mobilized about 300 Virginia militia and secured the assistance of an additional 200 militia from North Carolina. He also enlisted the help of Col. John Montgomery, who was on his way back to Kentucky with some Virginia regulars. These men marched to Long Island on the Holston, where Daniel Boone and his road cutters had started for Kentucky just four years before. Here they acquired boats, and on April 10 they headed down the river toward the Indian towns.

The march to the Chickamauga villages required ten days. When the militia reached their objective, they encountered very little resistance since many of the warriors were elsewhere. The attackers killed a dozen Indians who had remained to defend the village, scattering the survivors. Entering the village, the troops discovered British supplies, which had been cached for the proposed offensive. After taking what they wanted, they burned the towns and returned home. Colonel Montgomery and his men then proceeded on their way north to Kentucky.

Word of the attack caused Dragging Canoe's men to return to their homes. When they arrived at their towns, they found only ashes. As might be imagined, the burning of their villages stiffened the Cherokee resolve against the Americans. Seeking revenge at every opportunity, this Cherokee faction eagerly supported the British in the South, sending small war parties northward to harass the Virginia frontier.

Clark's victories at Vincennes and the Chickamauga campaign greatly heartened the beleaguered settlers in Kentucky County. Some even decided to leave the crowded forts and establish new settlements. Prior to 1779 the only new settlements had been Irvine's and Harlin's, but changes were to come rapidly.[8] Among the first to leave Logan's Fort was the family of William Whitley, who built a station at Walnut Flat Creek, about five miles from Logan's in the direction of the Crab Orchard. Whitley selected a site along the well-traveled Kentucky Road, on a land claim he purchased from Valentine Harmon.[9] Nearby (on his own claim) he later built what has been described as the first brick house in Kentucky. Later in the year about two dozen other small stations were started, many of them by settlers hoping to solidify their land claims.

Early in the spring of 1779, a new fort was built at the Falls, this time on the mainland, traditionally located at Twelfth and Rowan Streets in what is now Louisville. This move marked the date of Clark's founding of

Louisville, named in honor of King Louis XVI of France. When it was completed, a number of the civilians moved into the new stockade with the troops. One of the new settlers at the Falls in 1779 was Squire Boone, Daniel Boone's brother. That spring he brought his family down the river from Boonesborough "in two large canoes or pirogues lashed together."[10] His son reported that he purchased some town lots in Louisville and erected a cabin on the high ground near the mouth of Beargrass Creek.[11] But Squire Boone stayed in Louisville only a short while. In the following year he gathered several families and left to start his own station at Painted Stone near the present town of Shelbyville, thirty or so miles east of Louisville.

On April 15, twenty-five militiamen under En. Robert Patterson were sent from Harrodsburg to establish a station at some suitable place across the Kentucky River. Selecting a spot on the present site of Lexington, they planted some corn, built a blockhouse, and garrisoned it. A few of the soldiers who had been in Kentucky in 1775 noticed that this fort was only about 2,000 feet farther up a branch of the Elkhorn from one of Patterson's old cabin improvements. A year later this branch was to acquire the name of Town Fork.

In April 1779, George Bryan, accompanied by his brother Joseph, his cousin Daniel, and perhaps William Jr., emigrated to Kentucky to obtain land for themselves and other members of the family, erecting a small fort at the old Bryan settlement on Elkhorn Creek. Later in the year, as more people came to Kentucky, they enlarged the fort. It soon became one of Kentucky's largest, with forty-four cabins formed in a rectangle on a little hill adjacent to Elkhorn Creek. It was set back about a hundred yards north of a large buffalo road that ran between Lexington and Limestone Landing on the Ohio River (present-day Maysville). A hunter's path led from Bryan's Station northward to Ruddle's. When William Bryan Jr. was killed near the fort, many of the Bryan family members left Kentucky and returned to North Carolina.

Benjamin Logan's fort became a convenient stopping place for people traveling to Kentucky from the Holston along Scagg's Trace. Enlarged by 1779, it was still too small to accommodate its inhabitants without crowding. For this reason, some of the residents left before the end of April to start their own stations. Isaac Ruddle led a group that resettled John Hinkston's old station, which had been abandoned in the summer of 1776.[12] About two weeks after their arrival, they were joined by Ruddle's brothers, James and George, who brought several persons from Logan's

Fort. John Martin left Logan's Fort with a third party of settlers to establish a station on the left bank of Licking River not far from Ruddle's.

In May the Virginia legislature finally passed a land law for "ascertaining the terms and manner of granting waste and unappropriated land." The first and major provision was that all of Virginia was open for settlement except for the land north of the Ohio and southwest of the Green River, running from the head of the Green River in a direct line to Cumberland Gap. Forbidding settlement in this area would accomplish two things. It would provide reserve land that in the future could be used to pay veterans of the Virginia line. There was also the possibility that if settlers were allowed in this area, the Chickasaw Indians would mobilize and go to war against Virginia. Though the Chickasaw were not at the time exactly friendly, they were not in fact causing much trouble on the frontier.

Thomas Jefferson had suggested that Western land might be given free to settlers to provide new recruits to the class of sturdy freeholders he so deeply admired. He hoped that each man could be awarded fifty acres, but the Virginia legislature decided that they were too much in debt for such generosity. At the time, the Continental Congress did not collect taxes, so it had no revenue. Costs of the war were assessed against the colonies, which were hard-pressed to supply and pay the Continental troops.

The new land law recognized the rights of settlers but did not void the rights of veterans who had military surveys made under the king's proclamation of 1763. Thus the land surveyed by John Floyd, James Douglas, Hancock Taylor, and Isaac Hite between 1774 and 1776 was finally to be legally granted to these warrant holders. Practically all of the land in the vicinity of the Falls of the Ohio and a large proportion of that in the vicinity of Lexington, especially between Frankfort and Boonesborough, were owned by the officers of the French and Indian War, their heirs, or assignees. Thousands of acres were granted to such well-known Virginia leaders as Patrick Henry, William Christian, Bartholomew and Alexander Dandridge, William Preston, Hugh Mercer, Andrew Lewis, William Madison, and even George Washington. This land law was passed by the legislature while Patrick Henry was governor but took effect when Thomas Jefferson held the office.

The new land law satisfied most of the old settlers since it simply ratified property lines and boundaries most of them already observed by custom. When their claims were approved by the commissioners, they could pay the very low price of two pounds sterling and receive a certificate for 400 acres at their place of settlement, which they could immediately enter

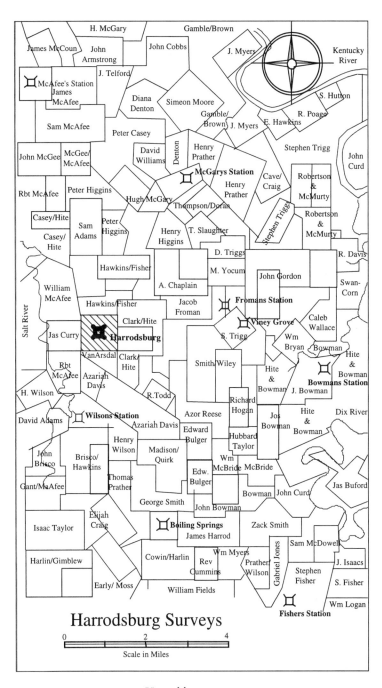

Harrodsburg Surveys

Scale in Miles

Harrodsburg surveys.

with the county surveyor. In addition, they could, if they chose, claim up to 1,000 acres adjacent to their settlements on a preemption warrant. This extra land would cost £200, still considered a reasonable fee at the time since payment was made with the inflated paper money or the equivalent in tobacco. Preemption land could not be entered until after May 1, 1780, thereby allowing those with settlement and military warrants the first choice of sites.

For a settler to qualify for the cheaper land, he had to have either raised a crop of corn or lived at the site for one year prior to 1778. If he established a settlement in 1778 or early in 1779, he could still qualify for a 400-acre tract, but the price was eighty pounds.

Those men who had come out before 1778 and marked a tract of "any waste or unappropriated lands, and built any house or hut, or made other improvements thereon" were also allowed a preemption of 1,000 acres for the price of £200. Those who had never been west, however, could purchase treasury warrants at the same price, locating their land on unclaimed sites. Those with preemptions had a slight advantage in that they were allowed to enter their claims before those men who purchased treasury warrants. It was estimated that the price of £20 per hundred acres was about the same as the old colonial price of ten shillings per hundred acres.[13] Within a few weeks after treasury warrants were first entered with the surveyors, their cost in Virginia money was raised from four shillings per acre to one pound, twelve shillings per acre, an 800 percent increase. This adjustment was made to compensate for the inflation of the paper money.

The word quickly spread throughout Virginia, Pennsylvania, and North Carolina that the commissioners intended to hold courts to hear the claims of settlers and preemptors. To facilitate what was already conceived as a potentially tangled process, the authorities divided the western counties of Virginia into four districts, and a commission (or court) was appointed by the governor to hear and determine all claims set up under this act. Many of the "outlyers" who had explored Kentucky in 1775 and 1776 rushed back with the intention of establishing claims. They searched the woods for the remains of their old unfinished cabins. If they failed to find a pen or cabin, they built another. Others thought it would be more profitable and convenient to sell their old claims, which were now bringing a fair price.

Not everyone was happy with the new land law. When William Fleming, one of the commissioners, was informed that some people in Kentucky would riot, he asked for protection from the sheriff of Kentucky and the militia while the commissioners held court in Kentucky. Although he did not mention the source of their greviences, the most likely reason was that newcomers who arrived on the frontier were given no special rights to public land, except to purchase it at the stated price, something that could also be done by rich Eastern speculators.

With the influx of new settlers, John Bowman, the ranking officer of Kentucky County, made plans for a campaign against the Northern Indians. Militia companies were assembled, and certain members were selected and made ready for the march. Early in May, the various companies assembled at the mouth of the Licking River. The largest company, which came up the Ohio from the Falls, contained ninety-six men. William Harrod served as its captain and James Patton as its lieutenant. The men in and around Boonesborough were collected by Capt. John Holder. Including Holder, they numbered fifty-eight. Benjamin Logan, with his brother John as his lieutenant, raised forty-seven men from his own and Whitley's Station. Harrodsburg sent two companies totaling seventy men, which were commanded by Silas Harlin and Levi Todd.[14]

Logan's company marched north, crossed Dick's River at the mouth of Hanging Fork, and the Kentucky just below the mouth of Hickman Creek. That night they camped at a spring in the valley of Clear Creek. The next morning they arrived at the newly founded and almost uninhabited Lexington. About twenty miles north of Lexington, they overtook the companies of Capts. John Holder and Robert Todd. Together they camped on the North Fork of Elkhorn Creek, having traveled about fifty miles in two days. Next day they marched along the Dry Ridge, the divide that separates the basin of the Kentucky from that of the Licking. They rested the next night along Mill Creek two miles north of Lees Lick, a western branch of the South Fork of Licking River. Continuing to the headwaters of Banklick Creek, they followed that stream to where it empties into the main branch of the Licking. A short march downstream brought them to the point of rendezvous. Colonel Bowman, with Harlin's company, had traveled to Martin's and Ruddle's Stations where they were joined by Lt. John Haggin and eighteen men. On May 27, Bowman's detachment joined the others at the mouth of the Licking.

With a total of 296 men Bowman crossed the Ohio on the following day. William Whitley and George Clark were selected as pilots as the march up the valley of the Little Miami began. Carrying their provisions on their backs, they marched for two days. Before dark on May 29 they stopped about ten miles from Chillicothe to eat. Because they had seen no

Indians, they assumed that their approach had not been discovered. Bowman decided to continue marching in order to surround the town before daylight and begin the attack at dawn.

About midnight the men reached a prairie to the southwest of the Indian village where Benjamin Logan deployed his company to the west of the town, between it and the Little Miami River. William Harrod stationed his men to the north and east side of the town, with his lines extended until they joined Logan's. With John Holder's men to the south, the town was completely surrounded. Bowman gave orders "not to fire a gun till day lite without we should be discovered."[15] As dawn approached, the Indian dogs discovered the Americans and began to bark. One of the Indians came out of the village to investigate, walking to within five feet of Captain Holder's line before he noticed them. As he shouted to give the alarm, Hugh Ross shot him and Jacob Stearns tomahawked him.[16]

To defend the town, the Indians had constructed a large two-story log building or council house at the center of the village. Upon hearing the shot, they quickly assembled inside this fortification. Before daylight, one group then charged the Americans but were driven back. When Bowman saw the strong fortifications at daylight, he decided that "we could not storm the place without sacrificing many a man."[17] He then ordered the militia to withdraw "a convenient distance" but to keep up the attack on the blockhouse while the men rounded up the Indians' horses. As this was going on, some of the troops entered another part of the town and started burning the empty houses.

During the withdrawal, several men, having taken positions behind an oak log about forty yards from the council house, were unintentionally left behind during the initial retreat. Seven soon lost their lives in an exchange of fire with the Indians. Running zigzag, the remaining eight reached a nearby cabin. Using some puncheons they found as protection, they safely left the combat zone.

From the council house came the loud voice of an Indian encouraging his braves, while another unceasingly beat a kettle drum. Those who heard the exhorter believed him to be Black Fish, the well-known Shawnee leader at the siege of Boonesborough. An escaped white prisoner later reported that actually the voice had belonged to one of the medicine men. Black Fish, the chief who had adopted Daniel Boone, had been seriously wounded at the outset and was unable to continue in command; he died a few weeks later.

During the attack the men captured a Negro woman, who informed them that Simon Girty and 100 Mingo Indians were in nearby Piqua. She also told them that a runner had been sent there for reinforcements. Hearing this, Colonel Bowman wisely ordered a retreat.[18] Before the day was out, the Indians had organized a counterattack. A band of Indians, that kept increasing in size, forced them to take cover and make a stand. In accordance with a prepared plan, the companies of Logan and Harrod formed the sides of a rectangle. Holder's company broke into two parts to close the ends. Lt. James Patton later wrote an account of the ensuing battle:

> We Marched about 6 miles on our Retreat and [were] Overtaken by a number of Indians which surounded us & fired on all quarters[.] [W]e had notice of their Coming and formed a line Round all our horses & plunder [and] soon were fired on in every Direction[.] Col Bowman a verry [*sic*] good Citizen but not Acquainted with Indian warfare submitted to his officers who were well Acquainted with Indian fighting; the officers ordered their men to Advance on the Indians at all quarters & we soon made them Retreat and pursued them near a mile—we killed their chief Red Hawk & wounded a number of Indians—we lost but one man killed and none wounded—we then marched in peace till we came to the mouth of Licking.[19]

Although some escaped along the way, the Kentuckians crossed the Ohio on June 1 with 163 mounts. For their efforts, each man received a share of the plunder worth £107 in Virginia deflated currency.

Colonel Bowman's attack on the Shawnee had the effect of diminishing chances of taking Detroit. Greatly cowed by the capture of Hamilton, the Northern Indians were not at all inclined to further warfare. They had been told by George Rogers Clark that the Big Knife soldiers had not come to fight them or take their lands but had wanted only a free road through their country to drive out the British. When the Virginians invaded their country and attacked their village, the Shawnee, realizing the whites could not be trusted, became more fully wedded to the British.

When news came to the Vincennes rendezvous that the 300 men Bowman promised would not appear, those assembled were disappointed. Clark reflected that disappointment in writing: "Instead of 300 men from Kentucky there appeared about 30 volunteers commanded by Capt. McGary. The loss of the Expedition [against Detroit] was too obvious to hesitate about it and it was abandoned."[20] Some of the troops remained to garrison Vincennes. Others were sent back to Kaskaskia and Cahokia under Mont-

Pencil sketch of Col. John Campbell, part owner of the land at the Falls of the Ohio. Campbell was captured by Indians, but returned after the war to claim his land.

THE FILSON HISTORICAL SOCIETY, LOUISVILLE, KENTUCKY

gomery, while Clark returned to the Falls of the Ohio with the remaining troops. Here, in accordance with an order he had sent the year before, the settlers on Corn Island had removed to the main shore where Louisville now stands and built a small fort at the west end of the proposed town surveyed by Capt. Thomas Bullitt in 1773.

In August, Lt. John Campbell, the co-owner of the property where the new "fort on the shore" was located, stopped at the Falls. Campbell probably approved of the fort location, which attracted settlers and in turn increased the value of his land.

A few weeks later, Col. David Rogers, a Virginian who had been born in Ireland, set off up the Ohio toward Pittsburgh carrying gunpowder. To protect his valuable cargo, Clark added an escort of twenty-three men under Lt. Abraham Chaplin. John Campbell also joined the party. On October 4, at the mouth of the Licking River, Rogers discovered a party of Indians. Thinking to take them by surprise, Rogers deployed his men on the Kentucky side of the Ohio. Instead, a party of Indians led by Simon Girty, in company with his brother George and British agent Matthew Elliott, ambushed them, and forty-two or so were killed, including Rogers. The Indians lost two killed and three slightly wounded. Girty, "the white renegade," later boasted that he had taken a fine brace of pistols belonging to Rogers. Among the fortunate survivors, Campbell was taken prisoner. Because he was treated well, many Americans believed he was a British sympathizer. It was well known that Campbell had been a friend and business partner of John Connolly and that the latter was a renowned Tory as well as a close confederate of the former governor Lord Dunmore. The settlers felt that only a Tory would have been spared by their enemies.[21]

In October, as provided under the land law, the Virginia land commissioners arrived at St. Asaph to hear the claims of settlers. The land court consisted of William Fleming, James Bourbor, Stephen Trigg, and Edmund Lyne. John William Jr. served as clerk. About the same time, George May, the appointed surveyor of Kentucky County, arrived and established his office at Wilson's Station, a few miles south of Harrodsburg. The arrival of the commissioners prompted numerous people to immigrate to Kentucky, either to present their claims or to search out unoccupied tracts that could be obtained with Virginia treasury warrants. A number of them had been influential in Virginia and would bring that influence to the Old Dominion's westernmost territory.

Col. James Barbour from Culpeper County had been a member of the House of Burgesses and had served for three years as a lieutenant in the Virginia Continental Line. While in Kentucky, he managed to acquire 13,500 acres of land.

William Fleming had recovered from his wounds suffered at the battle of Point Pleasant and had been active in the defense of the Botetourt County.[22] Stephen Trigg, from Dunkard Bottom on New River, married a sister of Col. William Christian; since Fleming was married to another of the sisters, they were brothers-in-law. The holder of a preemption claim on Harrods Creek, Trigg appears to have been in Kentucky in 1775. Likewise, in 1775 Colonel Fleming paid someone to come to Kentucky and make improvements for him on Beargrass Creek, adjoining the military survey of Colonel Christian, for which he obtained a preemption warrant.

Edmund Lyne, the son of William Lyne, from a distinguished Virginia family, was unmarried at the time of his appointment. Following the example of the other members of this commission, he too managed to obtain some Kentucky land, upon which he settled.

George May of Petersburg, Virginia, the surveyor, was one of several brothers who became prominent in Kentucky. They were sons of John May Jr. of Prince George County, who died in 1760, leaving nine young orphans to be reared by their mother, Agnes Smith May. George May attended William and Mary College and was thought by some to be one of the brightest young men in Virginia. His older brothers John, Richard, Stephen, and William were also very distinguished citizens. John May, who also moved to Kentucky in 1778, later became one of Kentucky's most active land speculators.[23]

John Floyd, who had been the Fincastle and Transylvania surveyor from 1774 to 1776, returned in the fall with his young wife and family. He was accompanied by several friends and relatives who were also seeking new homes in Kentucky. His first stop was Harrodsburg, where he noted the land fever prevalent there:

> The commissioners are here and I procured my certificate yesterday for 1,400 acres at Woodstock and was immediately offered six find [sic] young Virginia born negroes for it. You never saw such keeness [sic] as there is about land.[24]

The new arrivals brought horses and cattle, sleeping in tents until they completed building their new log homes on Beargrass Creek.

Most men who had explored Kentucky between 1774 and 1777 returned to claim preemptions at their "improvements," even if they had only been in Kentucky for a couple of weeks. A thousand acres around these old cabin claims could be obtained for 200 pounds, Virginia currency. But many of the early adventurers as well as some of the established settlers were involved in trading claims. Around the Harrodsburg area, land awarded to members of James Harrod's original company at their cabin claims was the exception rather than the rule. Of the thirty men who came to Kentucky with Harrod in 1774, only twelve received patents at their original improvements, the remainder having sold, traded, or abandoned the right to their original claims. Around Harrodsburg, one finds land granted to John Cowan, assignee of Silas Harlin; Silas Harlin, assignee of Andrew Gimblew; Alexander Robertson, assignee of Stephen Trigg; and Stephen Trigg, assignee of John Grayson—a succession of transfers that seldom left property in the hands of the original claimant.

Many who held old military warrants (awarded for service in the French and Indian War) also headed for Kentucky to stake claims on unoccupied land. Though some had served in the war, many others had purchased the warrants of the old veterans. They needed to find and enter a tract of land that the warrants had authorized. Rank determined the amount of land awarded for service, A private soldier, for example, was issued a warrant for

50 acres for each tour of duty, a sergeant 200 acres, a lieutenant 1,000 acres. Between 1774 and 1776, the Fincastle County surveyors had staked off 206,250 acres on military warrants, mostly in the Bluegrass and at the Falls of the Ohio, but another 272,592 acres on old military warrants was soon after entered with the Kentucky County surveyor.

Those veterans who had their land surveyed by John Floyd, Hancock Taylor, and James Douglas in 1774–76 were awarded the tracts without further effort on their part. The commissioners were furnished a list of these old surveys in order to avoid granting settlement or preemption claims on them. In spite of the obvious wording of the land law, many of the pioneers from Pennsylvania and the Monongahela area of Virginia found it difficult to believe that the old military surveys would be valid since the warrants had been issued by Lord Dunmore. Some of these "cabiners," as Floyd had called them, thought their old improvements would be superior to the military claims since these recipients had fought for the king. They were shocked to discover their error. Subsequently, many attempted to move their claims away from the old military surveys onto nearby land settled by men who had made improvements later than themselves.[25]

Many historians have assumed that most of those who came to Kentucky in the fall of 1779 and spring of 1780 were newly arrived land speculators whose intentions were to purchase the claims of the old settlers. The records indicate that some of the land claims were traded and sold, but many of the speculators were the old pioneers themselves, such as Squire Boone, Isaac Hite, and William and Francis McConnell. Some later arrivals such as Elijah, John, and Lewis Craig would, however, qualify as speculators. Members of the land commission also themselves seemed to be active participants. James Barbour acquired warrants for about 13,500 acres, William Fleming for 59,700 acres, and Stephen Trigg for 7,500 acres.

There were also the so-called absentee speculators, men who purchased warrants so that the men in the field could locate vacant tracts of land. For example, John May worked for several years in partnership with Samuel Beall, May being responsible for locating and surveying unclaimed land and Beall for supplying the land warrants. It should be remembered, however, that land speculators such as John May, living in Kentucky, were constantly exposed to the hazards of the frontier. Quite a few, including May himself, were eventually killed by Indians.

As might be expected, some applicants presented fraudulent claims, concealing the actual facts from the commissioners. For example, Isaac Taylor, who had fought with Clark in Illinois, acquired a preemption for

Indians capturing girls at Boonesborough.

building a cabin in 1774. Several individuals who arrived with Harrod that year later testified that Isaac Taylor was never in Kentucky and that the cabin upon which he based his claim was built by Silas Harlin, Taylor's brother-in-law. James Bryan, one of the founders of Bryan's Station, submitted a preemption claim for his infant son David, whom the commissioners assumed was full grown. The courts later discovered that not only was David underage, but that he had never been in Kentucky, nor had he made any improvements as required by law.[26] James Ray, the young man who had outrun the Indians in 1777 and who was soon to become an officer in the militia, also received a land grant from the commissioners, although it would appear that he was also underage. One prominent Baptist minister, Elijah Craig, credited by some with inventing Bourbon whiskey, stole a treasury warrant and fraudulently assigned it to another man, who then sold tracts to unsuspecting land seekers.[27] Several frontiersmen applied for and obtained land in both the Yohogania and the Kentucky district, thus obtaining twice as much land as the Virginia law allowed.

When it came to land acquisition, James Harrod, one of Kentucky's best-known pioneers, was not immune from skullduggery. Court records indicate that Harrod, while acting as an agent for his old companion Samuel Moore, after Moore's death fraudulently withdrew Moore's 1,000-acre preemption entry. Harrod then entered the same land in his own name on a treasury warrant and promptly sold it.[28] James Harrod, according to John May, was the most unprincipled man living and would swear to anything that was required so long as he made a profit.[29]

While the commissioners were hearing the settlers' land claims, Capt. James Shelby, the brother of Isaac Shelby, was having problems as the new commander at Vincennes. He reported that he had not received any supplies and was then without salt to cure meat that his hunters might bring into town. Until October the French occupants had furnished beef to feed the troops, but they were unable to supply any more. Shelby then suggested that the post be abandoned and requested further instructions from Colonel Clark.

By late summer, the leaders in Virginia learned that Spain, at the urging of France, had entered into the war against Great Britain in June. France in return had promised to aid in the restoration of Spanish Florida, Minorca, Gibraltar, and even Jamaica. Several patriots urged Congress to send an army southward and capture the British outposts in Florida, but Congress was unable to provide such an army. To his credit, the Spanish governor in New Orleans did not hesitate to take action. He collected a small force consisting of Spanish troops, French Creole militia, and allied Indians, quickly capturing the nearby British posts of Manchac and Natchez.

Although they continued to encourage and welcome Americans to purchase supplies in their ports, Spain did not become the ally of the United States, nor did it formally recognize the new republic until the end of the war. Congress was informed that "his Catholic Majesty deems of great importance to the interests of his crown" that Southern states should not make any conquests of lands lying on the east side of the Mississippi within the old proclamation line. Of course, this area included Kentucky, which had already been occupied by Virginians for four years. Congress rejected the request, but the Spanish government continued negotiations to establish themselves on the east side of the Mississippi.

When winter arrived at the end of 1779, Virginia citizens had the coldest weather anyone alive had ever experienced. Rivers froze solid from bank to bank, and accumulated snow did not melt. Game on the frontier became critically scarce and cattle and other livestock died in droves. Despite the severity of the winter, at first most frontier stations had adequate provisions. New settlers had brought a little corn, and hunters were out whenever weather conditions would permit. During the early part of the winter buffalo had not lost their fat, and a great many were killed. Wild turkeys could be found, but these soon became too scrawny to be of much value. Hunters managed to shoot a few bears and deer, but the supply did not last long. The cold weather kept most people, including the Indians, at home.

CHAPTER 6

✦

1780
The Land Rush

THE WAR IN THE SOUTH WAS NOT GOING WELL FOR THE AMERICANS. When the British general Henry Clinton, comfortable in his New York headquarters, received news that the French fleet had left the American coast, he decided that the time was ripe for a campaign in the Carolinas. Setting sail in December 1779, with 7,000 troops, he proceeded to Charleston, a city poorly prepared to resist an attack. Clinton landed on nearby John's Island February 11, 1780, and extended his lines to the Ashley River while the English fleet passed the forts and invested the city from the sea. Gen. Benjamin Lincoln, in charge of the American forces, made the mistake of undertaking the city's defense. In retrospect it was clear to everyone that he should have abandoned the water-locked city and maneuvered his army to defend the rest of the colony. Instead, he dug breastworks along the northwest edge of the city, using the Cooper and Ashley Rivers to guard his flanks.

On April 14, Col. Banastre Tarleton dispersed the American cavalry, which was posted north of Charleston at Monk's Corner under the command of William Washington.[1] This movement enabled Clinton to extend his lines to the neck of land between the two rivers and thus completely invest the city. General Lincoln surrendered his entire army soon after, the capitulation being signed May 12, 1780.

Content with his success at Charleston, Clinton embarked for New York, leaving Cornwallis with 4,000 men to complete the conquest of the colony. Having established sea bases at Savannah, Beaufort, Charleston,

115

and George Town, the British soon held posts in the interior at Camden and Rocky Mount on the Santee River, Cheraw Hill on the Pedee River, and Fort Ninety-Six in the backcountry.

Farther north, in Virginia and Kentucky, the severe winter brought suffering to men and animals alike. The temperature dropped below freezing before the first of the year and held. By February, horsemen could safely ride across the Kentucky River on two feet of ice. William Fleming reported that people moving to Kentucky had lost 500 head of cattle. The travelers were so distressed that "numbers of families not being able to get in were building huts on the road to winter in."[2] Unable to forage because of the snow, many wild animals died from starvation and prolonged exposure. Corn, the staple in Kentucky, was in short supply because of the increased population. With shortages came inflation, and soon the price of corn rose to thirty dollars per bushel. By December 1779, Floyd reported that he was unable to buy corn at fifty dollars per bushel.

During the winter, settlers usually stayed near the forts and stations, although there were very few Indian raids. The lack of food, combined with the lack of knowledge of proper sanitation, caused a great deal of sickness and death. Visiting the fort at Harrodsburg, Col. William Fleming, a physician, noted that the spring was situated in the lowest corner of the fort. He describes conditions around the spring as unhealthy in the extreme:

> [T]he whole dirt and filth of the Fort, putrified flesh, dead dogs, horse, cow, [and] hog excrements and human odour [all washed into it. Furthermore, the situation could hardly have been improved by] the Ashes and sweepings of filthy Cabbins [sic], the dirtiness of the people, steeping skins to dress[,] and washing every sort of dirty rags and cloths in the spring makes the most filthy nauseous potation of the water imaginable and will certainly contribute to render the inhabitants of this place sickly.[3]

In spite of the cold weather and danger from Indians, some enterprising men continued to earn a living during the winter by capitalizing on the people's eagerness for land. Nicholas Merewether, for example, was employed early in 1780 to "lay off, run & mark out land" for several landowners on Clear Creek. He hired chainmen and surveyed four tracts containing 5,134 acres. The required boundaries of the tracts were over twenty-two miles long. There is no record of his total profit for this work, other than his having received a land warrant for 666 acres from one of the participants. Others were not so lucky. On March 9 while working outside the fort at Boonesborough, Col. Richard Callaway and Pemberton Rowling were attacked and killed by Indians.[4] Two Negroes with them were captured. They had been working on a flatboat, which Callaway had planned to use as a ferry on the Kentucky River. The following day the Indians killed William Bryan Jr. at Bryan's Station, then attacked Ruddle's Station. There the settlers were able to escape injury by taking shelter in the fort. Though no individuals were harmed, all the cattle were killed and all the horses stolen.

The commissioners having closed the land court on February 26, the members prepared to return home when on March 19, 1780, they received word that their stay in Kentucky was to be extended through April. Because many settlers had been detained by the weather, the legislature granted them more time to submit their claims. William Fleming, Stephen Trigg, and Edmund Lyne assembled at St. Asaph on April 16 and made preparations to hold court again. During that month they heard another 134 land claims before ending the court.

When the commissioners finished their work, many new arrivals who had come to Kentucky to obtain cheap land began to realize that there was not much available. Those who had obtained settlements and preemptions were asking what many considered prohibitive prices, especially in populated areas. Even before the year opened, John Floyd reported that 1,400 acres of "poor land" on Beargrass Creek had sold for £300, and with the coming of spring, inflation caused another rise in land prices. When the state increased the price of public land from £20 to £160 per hundred acres, the price of private land went up proportionately. In April some of the landless people at the Falls were so frustrated that they decided to seize the land commissioner's records and burn them.[5] Fortunately, the records were then safe at Wilson's Station and were about to be sent to Richmond.

John May, the brother of the surveyor, was convinced that land, though selling at high prices, was still a bargain. He found that his trip of ten days from the Holston to Harrodsburg was very unpleasant:

[T]hrough an uninhabited Country the most rugged and dismal I ever passed through, there being thousands of dead Horses, Cattle on the Road Side which occasioned a continual Stench; and one Half the way there were no Springs, which compelled us to make use of the water from the Streams in which many of these dead animals lay: and what made the Journey still more disagree-

Kentucky frontier.

able was, the continual apprehension we were under, of an Attack from the Indians, there not being one Day after we left Holston, but News was brought us of some Murders being comitted [*sic*] by those Savages.

[He was also disappointed at what he found when he arrived.] I find that the Commissioners here have granted certificates for Settlements & PreEmptions for all the prime Land in this Country some of them having entered largely into the Land Business by purchasing Claims & then sitting in Judgement upon them; and granting Certificates to themselves; and in order to procure Land have admitted hundreds of Claims entirely out of the Letter & meaning of the Law.[6]

Warmer weather mitigated the crowding inside the old forts. New stations sprouted up with the crocuses that spring, about fifty of them, including ten or more around Boonesborough, nine in the Harrodsburg–Crab Orchard area, and seven near Louisville. But many of these stations were still crowded. William Fleming reported that Whitley's Station contained 22 men, 54 women and children; St. Asaph's, 25 men, 74 women and children, 20 blacks; Clark's Station, 10 men, 23 women and children; and Doughty's Station, 5 men, 16 women and children. Most heavily populated was the village of Harrodsburg, which contained about 400 people.[7]

John Floyd and his little party became the first settlers on Beargrass Creek near the Falls. When Floyd arrived, he discovered that eleven cabins had been built on his survey by men hoping to preempt the land for themselves. Outliers, land jobbers, and prospective settlers had built similar cabins on most, if not all, of the 1774 military surveys, hoping their claims would somehow win preference. In all but one instance, however, the commissioners ruled that settlement and preemption claims could not be established on tracts that had been surveyed earlier on military warrants.[8]

Floyd, with little help from his friends, spent the winter trying to establish a station on his old military survey. In cutting down the first tree, Floyd's only slave was injured when the trunk crushed his foot. Floyd did not take his place because he considered himself a gentleman, a member of a class of men who at that time were not expected to do physical labor. In a letter written on February 20, he assessed his situation:

I shall not be able to do much surveying this spring, as the hard winter and the loss of my Negro have prevented my getting one acre cleared on my place. We have but ten families with us yet, but I expect about fifteen in the whole, which I think will make us tolerably safe. Notwithstanding the severest winter that ever was known, I have lost one cow, & she died since the warm weather.[9]

A few Indians were seen along Beargrass Creek in March, and one party of travelers was ambushed on its way to the Falls. A man named Billy Easkins was killed. Another, Billy Breckenridge, was thrown from his horse but managed to escape. Roaming around in the woods for six days, he finally found shelter at Floyd's Station. About the first of April three men were killed and scalped near Levi Todd's station.

During 1780, John Todd was elected as a Kentucky County delegate to the Virginia Assembly. While serving in this capacity, he met and married Jane Hawkins. Levi Todd took on the responsibility of entering his brother's land claim at Mansfield.

By spring John Floyd had persuaded settlers at the Falls to build two more stations along the creek on his land, one called Hogland's and the other called Dutch or New Holland. Many of those in the Beargrass stations were Dutch families that had emigrated from Pennsylvania with a desire to settle together in order to preserve their language and religion. Another station was built near Floyd close by a large spring at the head of Beals Branch, afterwards called Spring Station. Asturgus Station was built on Col. William Christian's military survey, just to the west of Floyd.[10] Linn's Station was built on the next survey west. The station built to the south of Asturgus on the South Fork of Beargrass Creek became known as Sullivan's Station, later as Pope's Station.

About thirty-five miles east of Louisville on the waters of Clear Creek, Squire Boone, the brother of Daniel, established a station called Painted Stone. Among Boone's men were some of the Dutch immigrants. The name Painted Stone originated from the fact that Boone painted a sign on a large flat rock to establish a claim at that particular place. But the stone did not impress every pioneer who saw it. George Yount said that while traveling about in the woods he came upon it, and "the Stone was not bright; that this deponant [sic] heard the painted Stone spoken of as a notorious object and took the liberty of laughing at Squire Boone for speaking of the stone as a notorious object when it was so trifling [a] thing."[11]

John Fitch, one of the inventors of the steamboat, moved to Kentucky about this time. Born in Windsor, Connecticut, he, like many others, in-

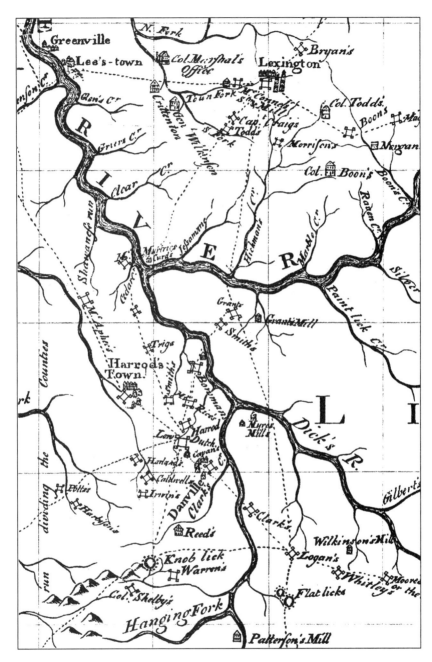

Filson's map showing stations.

Photograph of Spring House at Floyd's Station on Beargrass Creek near Louisville, taken in 1922. THE FILSON HISTORICAL SOCIETY, LOUISVILLE, KENTUCKY

tended to seek out some choice tracts of land. Exploring the area between the Salt and Green Rivers, he made several surveys. Unfortunately, his endeavors were short lived; he was captured by a band of Indians and taken to Detroit.[12]

The influx of new settlers and Spanish intervention in the war against Great Britain must have given George Rogers Clark a new sense of security. The Spanish army in New Orleans moved against the small British force in Mobile, defended mostly by Choctaw Indians. Many left for home after a short while, having a distaste for long sieges. When the Spanish fleet appeared in Mobile Bay on February 10, it was all over. In spite of storms, they had managed to bring 1,400 men ashore to confront the 300 British troops at Fort Charlotte. Gen. John Campbell, the British commander in Florida, sent 1,100 troops to reinforce Mobile, but they failed to arrive in time.

After Mobile surrendered, the Spanish hoped to move eastward to capture Fort George, the heart of the defenses at Pensacola. They collected ships and men at Havana, but on the first attempt, were driven back by storms. To block the land route, the British assembled over a thousand Indian allies to threaten their advance, but it was only the arrival of British warships that turned back the Spaniards' major attack. This development greatly relieved the American Tories who had moved to Florida, though this battle for the gulf ports was long from over.

Five hundred miles to the north, George Rogers Clark moved part of his regiment from the fort at the Falls of the Ohio to establish Fort Jefferson near the junction of the Ohio and Mississippi Rivers. His men started down the Ohio on March 14 to take advantage of the current. The leaders in Williamsburg ordered Clark to establish this base, believing that a fort at this location would protect the commerce between Kentucky and the cities of St. Louis and New Orleans. Clark also escorted a number of civilians to settle in a town site laid out near the fort, hoping that the civilians could furnish corn, vegetables, and other items needed to supply the garrison. Clark arrived at the mouth of the Ohio on April 19, soon after commencing construction of the fort.[13]

In early May, however, not long after Clark arrived on the Mississippi, he was informed that the British and their allied Indians were advancing for an attack on Cahokia and St. Louis. Without delay, he took part of his regiment and rushed northward, arriving only in "time enough to save the country from impending ruin."[14]

Following plans that Lieutenant Governor Hamilton had made the year before, the British projected a three-pronged attack. One army was to move from Pensacola against the Spanish in Louisiana to gain control of the Mississippi River. Another from Mackinac was to take St. Louis and the adjacent towns. The third was to attack Kentucky. The northernmost wing of the army, under Capt. Emanuel Hesse, consisted of 950 men, who had come down the Mississippi River. A smaller force under Charles Langlade traveled down the Illinois River. Indians made up the largest contingent of both forces. Appearing at the gates of St. Louis and Cahokia, these armies attacked the two towns but the defenders succeeded in repulsing both assaults. At St. Louis the Spanish authorities reported Hesse's casualties at twenty-nine killed and wounded and seventy prisoners. The British and American causalities at Cahokia are not known. The Indians, having been promised an easy victory, were both disappointed and hungry. As a result, many deserted and went home. This battle is said to have occurred on May 26.[15] Clark sent a little harrassing force under Capt. John Montgomery to speed them on their way; Mongomery's men chased the Indians as far as Peoria before returning to Cahokia.

Flat boat on the Ohio River.

Back in Kentucky, people had reason to be optimistic about the future of the settlements. As Floyd was able to report, numbers were beginning to tilt the balance in their favor:

> I think near three hundred large boats have arrived at the Falls this spring with families, and corn can be bought now for thirty dollars per bushel. We have six stations on Bear Grass Creek with no less than six hundred men. You would be surprised to see ten or fifteen wagons at a time going to and from the Falls every day with families and corn. I expect two hundred acres will be tended in corn this year at my place but very little of it will come to my share.[16]

During the spring of 1780 there were more Virginians in the Louisville area than could likely be mobilized for four or five years thereafter.

With the warmer weather, John Donelson and other settlers from Virginia and North Carolina headed west. On April 24 they arrived at French Lick on the Cumberland, now Nashville, Tennessee. There they started to build a station. Other settlers, following Donelson down the Tennessee rivers, soon discovered that traveling was very hazardous. Indians lured about thirty men, women, and children ashore, killing them when they disembarked with the hope of being given some corn. They had been hailed by a white man, who assured them that the Indians were friendly and advised them to come unarmed.

This settlement at Nashville was another extension of the frontier well beyond its former boundary. The land had been awarded to Richard Henderson's Transylvania Company as compensation for losing the territory they had purchased from the Cherokee in 1775. The settlement had also induced some dissatisfied Virginians to move southward from Kentucky County to the new Cumberland settlement, where they hoped that land would be cheaper.

At the time of these developments in Tennessee, the central part of Kentucky also experienced a spurt of sudden growth. Some of the newcomers ventured west to settle their old claims, others to find vacant land that could be acquired with treasury warrants, and yet others to purchase the claims of old settlers. Most landowners welcomed landless new arrivals, giving them favorable terms to live on their land as tenants. Some of the old settlers discovered that they were in great demand as guides or agents for newcomers possessing treasury warrants. In exchange for locating vacant land, they were offered either cash payment or a portion of the land warrant. At the time, most of the land seekers probably did not realize that those who were paid to locate vacant land might be obligated to make up for the acreage lost if they accidentally ran surveys on older claims.

Business boomed in the land office at Wilson's Station. Hundreds of men collected around the little fort, many sleeping in tents, awaiting their turn to enter their claims. In reference to the delays caused by the rush, John Floyd said, "I stayed at the Surveyors [sic] office till hunger drove me home before I could make an entry."[17] In early May the surveyor at the office entered over 100 claims per day, a number probably representing the maximum for clerks in the office to process.

Col. William Fleming, one of the Virginia land commissioners, had been staying at the home of his friend, Col. John Bowman. He decided to ride over to Wilson's Station to enter some land on a treasury warrant. Arriving, he was informed by the surveyor that everyone would draw lots to determine who would be the first to make his entry. Fleming was lucky enough to draw number 24 from the 300 tickets issued to those who arrived that day. One would have supposed that government officials, such as land commissioners and deputy surveyors, would have been given some special preference in making their entries, but the surviving letters and journals indicate otherwise. Colonel Fleming did have, however, access to the surveyor's official records. He disclosed that in the Kentucky district, certificates for 770,800 acres had been awarded to settlers, 423,000 acres for men who had improved land before 1778 (preemptions), and 135,450 acres to those who had made improvements since 1778.[18] A total of 1,328 men had claimed land, but some of them had purchased the claims of their friends and associates, significantly reducing the number who actually received land warrants from the commissioners.

Before winter set in, the surveyor also entered 2,531,779 acres of land on Virginia treasury warrants. These varied in size from just a few acres to a few very large tracts covering thousands of acres. Some men had numerous claims. For example, John Bowman and his partners managed to secure about 37,000 acres in twenty-five tracts, and John May, the brother of the surveyor, entered approximately 75,000 acres in about forty locations, but most Kentucky land was entered in tracts of less than a thousand acres made by less famous citizens.

When the weather warmed, hostile Indians lurked about the settlements, but no major invasions came from the Northern tribes. As Floyd wrote, "Hardly one week pases [sic] without someone being scalped between this and the Falls and I have almost got too cowardly to travel about the woods without company."[19]

In May the Virginia legislature passed an act establishing the town of Louisville. Boonesborough had already been chartered, so Louisville became the second official town in Kentucky. At the same time, the legislature passed an act to escheat several military surveys belonging to "British subjects," a total of 8,000 acres. The tracts at the Falls of the Ohio granted to John Connolly and Charles DeWarrensdorff were two of these surveys. Now made available, the land was used to establish the new city.[20] Capt. Thomas Bullitt had laid out a town at the Falls in the summer of 1773, and it is likely that the new streets and lots were based upon this old survey. In any event, according to Abraham Hite's copy of the original town plat, Louisville contained 300 lots and extended from First to Twelfth Streets, with the east-west streets being Main, Market, and Jefferson. The trustees of the new town included John Floyd, William Pope, Marsham Brashear, Stephen Trigg, John Todd, and George Slaughter.

Another of these echeated tracts, a few miles farther up the Ohio, belonged to Robert McKinzie, a good friend of George Washington during the French and Indian War. His property and another tract near Lexington owned by Henry Collins were sold, the money being used to start Transylvania College, the first college west of the mountains and one which later gave substance to Lexington's early claim as "the Athens of the West."[21]

The more or less peaceful conditions on the frontier changed as suddenly as the arrival of a summer thunderstorm. An enemy force of Shawnee and Canadian Rangers under Capt. Henry Bird had originally planned to move south in coordinated attacks on Cahokia and St. Louis. The original plan was to capture Clark's fort at the Falls, then to advance on central Kentucky. The Indian tribes on this expedition, however, considered Clark's fort too strong, and the plan was changed. Instead, the army took advantage of the flooded Licking River and moved southward by water, for the first time bringing artillery with them. They took Ruddle's Station on June 24 and Martin's Station the next day, the defenders realizing that their wooden forts could not withstand the firepower of British ordnance. In both instances, the simple threat of using the artillery was enough to upset the balance. Because the wood palisades were no match for cannonballs, both forts surrendered. According to one of the participants, Captain Bird had a force of "about 150 or 200 British regulars . . . and about 500 Indians."[22] About 60 fighting men and over 100 old men, women, and children from the fort were apportioned out in small parties among the Indians and escorted back to Detroit, many of them dying on the way, a number of them murdered by Indians whom Bird and his command were powerless to restrain.

In the meantime, Colonel Clark hurried back to Kentucky and arrived at Harrodsburg in time to hear news of the capture of these stations. Word of these events when it reached Harrodsburg on June 30 most likely created a furor. The closest station to the captured forts, Grant's Station, had already been attacked in May. With the loss of Ruddle's and Martin's, it was thought prudent to abandon it. Some of the inhabitants moved to Bryan's Station, others farther south to the Harrodsburg area.[23] Realizing their own vulnerability, the enemy retreated back across the Ohio, but the loss of the two forts made it clear that the British were still determined to win the war.

George Rogers Clark determined to punish the Indians as quickly as possible. With the cooperation of the various county militia officers, four out of every five militiamen were mustered in for duty between July 3 and 20.[24] Clark also ordered out a company of regular troops with artillery, a 6-pounder, to accompany the militia.[25]

The 6-pounder was a standard muzzle-loaded cannon with a smoothbore of 3.67 inches (93 mm) that used a pound and a quarter of powder to shoot a round ball weighing nearly seven pounds. It was a favored caliber for 250 years because of its mobility, and was used extensively from the time of the Thirty Years' War (1618) through the American Civil War (1865). The five-foot-long gun barrel, which weighed about 880 pounds, was mounted on a two-wheel, wooden carriage built with a heavy axial to support the gun and two beams extending backward to form the "trail." To transport the cannon, this trail was hooked onto another two-wheeled cart called the "limber," which carried the ammunition. The gunner and driver rode on the limber. The total empty weight for the gun, carriage, and limber was about 1,700 pounds. This combination was usually pulled by a team of six horses. Additional ammunition needed for the cannon followed in a wagon called the caisson, which often was two limbers hooked together. These vehicles had interchangeable wheels so that the wheels under the cannon could be easily replaced if damaged. In flat country the teams would cover five miles an hour, so they could easily keep up with the infantry.

These cannons could be brought into action very quickly by removing the trail from the limber. Elevation of the gun was accomplished by wedges or a screw mechanism, and its bearing was changed by sticking a handspike through slots in the trail and moving it sideways. There was no recoil mechanism, and when fired the gun jumped back, usually making tracks in the earth. The smoke created by firing was such that it was difficult to resight the gun, so when in a hurry, the men just realigned it by pushing it back up its tracts. Using solid shot, the maximum range was over three-quarters of a mile; one could not expect to hit a small target at that distance, but would have no trouble hitting the walls of a fort. Against enemy infantry, grapeshot was used when available. The addition of artillery, though it probably made Clark's march more difficult, was as much psychological as tactical, calculated to offset the perceived advantage of Bird, who had artillery with his attacking force.

When they were assembled, Clark marched them north. Though it has often been reported that Clark closed the office of the Kentucky County surveyor in order to muster the Kentucky militia, the land records indicate otherwise.[26] This force of nearly 1,000 men crossed the Ohio at the mouth of the Licking River on August 1. Clark distributed all that he had to supply the troops—300 bushels of green corn and 1,500 pounds of flour. Assuming the corn was in kernels rather than ears, this portioned out to around 20 pounds per man, though some of this food would have been needed for the horses.

On the way to the rendezvous, the detachment from Beargrass Creek suffered some casualties; as John Floyd wrote his wife on July 25:

> We are now [on the Ohio River] thirty miles above the mouth of Kentucky and all in high spirits. Captain Byrn [*sic*] and a party of about twenty men were out on the Indian side yesterday evening and were fired on by a party of Indians. They killed four of our men on the spot and wounded five more, of which number poor Byrn was one himself. He is to return to the Falls and by whom I write. I hope in one week to be in the towns and to return to you and little Billey as soon as in my power. Pray caution the people to be on their guard and do not yourself go out any where from the Fort as we see frequent signs of the Savages and perhaps some of them may visit you.[27]

Not expecting the rapid advance of the Americans, the Indians quickly evacuated Chillicothe. When Clark's army arrived, they torched the town as well as the corn crop they found in the adjoining fields. The Shawnee retreated to Piqua, closely followed by Clark's troops. In a letter to Thomas Jefferson, Clark described the battle:

> At half past two in the evening of the 8th, we arrived in sight of the town and posts, a plain of half a mile in width laying between us. I had an opportunity of viewing the situation and motion of the enemy near their works. I had scarcely time to make those dispositions necessary, before the action commenced on our left wing, and in a few minutes became almost general, with a savage fierceness on both sides. The confidence . . . the enemy had of their own strength and certain victory, or the want of generalship, occasioned several neglects, by which those advantages were taken to proved [*sic*] the ruin of their army, being flanked two or three different times, drove from hill to hill, in a circuitous direction, for upward of a mile and a half; at last [they] took shelter in their strongholds, and woods adjacent, when the firing ceased for about half an hour, until necessary preparations were made for dislodging them. A heavy firing again commenced and continued severe until dark, by which time the enemy were totally routed. The cannon playing too briskly on their works they could afford them no shelter.[28]

Most of the retreating Indians managed to evade Col. Benjamin Logan's encircling column, which could not advance quickly because of the terrain. During the short battle, the Americans suffered losses of fourteen killed and thirteen wounded. The pay records show twenty-two killed, suggesting that many of the wounded did not survive very long. The Indians managed to carry off most of their casualties, so their exact loss could not be determined. The dead in Clark's army included Capt. William McAfee, one of the company commanders; Samuel Moore, one of the original members of the 1774 Harrodsburg company; and Joseph Rogers, the cousin of George Rogers Clark. Rogers had been captured after helping his famous cousin bring in the gunpowder in 1776. When he tried to reach the American lines, he was mistaken for an Indian and shot. He is said to have died in Clark's arms.

Clark followed up the destruction of Chillicothe by looting and burning the town of Piqua and its cornfields. By this time the army's meager supplies were running short, so Clark started back to Kentucky. Upon their return they heard the bad news that Charleston had fallen to the British.

After the surrender of Charleston, South Carolina, by General Lincoln, Congress selected Gen. Horatio Gates to lead the forces in the South. He was joined by Gen. Baron de Kalb, who had already been sent south with the Continental troops from Maryland and Delaware lines and a regiment of artillery. Gates advanced directly upon Camden, South Carolina, where the main British army, commanded by Lord Rawdon, was posted. He was about fifteen miles north of Camden on August 13, the same day that Cornwallis, arriving from Charleston, joined Lord Rawdon at Camden. By coincidence, both Gates and Cornwallis set out at the same hour of August 15 to surprise the other by a night attack. To their mutual surprise, they encountered each other short of their destinations. In the battle of Camden, which followed at daybreak, the American militia fled from the field with Gates leading the mob. He retreated to Charlotte and then to Salisbury and then to Hillsboro. The Continental troops under de Kalb, however, maintained their position until they were overrun by superior numbers and de Kalb killed.

When the news of the disaster at Camden reached Philadelphia, many realized that the politicians had blundered again. Congress had a very poor record for picking generals in the South. First they had chosen Robert Howe, who had lost Savannah and all of Georgia. Then they had selected Benjamin Lincoln, who had lost Charleston and South Carolina. Finally, they had appointed Horatio Gates, who had lost the rest of the South

Frontiersman shoots Indian.

along with his army. They decided to entrust the choice of his successor to George Washington, who appointed Gen. Nathanael Greene to supersede Gates, a wise choice.

After his victory at Camden, Cornwallis sent Maj. Patrick Ferguson with a force of mounted "American Volunteers" into the western part of the Carolinas to recruit more loyalists for his army. Somewhat successful in this operation, he sent word to the backwoodsmen that if they did not desist from opposition to the king he would march over the mountains, hang their leaders, and lay waste their country with fire and sword. This message had the same effect as throwing gasoline on a fire.

The militia units from the western counties were called up and organized. Isaac Shelby brought Virginia troops. John Sevier, William Campbell, Benjamin Cleveland, and Charles McDowell mobilized the North Carolina militia. By September 25 they had all assembled at Sycamore Flats on the Watauga River. Outnumbered, Ferguson thought it expedient to retreat. The Americans were mostly mounted, and they gathered several hundred more recruits as they pursued, eventually reaching 1,400.[29] Ferguson with about 1,100 men decided to take a stand on King's Mountain, a steep, rocky knob about 500 yards long by 75 yards wide, located in South Carolina. The Americans completely surrounded the British, and the fighting began.

The terrain favored the American riflemen over the defenders who held their positions with muskets and bayonets.[30] As they advanced up the hill, the frontiersmen had no trouble finding trees and rocks for protection. Once they were near the top, the British would charge with the bayonet and force the Americans back down the hill only to have another group reach the top and fire at them from a different direction. Many patriots, determined to avenge the death of friends by the Tories, continued shooting even after the British had surrendered. When the leaders stopped the battle, Ferguson, along with 156 of his men, had been killed. One hundred and sixty-three had been wounded, the remainder captured. Afterwards, military courts tried some of the captured troops for various crimes and hanged them.

The victory had the overall effect of raising the spirits of the Americans and discouraging future Tory activities in the South. Cornwallis immediately retreated westward with his main army to Winnsborough, South Carolina, where he encamped and awaited reinforcements. His position was strong because he still held Camden on his right and Fort Ninety-Six on his left. General Greene wisely decided to maneuver his army to threaten the British rather than to seek a decisive battle against what was obviously a superior force.

To the west, on the Mississippi River, 200 Chickasaw attacked the Virginia troops and militia at the newly constructed outpost called Fort Jefferson. The attack, occurring on Monday morning, was directed at the far end of the new town. The initial fire instantly killed three of the defenders, but there was a log blockhouse built at that end of town, equipped with a swivel gun. This fortification, containing five soldiers and five militiamen, went into action and commenced firing. The skirmish lasted two and a half hours before the Indians were finally driven off after killing most of the livestock. Capt. Robert George, the commander of Fort Jefferson, worried afterward about his depleted food supplies, "having about two hundred mouths to feed daily."[31]

On Sunday morning, August 27, another enemy force arrived at Fort Jefferson. Lt. John Whitehead, who had been detached from the British regiment in Pensacola, Florida, commanded these troops. The Indians ambushed some slaves working in a cornfield and then began firing at the fort. After firing a few rounds, Lieutenant Whitehead hailed the defenders and demanded their surrender. They refused, but the next day James Colbert, a Scottish-Chickasaw chief, met with Capt. Leonard Helm under a flag of truce and made the same demands. Again the defenders turned down the offer, but as Helm walked off, Colbert was shot by some of the allied Kaskaskia Indians, who were visiting in the village. The Chickasaw then attacked the town and fort but did little damage. The next morning they departed. This fort, which gave the Americans a claim to the territory along the Mississippi, was eventually abandoned.

Back in Kentucky in October, Daniel Boone and his brother Edward went hunting on Grassy Lick Creek. While Edward was cracking walnuts, Daniel went to the lick and shot a bear. Almost at the same time, he heard gunfire behind him and turned to see his brother shot by Indians. Since his gun was unloaded, he ran in the woods and through some canebrakes to escape. Unfortunately, the Indians had a dog that continued to track Daniel until he finally managed to reload and shoot it.[32]

Eluding capture, Boone made his way back to his station where he recruited a company of volunteers to pursue the Indians. This particular militia group was under the command of Capt. Charles Gatliff, not Boone. Among the company was James Ray, the young man who had outrun a party of Indians in 1776. The militia was able to follow the trail of the Indians all the way to the Ohio River. Discovering that the Indians had already crossed the wide expanse, they gave up the pursuit.[33]

On the Southern front, Joseph Martin, a Virginia agent who lived with the Cherokee, informed the governor that the tribe had been induced by British agents to join an offensive against the Americans. The militia from Virginia and North Carolina, which only a short time before had defeated Ferguson at King's Mountain, mobilized again and started westward. Col. John Sevier led 300 Carolinians on a forced march to the French Broad River, where they skirmished with the Indians on December 16. A short time later, they were reinforced by 400 troops from Virginia under

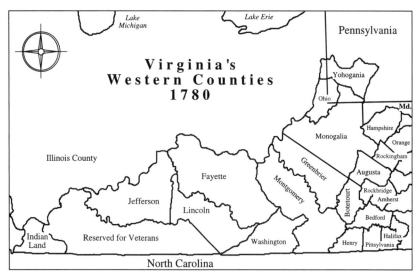

Virginia's western counties, 1780.

Col. Arthur Campbell. The combined force marched to the Cherokee town of Chote without opposition and destroyed the village. They continued on to the Chickamauga town, at which time the fatigued North Carolina troops went home. Campbell and his men continued, burning villages and threatening the Cherokee with permanent occupation if they did not come to terms. From the militiamen's viewpoint, the campaign had been a success. Their leaders estimated that they had burned over a thousand Indian houses and destroyed about 50,000 bushels of corn.[34]

At year's end, the Virginia frontier still held against the pressure of the British military effort but perhaps only because of the increase in population. In fact, the influx of settlers had been so great that in November, Virginia's most westerly county, Kentucky, was divided into three new counties—Lincoln, Jefferson, and Fayette. Benjamin Logan, John Floyd, and John Todd, were, respectively, the top officials in these counties. The new arrangement displeased James Harrod because he was only offered the rank of major in the Lincoln County militia. Miffed, he refused the commission and subsequently served as a private.

Of course, these were not the first new counties created by the legislature.[35] In 1777 alone, Rockbridge, Greenbrier, Fluvanna, Powhatan, and Rockingham Counties had been established. Because of the efforts of the Commonwealth to support the war by selling public land, the tide in the West had started to turn.

CHAPTER 7

1781
A Quick End to
the War in the East

On January 3, 1781, the then-famous traitor Benedict Arnold, having switched sides, landed with about 1,600 British and Tory rangers at Hood's Point, near Richmond, Virginia. After his defection, Arnold had been promoted to brigadier general by the English. On this campaign he was accompanied by Colonels Dundas and Simcoe, two experienced and reliable officers. After a brief skirmish, their troops were moved to Westover and then marched to Richmond, arriving unopposed on the fifth. Without firing a shot, the few militia guarding the city fled. Continuing up the James River, the British destroyed a powder factory and five tons of gunpowder. They then retreated to Portsmouth where they set up an encampment. During the ensuing weeks, Simcoe's British rangers continued to harass the Virginia militia by raiding nearby villages.

By February the Virginians on the frontier also felt the pressure of the British offensive. Hunting during the winter, the men in Kentucky had managed to acquire a large quantity of meat, which they hoped to salt down or "pickle" to serve Colonel Clark's army through the summer. Squire Boone stored one supply of over 100,000 pounds at his station. Another load of about 60,000 pounds was stored along the Kentucky River in the deserted cabins at Leestown. Evan Hinton, Squire Boone's associate and close friend, agreed to haul a load of salt from Linn's Station to Boone's Station. On February 6, he and two others were captured en route; the wagon was destroyed and the salt dumped out. As a result, most of the meat spoiled.

The remaining beef was also lost. John Floyd explained what happened:

> I have been more unfortunate in my little hunt last winter than
> the rest. I hired seven or eight men, went to Lees cabins with
> horses loaded with salt, gave £1000 for building canoes, killed &
> saved 54 buffalo, 4 elk & 2 large wild hogs & brought it safe
> [down the Kentucky and Ohio Rivers] to between Goose Creek &
> Beargrass where my vessells [sic] were overset by a gale of wind and
> sunk my whole cargo to the bottom.[1]

George Rogers Clark rose in rank from colonel to brigadier general in
Virginia's regular army on January 22, 1781. This promotion probably
gave him more prestige than he had with the rank of colonel since most of
the ranking county militia officers also obtained the rank of colonel. Clark
spent most of the early spring recruiting new men for the regular Virginia
regiment. Apparently, the general paid bounty money to the new recruits
out of his personal account, though the state later reimbursed him with a
land warrant for 560 acres, which he located south of the Falls.[2] Equipping
these troops was more difficult because their officers had to rely on Virginia's credit, which was not very good. The inflated money also caused
some discontent.

Some Tory sentiment had always existed on the Virginia frontier, but
during 1781 disaffection reached serious proportions in Hampshire
County. Here, on the headwaters of the Potomac River, a man named John
Claypool refused to furnish any material aid to the Virginia government.
Even worse, he and his friends drank to the king's health and publicly
damned the Continental Congress. When the sheriff tried to the serve the
warrant issued for his arrest, he found himself confronted by sixty angry
Tories.

Armed opposition, the chief object of which was "to be clear of Taxes
and Draughts," flared up in other parts of Hampshire County. On May
22, 1781, an urgent plea was made to Frederick County for 300 militiamen to protect the remaining patriotic Hampshire County citizens. On the
preceding day the militia had been fired upon and two of them taken prisoner. Worse still, Claypool was rumored to be assembling an army of a
thousand men in the Lost River area.

Four companies of infantrymen from Frederick County and other recruits under Daniel Morgan eventually dispersed the rioters. Forty-two of
them, including Claypool, either surrendered or were captured. Upon the

approach of Morgan's army, however, most of the Tories fled over the mountains to Pennsylvania.

After his capture, Claypool elicited considerable sympathy from the other inhabitants, who also felt they were being overtaxed by the state. Many of his neighbors vouched for his character. Even Daniel Morgan rose to his defense, calling attention to the isolation and ignorance of the people of Hampshire County. He also declared that the requirements of humanity dictated leniency since Claypool's family consisted of a wife and fourteen children, "chiefly small," who were dependent on him. Eventually Claypool and most of the other participants were pardoned, and several later served in American armies.[3]

In the Southern theater, Gen. Nathanael Greene began recruiting troops to oppose the 4,000 men commanded by the Earl of Cornwallis. Greene's little army consisted of 1,500 poorly equipped soldiers—no match for the British. Arthur Campbell, representing the Virginia militia, anticipated that many of the frontiersmen would volunteer to join Greene, but he worried about the possibility of a Cherokee invasion during their absence. To counter this threat, General Greene appointed eight prominent men from Virginia and North Carolina to negotiate a peace with the Cherokee. Before any negotiations began, however, Cherokee warriors began raiding frontier settlements in both colonies. Without delay, John Sevier collected 150 North Carolina militia and attacked the middle towns, while Joseph Martin raised 200 Virginians to threaten those living on waters of the upper Tennessee River. Both attacks were successful.

In Florida the commander of the British forces, Gen. John Campbell, recruited Choctaw warriors to harass the Spanish at Mobile Bay. A force of about 400 British-led Indians had some initial success, but the Indians withdrew to Pensacola when the British officer in charge was killed in a counterattack.

In spite of the continuing Spanish threat to his only remaining base in West Florida, Gen. John Campbell dismissed about half of the 700 warriors under his command. When the Spanish fleet appeared off Pensacola in early March, he found his army of 1,500 regulars and 500 Indians greatly outnumbered, with time on the side of the Spanish invaders. The Spanish summoned reinforcements from Havana and New Orleans until their army numbered up to 7,000 men, more than three times that of the defenders. A cannonball into the British powder magazine brought the contest to a close; on May 8, the British capitulated to the Spanish. General Campbell's surrender meant more than the loss of a single outpost. It ended the presence of the British in West Florida and any effective functioning of the Southern Indian Department under Alexander Cameron, the successor of John Stuart.

Despite the fact that British troops were then threatening Richmond, Virginia's western counties made an effort to supply those defending the Kentucky country. Local leaders supported George Rogers Clark's proposal to raise 2,000 militia for a campaign to capture Detroit, an enterprise endorsed by both Thomas Jefferson and George Washington. The plan was for Clark to assemble his main force at Pittsburgh, move down the Ohio to join with the Kentucky militia on March 15, then strike northward through the Indian towns to the British outpost. In this way, he planned to crush all Indian resistance before encountering the British troops. Clark had traveled back to eastern Virginia to confer with Jefferson, but Benedict Arnold's invasion undermined their hopes for the Western campaign.

For a time the Kentucky leaders still hoped that they could launch the proposed campaign against Detroit. But favorable signs were few. Rumors held that the British and Indians at Niagara were planning to attack Pittsburgh and Wheeling and that another force might even attack the fort at Louisville.

On March 1 a party of Indians did attack Strode's Station, lingering around the fort for three days. A few days later, Capts. John Tepton, William Chaplan, and William Linn were killed on the Beargrass trace while traveling to Louisville to attend court. Floyd informed Governor Jefferson that during the first three and a half months of the year forty-seven people were killed in Jefferson County alone. In mid-May the Indians attacked the lower McAfee's Station on the Salt River, but they were soon driven off by some of the neighborhood militia under Capt. Hugh McGary.

As summer approached, the situation did not improve. At Louisville it was necessary to send troops out to guard the men cutting timber for boats. In June, Colonel Montgomery was compelled to give up the outposts on the Mississippi, unable to purchase supplies in Illinois or St. Louis because Virginia's credit had run out. On June 8 he abandoned the forts and brought back sixty starving men, all the troops that remained at Fort Jefferson and Kaskaskia. This left only forty Virginia soldiers north of the Ohio River, the men that had remained to garrison Vincennes. The others traveled up the Ohio to the Falls but found the government credit no better in Kentucky than in Illinois. In order to feed his men, Colonel Montgomery billeted his troops in small squads throughout Lincoln County so they could provide their own food.

Virginia's credit had been deteriorating for some time. In the latter part of 1779 the state began to sell public land for the price of four shillings per acre. In May 1780 the official price was increased to one pound, twelve shillings per acre (thirty-two shillings) because of inflation. To put the cost in perspective, tobacco at the same time was selling for forty-five pounds per hundred pounds, in Virginia paper money. In November 1781, the Virginia legislature passed an act that allowed the surveyors to collect their fees in tobacco. Its purpose was to ensure that surveyors' fees would not be affected by the depreciation of paper money. The inflation of the paper currency continued until the average person refused to sell anything to the state, realizing they would be paid with deflated currency. In 1778, soldiers in Clark's Illinois regiment were earning one and a third shillings per day at a time when one pound was officially equal to three and a third dollars. Although inflation increased the price of land, the soldiers' pay rates remained the same. In the summer of 1782, horses were valued at between ten pounds and thirty pounds, a saddle at slightly over one pound, a gun at six pounds, and an army blanket at one-half pound, in specie. But very few citizens had any of these old silver coins, their primary medium of exchange being the worthless paper money issued by Virginia.

In November the legislature authorized a land office to process warrants for Virginia veterans of the Revolutionary War. Soldiers or their heirs were given land warrants and could find and select tracts in that part of Kentucky southwest of the Green River or in Illinois. Nothing was done immediately, and the first warrants were not issued until the summer of the following year.

In 1781 the Virginia assembly finally gave in to the pressure of the Northern colonies and offered to cede their territory north of the Ohio River to Congress. The ultimate result of this concession was for the Virginia government to cease supporting military efforts in that area. If it was not to be part of Virginia, why should the Commonwealth defend it? Soon all the troops in Vincennes were also recalled and marched back to Kentucky.

By October most of the men who had recently migrated to Kentucky, especially those who had hoped to obtain land in the Bluegrass area or at the Falls of the Ohio, were very disappointed. They discovered that all of the land on Elkhorn Creek between Leestown and Lexington, and beyond, extending along the headwaters of Stoners and Hinkstons Creeks, was claimed either by the gentlemen who had warrants issued by Lord Dunmore for service in the French and Indian War or by the early settlers and

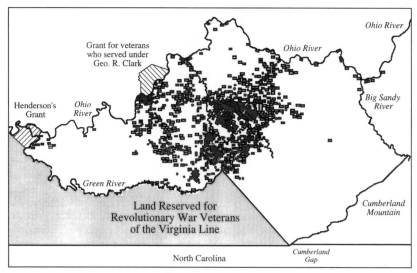

Settlement, preemptions, and military claims in the Kentucky district of Virginia.

land jobbers, especially the "Macs" who had come down the Ohio in 1775 and 1776.

Likewise, all the land on the south side of the Ohio, extending out fifteen miles from Fort Nelson at the Falls, had been surveyed and was claimed by gentlemen with these old military warrants. Surveys made with warrants for service during the French and Indian War covered nearly a half million acres. Beyond these surveys were claims by many prosperous gentlemen, such as Isaac Hite, Abraham Hite, Henry Clay, James Madison, Grandville Smith, Francis Taylor, Charles Minn Thruston, Cuthbert Bullitt, and John Mays. Along the road from Louisville to Painted Stone, Alexander Breckinridge had over 7,000 acres; John Madison, 5,000 acres; Joseph Kemp, 12,250 acres; and John Lewis, 22,000 acres; nearby, John May could claim 10,000 acres; Samuel Beall, 5,000 acres; Peachy Purdy, 3,000 acres; and Joseph Patton, 30,000 acres. Squire Boone also had in excess of 7,000 acres in the vicinity of his station. Much of the land was for sale, but at very inflated prices. Most new arrivals found they had no opportunity to obtain farm sites anywhere in these areas. Thus many took the only option available, settling on the good land as tenant farmers or deciding to live on a lot in one of the new towns such as Louisville or Lexington.

The new arrivals at Louisville found conditions especially bad in that there seemed to be Indians everywhere they went. Another serious problem at the Falls was the malaria caused by mosquitoes. John Floyd reported that there were about 300 men of militia age in Jefferson County, but 100 of these were making plans to move to Harrodsburg or other places that were safer, "and many others would follow their example, but are unable to remove by land having lost most of their horses already, by the savages, and the Ohio [River] runs the wrong way."[4]

On the East Coast, Virginia citizens were more concerned about their own problems than those in Illinois. The British were present in force. To relieve the Virginia militia and punish Arnold, General Washington detached 1,200 men under Lafayette to march southward to support Gen. Friedrich von Steuben, who was in charge of the Continental forces in Virginia as well as the militia under Muhlenberg, Weedon, and Nelson. Before Lafayette could arrive with his troops, Gen. Benedict Arnold again advanced up the James River, destroying everything of value. Muhlenberg's men resisted at Blanford but were soon driven off, retreating to Chesterfield Courthouse. The British again occupied Petersburg, which was undefended. A skirmish occurred there on April 24, 1781.

The expedition continued without substantial and effective opposition. The British followed the Americans to Chesterfield Courthouse, where they burned the barracks, 300 barrels of flour, and other stores. At the same time, General Arnold led the 76th and 80th British regiments, the Queen's Rangers, some jaegers, and a force of American Tories to attack a small naval force below Richmond. He succeeded in wrecking four ships, five brigs, and several smaller vessels. The two British forces then combined and marched to Manchester, burning thousands of hogsheads of tobacco along the way. After this little campaign the British returned to Petersburg.

Lafayette with 1,200 Continental troops arrived at Richmond on April 29 and held the north bank of the James, British troops holding the other side of the river. The tide turned on May 20 when General Cornwallis arrived to take charge. He had with him one Hessian and four British regiments augmented by Tarleton's Legion and Hamilton's Tories, about 1,500 men in all. A few days later, more troops arrived from New York, increasing the British army to 7,200 rank and file. Lafayette, meanwhile, received additional forces, bringing his army up to about 3,000. Lafayette realized that he could not defeat the British but was determined to stay close and harass them with skirmishes.

On May 24 Cornwallis crossed the James to Westover. On June 1, he camped at Hanover Junction and then sent Tarleton and Simcoe north to scout. Lafayette was forced to retreat to Dandridge's on South Anna River to await reinforcements from General von Steuben. The Americans under von Steuben fell back to the Rapidan River, where they were attacked by Simcoe's Rangers, who captured about thirty men. After they had crossed the Fluvanna River, the retreating Americans could not be pursued because the British had no boats.

On June 4 General Cornwallis dispatched Colonel Tarleton with 180 of the legion's cavalry and 70 mounted infantry against Charlottesville, where the Virginia legislature was in session. On the way he came upon a train of twelve wagons carrying much-needed clothing for Greene's army. After burning the supply wagons, he went on to Charlottesville, where he narrowly missed capturing Governor Jefferson, who was warned at the last moment by Jack Jouett, who made his famous ride to warn Jefferson at nearby "Montecello." Daniel Boone, on the other hand, was captured but released the next day. Boone's son Nathan recalled his father's capture during an interview in 1845:

> I have heard that when Jack Jouitt [sic] gave notice of Tarleton's approach, my father and some others remained, loading up on wagons some of the public records, until some of the light horse entered the town. My father and Jouitt started off in a slow, unconcerned walk when they were overtaken by the British, questioned hastily and dismissed. Then father, who had probably been first examined, walked on leisurely. But when Jouitt was through, he called out "Wait a minute, Captain Boone, and I'll go with you." Then said the British officer, "Ah, is he a captain?" and at the same time ordered him to stop and took him into custody.
>
> Father was conveyed to the British camp and put into a coal house and kept all night. It was rainy, so he presented a dirty appearance the next morning. Then he was taken before Colonel Tarleton and examined, either then or the next day, but they released him. He very probably explained his title of captain by referring to his old Dunmore commission. My father also may have pretended contentment and sung songs while confined.[5]

About this time General Arnold was recalled to New York. On June 7 Cornwallis retreated toward Richmond with Lafayette at his heels. He reached Richmond on June 16 but stayed only four days, leaving on the twentieth. During these maneuvers Col. Richard Butler's men fought a brief skirmish with Simcoe's rangers at Spencer's Ordinary. On his way toward Williamsburg, Layfayette decided to strike the British, who were crossing the James River. The attack occurred at Green's Spring with the result that the Americans were beaten back but not destroyed. Clinton ordered Cornwallis to hold Old Point Comfort and Yorktown, but the former was not a defensible place, so Cornwallis proceeded to fortify Yorktown.

In August, the famous Iroquois Indian leader Joseph Brant paid a visit to western Virginia. His war party included two white men, George Girty and Cage Callaway. Discovering that General Clark was bringing troops down the Ohio from Wheeling, they made plans to attack him en route. Clark, together with Col. Archibald Lochry of Westmoreland County, had been recruiting men in that area and intended to make the trip together. Unfortunately, Lochry did not appear at Wheeling at the designated date, and Clark, supposing that Lochry's recruiting was unsuccessful and finding his own underpaid recruits deserting, started down the river to the Falls. On August 8, only twelve hours after Clark had departed, Lochry finally arrived with over 80 men. The two commanders communicated with the aid of scouts. Between them, it was decided that Clark would slow his advance to allow Lochry's force to catch up.

Lochry and his men then started down the Ohio in seven boats. Another small party followed along the shore with the horses. On August 14 these men encountered sixteen deserters from Clark's detachment and forced them to accompany them. The following day, Lochry reached three islands near the present Manchester, Ohio. There Clark had detached Maj. Charles Craycraft with a horse boat. The horses were then loaded and the entire company proceeded down the river. Afterwards Craycraft and six men boarded a small boat and went ahead to inform Clark of Lochry's progress.

In the meantime, the Indians were planning to ambush Clark on the river. Joseph Brant led his force to what is now called Laughery Island, which is located about ten miles below the mouth of the Miami River. He intended to attack General Clark's boats from both sides of the river and from the island, thereby having two-thirds of his warriors within rifle range, regardless of which side of the river Clark traveled. When Clark's boats came in view, however, the Indians realized that they were outnumbered and outgunned, Clark having mounted a swivel gun on one of his boats. Brant became exasperated with his warriors' lack of courage. But a day or two later they managed to capture Major Craycraft's party, from whom they learned that Lochry's boats were following Clark.

Brant did not need to adopt any war plan to defeat Lochry. On the morning of August 24 the colonel ordered his men to land to cook some buffalo meat and to feed and water their horses. Unknown to them, their landing place was very close to Brant's camp. Spotting the force coming ashore, the Indians quickly organized an attack. Catching Lochry's men by surprise, the Indians drove them onto a sandbar in the river, where they attempted to defend themselves from behind the boats. Finally, the survivors were taken prisoner after Colonel Lochry felt compelled to surrender. The Indians eventually killed Colonel Lochry and most of the wounded prisoners.

Butler's Rangers and more warriors under the command of Capt. Alexander McKee soon arrived to reinforce Brant's force. The leaders attempted to organize an attack against General Clark's base at the Falls, but most Indians, wary of the magnitude of the venture, were not willing to make a direct attack on the fort. Subsequently, most of them crossed the Ohio and moved south in small war parties.

After reaching his base, George Rogers Clark called a conference of the nearby county militia officers to decide the best course of action. John Todd of Fayette County and Benjamin Logan of Lincoln thought it "best to decline an Expediton [sic] this season Altogether."[6] Instead, they urged that a fort be constructed at the mouth of the Kentucky River to protect the interior settlers of their counties. John Floyd of Jefferson County favored another expedition up the Miami River against the Shawnee. He reasoned that such an expedition would force the Shawnee to offer terms that would pave the way for other tribes to "Come in." Colonels Trigg, Cox, and Pope agreed.

At the nearby Squire Boone's station on Clear Creek (also called Painted Stone) the settlers frequently began to observe Indian signs. Their leader having been seriously wounded in the spring, they decided to abandon their homes and seek refuge in some of the nearby Beargrass stations, which they felt would be safer. When they requested an escort, Floyd ordered out eight militiamen under Lt. James Welsh, and Clark sent twenty-four dragoons from the Illinois regiment under Lt. Thomas Ravencroft. When the troops reached the station, they found that the Indians were already near the fort. A skirmish followed in which one man was killed. Their leaders decided to evacuate the station before a general siege developed; the settlers left in convoy with the militia. Only the injured Squire Boone and the widow Hinton remained behind.

As the settlers traveled along the wagon road, the families became strung out. After going nine miles, Lieutenant Welsh became ill, and the militia halted so that he could recover. They were bringing up the rear of the column, believing that in this position they could protect the settlers. Three miles farther along the road, near a stream called the Long Run, the Indians attacked. Although some of the men dashed for safety, others dismounted and fought bravely. Many cut the packs from horses and put their women and children on the animals so they could escape. A running fight developed, with the white settlers retreating along the trail and the Indians following closely, cutting down those who exposed themselves. Most of the settlers eventually managed to reach Linn's Station, situated about twelve miles away on the headwaters of Beargrass Creek. The Indians managed to kill about a dozen, including women and children.

When news of the massacre reached Col. John Floyd, he immediately mobilized all the mounted men at the Beargrass stations and rode to Linn's Station, where he surmised that the next attack would come. His force was smaller than he had hoped, for that very afternoon Indians had stolen twenty-five horses from the Dutch Station. Early the next morning, on September 14, Floyd gathered twenty-seven men and headed for Long Run.[7]

Floyd, having spent some time training this mounted militia, believed that his men could effectively handle the enemy. Like most of the leaders in Kentucky, he was still a relatively young man, prone perhaps to overconfidence. The following morning the twenty-seven "Horse Militia" rode out in three columns, with Colonel Floyd at the head of the center column, Capt. Peter Asturgus leading the right, and Lt. Thomas Ravenscraft leading the left.

Samuel Wells Sr. and Samuel Wells Jr. rode out with Floyd. The elder Wells had led parties to the Licking in 1775 and 1776 to preempt land; he had brought back his family to make his claim but apparently too late to see the commissioners. Eventually, his family had obtained a 1,000-acre preemption by applying to the county courts. In 1780 Lt. Samuel Wells had been second in command of a militia company from Jefferson County during Clark's invasion of Ohio. On this occasion, John Floyd apparently called up the same company. For some of the troops, including Samuel Wells Sr. (who had previously been convicted of beating his wife), this was to be the last day of their lives.

The cavalry followed Boone's wagon road over the ford of Floyd's Fork and along the top of the ridge beyond. Approaching the next little creek called Long Run, Floyd's columns ran headlong into a party of 200 Indians. A short battle began, with the militia on the defensive. Within a few minutes Floyd's troops were down to nine men, all of them fleeing for their lives. Sam Wells Sr. was one of those killed. Floyd was wounded in the foot or leg, and his horse killed. As he was being closely pursued, he was given another horse by Samuel Wells Jr. upon which he made his escape. When the survivors returned to Linn's Station, Colonel Floyd dispatched a note to General Clark at the Falls:

$^1/_2$ past 10 O'clock

Dear General:

I have this minute returned from a little Excur[s]ion against the enemy & my party, 27 in number, are all dispersed & cut to pieces except 9 who came off the field—with Captain Asturgus mortally wounded and one other slightly wounded. I don't yet know who are killed. Mr. Ravenscroft [sic] was taken prisoner by the side of me. A party was defeated yesterday near the same place & many Women & Children wounded. I want satisfaction: do send me 100 men, which number with what I can raise will do.[8]

The fact that the mounted militia company was so quickly surrounded and defeated led everyone to believe the Indians had prepared an ambush. Bland Ballard's statement that "he could not persuade Floyd not to pursue" later reinforced this version:

He was decoyed onto a ridge in pursuit of some indians that showed themselves and the indians just fired on them from both sides, their shot crossing up the hill. His men would have been, as many of them were, just shot down, but they charged through the ranks [of the enemy]. Floyd was wounded but 6 or 7 men brought him off.[9]

In fact, more careful study reveals that the Indians were more surprised to meet Floyd than he was to meet them.[10] Most of the Indians were off the road, collecting the goods discarded by the settlers the day before. On seeing the militia riding along the ridge, they were able to attack from both sides and the rear. Being greatly outnumbered, the only chance for Floyd's men to survive was to wheel about and retreat through the enemy.

Floyd's men had killed only three Hurons and a Miami, but one of the Hurons was their chief. This man was their principal warrior and had been a great supporter of the British efforts to keep the Indians organized against the Americans. Alexander McKee tried to persuade the Indians to follow up on their success, but the Huron would not listen and started for home. McKee and most of the Miami, deprived of much of their party's strength, were obliged to follow.

A day or two after Floyd's defeat, a force of about 300 men—some of them Virginia regular troops—returned to the site of the battle. Finding the Indians gone, they buried the dead. Soon after, Squire Boone and the widow Hinton were rescued from the Painted Stone Station. Vacated, it was later burned down by a party of Indians.

While Floyd was recovering from his wound, Gen. George Washington moved his army southward against Gen. Charles Cornwallis at Yorktown. He secretly began to march his troops south on August 21. By September 6 they had passed through Philadelphia and reached the head of the Elk on the Chesapeake. There the men were loaded onto ships, the last ship sailing on the eighteenth. After a short voyage by sea, the ships put the army ashore at Williamsburg on the twenty-sixth.

As Washington moved south, Lafayette marched his men by land and camped near Williamsburg. Gen. Anthony Wayne's detachment was posted at Cabin Point on the James River. These troop movements were designed to keep Cornwallis penned up in Yorktown. Next, the French fleet (twenty-four ships of the line and six frigates) under Grasse arrived outside of Hampton Roads. By the end of August, General Cornwallis was not only surrounded but outnumbered on land and sea. To make matters worse for Cornwallis, on September 5, 3,000 French troops under Marquis Saint Simons disembarked to reinforce Lafayette. About the same time, the French and British fleets went into action. The French had twenty-four major ships, the British nineteen. The ensuing battle lasted two hours and resulted in five British ships being heavily damaged. Defeated, the British ships broke off the action and sailed back to New York, leaving Cornwallis to his doom.

When Washington's force combined with Lafayette's and the Virginia militia under Thomas Nelson, it numbered 8,845 men. The French under General de Rochambeau had 7,800 soldiers. To oppose them, the British had about 7,300 troops, including Hessians and Tories. When Washington marched from Williamsburg to Yorktown on September 28, Cornwallis abandoned the outlying redoubts and consolidated his position. The siege lasted less than a month, and Cornwallis, realizing the futility of further resistance, surrendered on October 19, 1781.[11]

With a truce in the East, Washington sent Brig. Gen. William Irvine to Fort Pitt to manage the Western theater. There he was to command a ragtag little force consisting of the 8th Pennsylvania and the 7th Virginia. These 300 troops had not been paid for two years. Their numbers had been depleted by disease and desertion. General Irvine wrote General Washington, candidly describing their condition, "No man would believe from their appearance that they were soldiers; nay, it would be difficult to determine wheather [*sic*] they were white men."[12]

Soldiers in General Clark's Virginia regiment did not fare much better. In December, Capt. Robert Todd wrote to Gov. Thomas Nelson:

> [I]t becomes a part of my duty to represent the wretched situation of the few troops remaining Westward. Many of them have been in the service for two years past and have never received a Shoe, Stocking, or hat, & none of them any pay. What other clothing not here mentioned rec'd at fort Jefferson, are now worn out.[13]

To those in the higher command, unpaid troops provided no great cause for alarm. Many correctly believed that the victory at Yorktown would end the war. The question was when. Peace commissioners were appointed, and on November 30, 1781, they signed provisional articles to end hostilities. The final peace treaty, however, would not be concluded for nearly two years. In the meantime, Virginia's war in the West continued.

CHAPTER 8

1782
Cornwallis Surrenders
but the War Goes On

THE SETTLERS ON VIRGINIA'S FRONTIER DESPERATELY HOPED THAT THE war they had endured since 1776 would soon come to an end. The few regular Virginia soldiers that remained had not been paid for months. Their meager supplies were nearly depleted. The state's credit was at an all-time low, and Gen. George Rogers Clark was having great difficulty simply keeping his men fed.

Early in February the Indians started their offensive by attacking settlements in Monongalia County. The county lieutenant, John Evans, asked the governor to send him reinforcements since the local militia contained only 350 men, and they were settled along a line eighty miles in length. Without reinforcements he was afraid the people "will be under the necessity of vacating the Country—Colo. Clarke's Expedition falling through, and so many men falling into the Enemies hands have encouraged them so that they are constant in our Country."[1]

Despite the dangers, people were still moving west. One party, led by Jacob Baughman (or Boofman, a different man from John Floyd's former chainman of the same name, who died circa 1778), was attacked on Scagg's Trace south of William Whitley's station, and several of the new-comers were killed. Whitley reported that he first learned of the attack when "Mrs. Hammons came into Crab Orchard in her linsey-wooley wounded in the head with an arrow."[2] This woman was the wife of Philip Hammon, who earlier had beer one of the two men who ventured out of Fort Henry to warn the Greenbrier settlements.

149

The Virginia House of Delegates turned down Clark's plans for an offensive spring campaign. They decided that such an undertaking would require 2,000 men, 1,900 packhorses, 1,200 pounds of powder, 2,400 pounds of lead, and 4,000 bushels of corn plus the flour and salt then on hand. There was then available 200,000 pounds of flour, 8,000 pounds of powder, 1,600 pounds of lead, and between 600 and 800 bushels of salt. Because the state could not muster the men and supplies, the legislature decided that the frontier might be defended by keeping garrisons at new posts along the Ohio. Governor Harrison wrote Clark that he should call out militia from Fayette and Lincoln Counties as necessary to reinforce the regulars to the number of 304 men, stationing 100 at Louisville, and 68 at three new posts, to be established at the mouth of the Kentucky, the Licking, and Limestone Creek. The governor also ordered Clark to build three or four gunboats and promised to send cannons to Fort Pitt to be used in the forts and boats. Clark could arrange to have them shipped where they were needed. The governor added that he hoped these orders could be accomplished by Clark without money, as there was none to spare.[3] This was not an exaggeration; Virginia had only two shillings in the state treasury in April![4]

Though Clark had hoped for a spring campaign against the Indians, as mentioned, the Indians made the first move. Another attack occurred in March when a war party of Wyandot invaded Fayette County. On the first they attacked Strode's Station, killing two men. On March 19, the inhabitants of Boonesborough, spotting empty rafts afloat on the river, immediately sent a warning to nearby Estill's Station. Capt. James Estill raised twenty-five men from his own and nearby stations to go in search of the Indians. While they were gone, the Indians surrounded the station, killed and scalped a young woman, and captured Monk, James Estill's Negro slave. Monk quick-wittedly told the Indians that the fort was well manned and prepared for an attack. This erroneous information so discouraged the marauders that they withdrew and headed for home.

After they had left, Capt. James Estill and his militia company started in pursuit. A brisk battle ensued on March 22 when the two forces met in a woods near Little Mountain Creek, not far from the present town of Mt. Sterling. Though the forces were initially about equal in number with about twenty-five men on each side, during the battle Lt. William Miller and six others fled, leaving Estill's remaining force outnumbered. The fight lasted two hours. Estill was covered with blood from a wound received early in the action, Lt. John South and nine of his men were dead, and four others were too disabled to fight.[5] When the fighting men were reduced to four, an Indian rushed Captain Estill and buried a knife blade in his chest. At the same time, Joseph Proctor shot and killed the offending Indian. With their leader and most of the company killed, the remaining Virginians retreated. Reports stated that Proctor aided a wounded friend in making his way back to the station, a trip of thirty miles. During the battle Monk escaped from his captors and was later freed for averting an attack on the station.

About the time that this party of Wyandot invaded Kentucky, a troop of 100 mounted men from Pennsylvania under Capt. David Williamson crossed the Ohio and rode to the Indian village of Gnadenhutten, a town occupied by friendly Delaware. Moravian missionaries had succeeded in converting the town's ninety inhabitants to Christianity. During the war, the Indian inhabitants had lived peacefully in their village, raising their families and tending their crops. Nevertheless, Williamson and his volunteers rounded them up and confined them in some outbuildings while these Pennsylvanians voted to determine their fate. Eighteen men wanted them spared or made prisoners, but the others demanded death. The Moravian Indians, including women and children, were then brutally killed one or two at a time, many of them with a mallet. The white men then proceeded to gather up anything of value, including the Indian horses, as spoils of war, then burned the town.[6] Two boys miraculously escaped to tell the story.

Many Pennsylvanians and almost all of the Virginians immediately condemned the murders, one of the most senseless atrocities of the war. Even so, another punitive expedition consisting of 488 Pennsylvania militiamen was organized a few weeks later. Their expressed purpose was to march west and burn the Indian towns along the Sandusky River. Col. William Crawford, a distinguished veteran of the war in the East, was elected to lead them. This army set out on May 25. Captain Williamson, by then famous for his massacre of the Moravian Indians, brought his men along, and they served as part of the army. Although the Pennsylvanians were on horses, their progress was slow. Their slackened pace allowed the British Rangers to assemble the Indians and organize their defense. On June 4 the two forces clashed. The odds were about even, and the first day's engagement ended in a draw.

The following morning the men on both sides cautiously began to engage each other from cover, but no charges were made. The Indians were content to keep the whites in place, since they knew that Alexander McKee and 150 Shawnee reinforcements were on their way. By afternoon, Colonel

Crawford and his officers, realizing that they were being outnumbered and surrounded, decided to form into small groups and retreat at dark. The retreat turned out to be a rout as the Indians killed and captured large numbers of the Americans. Still furious at the atrocities committed on the peaceful Christianized Delaware at Gnadenhutten, the Indians enacted their justice upon the captured whites. Most of the captured prisoners, including Colonel Crawford, were tortured and burned at the stake. David Williamson, Crawford's second in command and the man who had earlier condoned the murder of innocents, managed to escape. These two campaigns conducted by the Pennsylvania militia were probably the most humiliating of any on the frontier up to that time. But they were not to be the last.

In western Virginia, people were still thinking about defense, as reflected in these statements of John Todd, who oversaw the building of more elaborate fortifications at Lexington:

[To] build a new Fort upon the very advantageous Situation at this place & make it proof against Swivels & small Artilery [sic] which so terrify our people. I laid off the Fort upon the simplest plan of a Quadrangle & divided the work equally among them to employ Workers from this and the neighboring Stations & assuring them of their pay myself. [He managed to complete the fort in twenty days by rewarding the men with liquor] which proved to be a powerful incentive to Industry.[7]

Thus Todd turned the little blockhouse at Lexington into a fort. John Floyd, the leading Jefferson County official, wrote to General Clark concerning the orders from the Virginia House of Delegates to build three more forts and have two gunboats at each fort, including Fort Nelson:

I have seen no person yet qualified for the purpose of boat-building except old Mr. Asturgus who seems willing & even desirous of building one, but [he has] no person about him to wait on his wounded son, & to do the drudgery about his plantation. I wish you could get him as he appears to understand every part of the business. It will, I find, be a great mortification to the inhabitants in general if no Post is erected on the Ohio above the Falls.[8]

The question of building another fort for defense had been discussed previously. In October 1781 John Todd and Benjamin Logan wrote General Clark, stating that the militia of their respective counties were unable to build a fort on the Ohio because they had no entrenching tools and their ranks were too thin. They believed that if they had one they could better defend themselves closer to home. As mentioned, Todd did manage to build a fort near Lexington. About a week later, Todd wrote the governor, suggesting that Clark take it upon himself to build and garrison another fort at the mouth of the Kentucky River, using the troops he then had stationed at the Falls of the Ohio. He insinuated that the fort at the Falls had little value other than to protect the Beargrass stations, and these could be abandoned if necessary.

Back at the Falls, Floyd eventually hired men to build the galleys, but he had difficulty finding the material for sails and riggings. In another note to Clark, Floyd wrote that he would search all the houses in the neighborhood for hemp, though he did not expect to find much. For this reason, he employed some men to make rope of water-soaked papaw bark instead of hemp, hoping it would serve just as well.

By early May, Indians were raiding along Beargrass Creek. The settlers at Spring Station would not venture outside their fort to plant corn unless furnished with a militia guard of fifteen men for one week. They informed Floyd that if he furnished the guard, they would send fifteen men down to the river to work on Fort Nelson when they had finished planting. On June 16 Floyd reported that his rope makers were slow but had managed to make thirty fathoms of good rope per day, and "that the galley is likely to answer your expectation." Colonel Floyd reported with embarrassment that it was necessary to order out all of the Jefferson County militia for two weeks in two shifts to work on Fort Nelson.

Clark's galley was seventy-three feet long. It was built to have forty-six oars, 2 men to an oar, with a total crew of 102 men. It was designed to hold four cannons, these being 6-, 4-, and 2-pounders.[9] It possessed a novel feature, hinged gunnels that could be raised in case of attack to protect the rowers from rifle fire. No description of the rigging survives, but sails were provided to propel the vessel when the wind was favorable.[10] Clark believed that ships of this type would provide better protection against Indian raids than forts along the Ohio. The boats could sail down to any crossing place and defeat the invaders regardless of their direction of travel, either during their advance or retreat. This would have been an ideal solution if the boats had well-trained and dedicated crews. Unfortunately, they didn't.

Artillery officer Capt. Robert George commanded the first galley on its maiden voyage. The crew consisted of militia from Fayette County under Robert Patterson. But, according to Captain George, this type of duty displeased the militiamen:

> [T]here has been nothing but murmouring [sic] and grumbling on their part; first they insisted on being allowed double Rations of Flour—this was granted them—then they must be allowed to march on the shore and not work at the boat—that was granted them; . . . at last this morning they have determined to go off at all Events, altho thier [sic] Tour is not out this seven days.[11]

In the meantime, Jacob Pyeatt began to recruit a company of "marines" for the boat, mostly from men who had been discharged from Crockett's regiment. He promised them ten dollars per month and a "suit of Cloaths [sic]." He asked General Clark to furnish the other "Necessaries" since it was impossible to purchase anything on state credit.

Nevertheless, even without the militia and the marines, the undermanned galley did patrol the Ohio where Indian scouts soon observed it. Capt. Robert George still had his faithful company of twenty Virginia regulars, among whom was John Oakly, one of the three gunners. Because it would be difficult for twenty men to handle a forty-six-oar galley, other crew members must have been added. The Indians, not realizing that the sailors on this galley were inexperienced, interpreted the presence of such a large boat as a prelude to an invasion by General Clark. They rushed back to the Miami towns to report the news that they had invented.

On July 3 a force of about 200 Seneca struck at Hannastown in Pennsylvania. Located twenty-five miles east of Fort Pitt, this settlement was a place that few would ever regard as being on the frontier. The town was burned, and about thirty people were either killed or captured.

In Louisville, George Rogers Clark received news that Gen. William Irvine at Fort Pitt was scheduled to recruit 700 Pennsylvania militia to go on the offensive. On August 10 he wrote Irvine, saying that he had learned of Irvine's intention to launch an attack on the Indians in the fall. He requested more information so he could lend assistance if possible. What Clark didn't know was that Gen. George Washington was having doubts about Irvine's proposed offensive. Leaders in the East were mistakenly beginning to believe that the war was over. They would be proven wrong.

Toward the end of July, British agents Capts. Alexander McKee and William Caldwell had assembled "eleven hundred Indians on the ground and three hundred within a days march of me [i.e., McKee]" at the "Priowee Village" with the intention of going on the offensive. McKee and Caldwell had considered an attack on Wheeling until some of their spies spotted the large galley on the Ohio near the mouth of the Licking River. The spies reported that General Clark had begun another invasion of the Indian country. When the rumor proved false, many of the Indians left for home. McKee and Caldwell convinced the remainder, "upwards of three hundred Hurons and Lake Indians, few of Delawares, Shawneese [sic] or Mingoes" to march to the Ohio.[12] After sending out scouts toward Louisville, the remainder crossed the river, marched to the heart of the Bluegrass, and surrounded Bryan's Station (now part of Lexington). They surrounded the station on the morning of August 16 and "tried to draw them out by sending up a small party to try to take a prisoner and show themselves, but the Indians were in too great a hurry."[13]

Ordinarily, Capt. Robert Johnson commanded the militia company at Bryan's Station, but he was away serving in the Virginia legislature, so Capt. John Craig had taken charge in his place. Two of the most active land speculators on the frontier, these men individually and in partnership had patented over 144,000 acres on the Virginia frontier. Johnson's wife, who did not go back to Richmond with her husband, was present during the siege as were her five children. Richard M. Johnson, their son who later became the vice-president of the United States, was still an infant in a crib. It was later claimed that a flaming arrow hit the crib but was quickly pulled off by his young sister, Betsy.[14] One of the militiamen on hand was twenty-two-year-old John Hammon, who had arrived in Kentucky during the summer. An experienced veteran who fought at King's Mountain, Hammon epitomized the thousands of landless people who migrated west during this period. He later earned his living as a steamboat carpenter.[15]

A few days earlier, another party of Indians, probably not part of the group described, had captured two boys near Hoy's Station, one of them William Hoy's son. Hoy's Station was located on the ridge west of Holder's Station, which was on Otter Creek about four miles above Boonesborough. As he passed these settlements in pursuit of the kidnappers, Capt. John Holder quickly gathered additional militia from his own station, Boonesborough, and Strode's and McGee's Stations. The pursuit followed the Indians northeast to the Upper Blue Lick, and a few miles farther on what was later to be called Battle Run. There, the Indians ambushed Holder's men, who lost one killed and three wounded. Although Holder's company probably outnumbered the Indians, they hastily retreated after the ambush, leaving their wounded on the field. One who was left to die was Billey Buchanan, a friend of John Floyd.[16] Several days later his brother went to the battle site to search for him and found him in the woods. He was barely alive and, to his brother's dismay, lived only a few more hours.

At about the time Holder's men were pursuing the Indians, another well-known settler was killed. Indians waylaid and shot Nathaniel Hart, one of the original members of the Transylvania Company who had moved to Boonesborough in 1775. Hart was searching for a stray horse near White Oak, his station on Otter Creek. He had been one of Daniel Boone's best friends. Despite that fact, several years later his children sued Boone over a survey he directed for their widowed mother.[17]

Back at Bryan's Station, the attackers were frustrated. According to tradition, the British and Indians permitted the women to go to the well and fetch water, hoping to ambush the men when they left to tend their crops. Though often repeated, this story has not been confirmed by any contemporary account. Research reveals that two springs were near the fort, on the northeast side near the creek, and the other south of the gate. It is likely that any Indians lying in wait around it could have been seen and shot from the corner blockhouses. More likely, the Indians permitted the women to go to the spring because they respected the defenders' marksmanship and kept out of rifle range. At least one fact emerges with certainty through the apocryphal mists. When the Virginians discovered the Indians in threatening numbers, they dispatched two men on horseback to ride to nearby Lexington for assistance.

Bryan's Station, the largest station in the three Virginia counties, had forty-four riflemen to defend it. Six hundred feet long by 150 feet wide, it contained twenty cabins and a blockhouse at each corner. The population consisted of ten or twelve families, plus a number of single men, for a total of ninety people. Most cabins at the time were about sixteen feet on the longest side.[18] If this description is correct, subtracting the cabins, blockhouses, and gates, the fort would still have 1,036 lineal feet of walls, proportions that seem somewhat excessive. Each of the forty-four riflemen would be required to defend over thirty feet of the palisades. One would think that the builders would have had more common sense than to construct a fort of these dimensions. As described, the walls between the cab-

Women getting water from spring at Bryan Station, 1782. OUR PIONEER HEROES AND THEIR DARING DEEDS, D. M. KELLEY. H. W. KELLEY PUBLISHER, 1854

ins in this fort would average thirty-six feet long, as the end walls had no cabins. In deploying the forty-four defenders, if two men were placed on the second floor of each blockhouse to shoot along the walls and the others were positioned on the walls, there would be only a single man between the cabins, with only five on the long-end walls. Because the end walls were about 150 feet long, each of these men would also be required to defend 30 feet of wall, and the men between the cabins, 36 feet of wall. Perhaps this pioneer station was not as large as past historians have suggested.

When the Indians concluded that the white men were not coming out to meet them, they did eventually show themselves. The Lake Indians rushed up to the stockade and set several outbuildings on fire. Fortunately for the settlers, these sheds were too far away to ignite the fort, especially since the wind was blowing the flames in the opposite direction. While the buildings burned, the engagement between the settlers and Indians continued.

Toward the middle of the day, the relief company that Capt. Levi Todd had mustered arrived, having marched about five miles out the old buffalo road to Bryan's. On the trail the original party of thirty met another ten men from Boone's Station. These men joined them. Well aware that the Indians had surrounded the station, seventeen men who had horses galloped at full speed into the fort, followed by the remaining twenty-three militia on foot. Because they had not been expecting the relief to arrive so soon, the Indians were spread around the fort. Those on the west side soon formed a battle line in a cornfield and engaged the new-comers, who were marching up the road protected by two parallel fences. After the Indians killed one Virginian and wounded three, Captain Todd's foot soldiers withdrew to Lexington to gather a larger force. One of those wounded was William Hays, the son-in-law of Daniel Boone.

With firepower inside the fort increased from the forty-four guns to sixty-one, the attackers began to sustain casualties. By nightfall, the tally of killed or wounded had risen to five. At about 10:00 A.M. the next morning, the British Rangers and Indians left the fort and marched to the unoccu-pied Ruddle's Station about twenty miles to the northeast. Here they di-vided, with about a hundred Indians going back by the way they had come to retrieve some baggage left down the river. The remainder marched east-ward along some old, well-established buffalo roads to the Blue Lick, a route that "was nigher and the ground more advantageous in case the enemy should pursue us."[19] They reached the Lower Blue Lick on the eighteenth and camped for the night.

By the morning of August 17 the militia of both Fayette and Lincoln Counties had been called up. That evening several companies totaling 182 men, mostly mounted troops, reached Bryan's Station. The ranking officer was Col. John Todd of Fayette County. Lt. Col. Stephen Trigg brought 130 men from Lincoln County, and Lt. Col. Daniel Boone commanded about 50 men from Fayette County. More men were expected from Lin-coln County, where Col. Benjamin Logan was collecting the remaining companies.

At the time Lincoln County had a much larger population than either of the adjacent counties, Jefferson and Fayette. Not only could Lincoln County raise more troops, but its commander, Benjamin Logan, was the highest-ranking officer. During the officers' conference Logan's superior rank created a dilemma. The 182 mounted troops could start the next morning and most likely encounter the enemy on the road, or they could wait for more men and possibly allow the enemy to escape over the Ohio. If they chose the first option, their commander would be Col. John Todd of Fayette County, though most of the troops were from Lincoln County. Only forty or fifty were from Fayette County. Under the second option, the larger army would be commanded by Col. Benjamin Logan.

The officers at Bryan's Station disagreed about the best course of action. Maj. Hugh McGary, from Lincoln County, originally opposed an immediate chase, advising Colonel Todd to wait for Logan and the other companies to arrive. But Todd disregarded his advice, saying that a single day lost would enable the Indians to cross the Ohio River and escape. When warned that the Indians might outnumber his force, Todd replied that this talk of numbers was nonsense, and even if they had more men, the more the merrier. He apparently insinuated that he had enough brave men with him to go ahead without McGary.

Early in the morning the mounted militia began the pursuit on the trail of the enemy. They rode all day, passing Ruddle's deserted fort and continuing eastward along the old trail. The distance between Bryan's Station and Ruddle's was approximately twenty miles and another twenty miles to the Lower Blue Lick. One would suppose that the trip could be made in ten hours, but the troops probably made numerous stops while their advanced scouts rode ahead to avoid an ambush. Their exact stopping place is not known, but by the time the militiamen made camp, they were not far from the river crossing at Lower Blue Lick.

Capt. William Caldwell, assisted by Alexander McKee and the white renegade Simon Girty, led a force consisting of a few Canadians of Butler's Rangers and about 300 Indians, most of them Wyandot. The Indians and British Rangers had camped at the Licks on the evening of August 18. By the next morning they knew the whereabouts of their pursuers. To meet the Kentucky militia, Caldwell placed his men on both sides of a ridge, about 3,500 feet north of the ford. Adjacent to the ford was a broad expanse of flat bottomland containing the salt licks. The ford itself was located at the bottom of a U-shaped bend in the Licking River.[20]

Captain Caldwell realized that he had gained an ideal defensive position since retreat could be effected with ease for the defenders but not for the attackers, whose exit route would be blocked by the river. Holding the high ground gave the British and Indians another advantage, especially because the top of the hill was wooded, whereas the lower land adjacent to the licks was clear of vegetation. The defenders had one other advantage. On the east side of the buffalo trail was a razorback ridge with a steep descent to the river. Men stationed just behind this ridge could easily advance and fire down upon anyone coming along the road.

In the morning the militia broke camp. After traveling a short distance, they came to the hill on the south side of the ford. The advanced scouts sighted some Indians on the other side of the river, moving away

from them up the hill at a casual pace. The Americans halted, and the officers conferred to decide their course of action. Daniel Boone wisely advised
against proceeding, intuiting that the Indians would ambush them where
the timber began. He stated that it would be better to stay there and wait
for the reinforcements under Logan. If they were determined to press the
attack, the best plan would be to use another trail along an upstream bend
in the river to get beyond the enemy's position and attack from the rear.
The rear of the enemy could be reached by traveling about two miles, during which time their movements would be screened by the terrain. To
reach the trail behind the enemy would be an easy trip by horseback.

The other officers seemed inclined to follow Boone's advice, but Maj.
Hugh McGary, still fuming about his treatment at Bryan's, cursed them for
a set of cowards and swore that as they had come so far for a fight they
should have it, or he would disgrace them. He then mounted his horse,
headed for the river, and called upon all who were not cowards to follow
him. Thus Major McGary, rather than Colonel Todd, actually made the
decision to fight the Indians at that place and time.

The Kentuckians followed McGary, but in an orderly fashion, not as a
mob as some have suggested. They advanced up the trail until they were
nearly to the top of ridge about 200 yards in front of the Indians' position. Then they dismounted and formed a line of battle, after fastening
their coats and other clothing to their saddles. The time required to deploy
allowed the officers sufficient time to organize and form their companies.
Those from Fayette County under Boone moved to the left or western side
of the line. Major McGary's Lincoln County company formed the center,
and Colonel Trigg with the second company from Lincoln County formed
on the right or east end of the line. As was customary, every tenth man
stayed behind to hold the horses. Thus the three companies in line consisted of about 130 men. The length of this line would have been about
600 feet long with the men spaced about 4 feet apart. Where the men
lined up for battle, there is a distance of 2,000 feet between the riverbanks.
The Americans formed their ranks in the open and could be observed by
their enemies, most of whom were concealed by the adjacent forest.

The battle began when Major Harlin with an advanced party of horsemen charged the Indians' position in an attempt to break their line, but
most of the Americans were shot down.[21] Boone's company on the left engaged the enemy about the same time and pushed the Indians back about
100 yards. Daniel Boone did not lead his men carrying a sword, but instead carried a shotgun loaded with three rifle balls and sixteen buckshot.

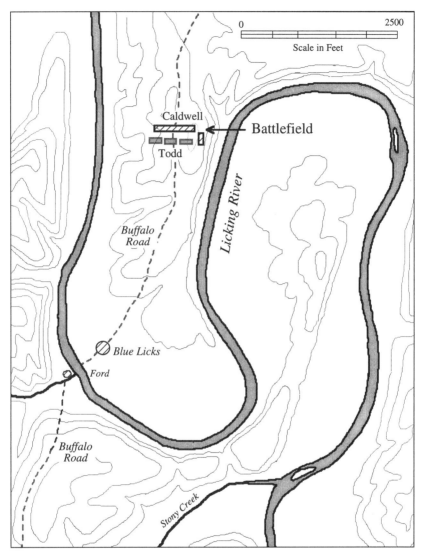

Map of the battle of Blue Lick.

During the advance he killed an Indian and passed by his body during the attack. Though Boone believed he had killed Indians on other occasions, he affirmed that he was positive only of having killed this one.[22] Subsequently, when he learned how the battle had gone, Boone concluded that the Indians had probably executed a feint to draw his wing into a trap. His

Battle of Blue Licks, from Adventures of Daniel Boone *by Henry Weiman, an old book whose publication date is unknown.* MISSOURI HISTORICAL SOCIETY LIBRARY AND ARCHIVES, ST. LOUIS, MISSOURI

men had pushed the Indians back from a ravine that ran perpendicular to the riverbank.

Jacob Stevens, a private from Lincoln County, dismounted with his comrades, and the company formed behind some sapling trees. When the firing started, he noticed that George Corn was shot in the mouth, the bullet having done considerable damage:

> taking away all the upper and lower teeth in his right jaw. I saw him spit the ball in his right hand, and though he was shot in the breast, such was the quantity of blood. . . . Jim Hays, on the other side of me, said he be dammed if he didn't shoot one. I told him to take care or he would get it next, and had scarce said it when he recived [*sic*] a shot in the collar bone. Both of these fell down and as soon as they could, crept back, got on horses, and got to Bryans

Station that same day. I had fired three time was just priming for the fourth when the word was given for to retreat.[23]

On the right, the Indians came over the ridge parallel to the road and appeared on the flank of Trigg's men. Either the inexperienced Trigg was one of the first killed or else he did not react quickly enough to maneuver his men to meet the flank attack. Colonel Todd rode into battle on his horse and almost immediately received a wound. In about two minutes it was all over. Seeing that they were outflanked, the Lincoln County militia began retreating from right to left, the Indians in full pursuit. By then, the Fayette County company had advanced beyond the little ravine on their front and were unaware that the battle had been lost.

Within five minutes, Major McGary came riding up to Boone and shouted, "Colonel Boone, why are you not retreating? Todd & Trigg's line has given way, & the Indians are all around you."[24] Colonel Boone ordered his men to collect together and, in a body, break through the enemy, for he had discovered that the Indians were already in his rear. Upon reaching the horses, each man took the first within his reach and looked for an escape route. Daniel Boone had the unfortunate experience of seeing his son Israel killed just as he mounted his horse. Instead of heading south to the main ford, Colonel Boone and most of his men went west, descended the hill, and swam their mounts across the river a half mile below the ford. Boone lost only fifteen of his men, compared to over fifty lost among the Lincoln County militia. Another of those killed was Andrew McConnell, whose twin sons had been captured at Leestown in 1776.

Daniel Boone's nephew, afterwards called the Preacher Squire Boone, was wounded, with his thigh bone broken. A young man, "scarcely grown," named Samuel Brannon stopped, dismounted, put young Squire on his horse, and jumped on behind him. Riding together they both made their escape over the river, but while climbing the hill on the other side, an Indian shot and killed Brannon. Squire made the trip alone back to Boone's Station with the injured limb dangling. Slowed down by his wound, the journey took three days.

On the right flank there was chaos. The Virginia leader, Col. John Todd, had been killed as had Col. Stephen Trigg, the commander of the Lincoln County company on the right. The Indians had already worked their way behind many of these men, racing them to the ford. Maj. Levi Todd described the scene a few days later, "He that could remount a horse was well off, and he that could not saw no time for delay." In making their

retreat, the survivors of the Lincoln County companies had very few options. The terrain forced the defeated men on the right flank to make their
way down the hill to the south and cross at the ford. Those who recovered
their horses generally succeeded in crossing the river, but the men on foot
were mostly cut off by Indians who caught some of the loose horses and
rushed to the ford to prevent their escape. During the retreat many men
lost or threw away their weapons. The Virginians lost at least twenty-three
horses, many taken by the Indians.

Just when complete disaster seemed inevitable, an unlikely hero appeared from the ranks of the militia. Benjamin Netherland was perhaps
one of the first to leave the battle. He had been one of the lucky ones to
reach the south shore of the Licking River unharmed. There he climbed
the hill where he had the protection of the forest. Looking back at the
clearing behind the battlefield, he could see that many of his comrades
would not make it across the river because they were being cut off by the
Indians. Instead of continuing his retreat, he turned around and began to
rally the others. "Let's halt boys, and give them a fire."[25] They positioned
themselves on the high ground above the ford where they began an effective fire to drive back the Indians. This rally undoubtedly enabled many to
escape who would have otherwise been killed.

The Indians did not follow the Americans very far. In fact, only a few
of them even crossed the river. There were too many valuables and too
many scalps on the battlefield to pass up. The victors gathered about 100
rifles in addition to many horses. Seventy-seven Virginians had been killed,
including a disproportionately high number of their leaders. In addition to
Cols. John Todd and Stephen Trigg, Majs. Silas Harlin and Edward Bulger,
Capts. John Bulger, John Gordon, Joseph Kincade, John Beasley, William
McBride, Joseph Lindsay, and Clough Overton were killed. The only ranking officers to escape were Col. Daniel Boone; Maj. Levi Todd, the brother
of Col. John Todd; and Capts. Robert Patterson and Samuel Johnson from
Fayette County, and Maj. Hugh McGary and Capt. William Ellis from
Lincoln County.

The man whose loss was mourned most was John Todd. He had numerous friends, not only in the rank and file who served under him in the
various skirmishes and campaigns, but in many of the leaders in Virginia as
well. He was close friends with men as diverse as John May and Daniel
Boone. Todd had moved to Kentucky with John Floyd in 1775 and established a home called Mansfield, a few miles northwest of Floyd's farm
called "Woodstock." He had returned to Virginia but was back in Ken-

tucky in time to assist in its defense in 1776–77. Wounded twice in Kentuky he also had been in Illinois as a county lieutenant. After his marriage to Jane Hawkins, he then returned to Kentucky and became the leading civil official and ranking militia officer in Fayette County. Had he defeated the Indians and lived, he may have been the first governor of Kentucky. But the Blue Licks was unlucky for John Todd. By eerie coincidence, he had also been defeated by Chief Pluggy in nearly the same place on Christmas Day 1776. When he died, his widow and infant daughter inherited various and valuable tracts of land that he had accumulated and were said to be the richest women on the frontier.

Before the end of the day, twenty-five of the retreating men came upon Colonel Logan's regiment on the main buffalo road. Their column had advanced only five miles beyond Bryan's Station. It is thirty-two miles from the battlefield to Bryan's Station, so there is no doubt that their horses were, by then, tired. After hearing the news, Logan turned his troops around and went back to Bryan's Station. For four days the militia stayed there, stunned, depressed, uncertain what to do. Each day the number of the reported enemy force increased as more stragglers appeared. The original number was thought to be 200, then 300, and finally 500. Cautious and not wishing to risk another disaster, Logan decided to keep his army in place and recruit more men. Four days later, he had 470 men under his command, at which time he felt it was safe to return to the Lower Blue Licks and confront the enemy.

When the militia from the two counties reached the battlefield, they were too late to find any Indians. Caldwell and McKee waited only a day for Logan's arrival, then returned to their villages north of the Ohio rather than tempting fate by fighting another battle.

Around the Blue Licks the militia counted about forty bodies, all of them mutilated. They had been scalped, and some, including Col. Stephen Trigg, had been cut up. After the Indians left, the wolves and vultures fed on the remains, and it took a man with a strong stomach to identify a friend or relative. With few exceptions, those burying the dead simply collected the unidentified bodies and interred them in a sink hole on the top of the hill. The bodies of those who had died crossing the river were never recovered.

After the battle, which came to be described as one of the worst defeats suffered by Americans on the Kentucky frontier, many of the participants and a few Virginia politicians wrote the governor explaining why this catastrophe had occurred. Some of the settlers in Fayette and Lincoln Counties blamed Gen. George Rogers Clark, alleging that the disaster was the result of Clark's failure to build additional forts along the Ohio River as protection for the inland settlers. Arthur Campbell, who had not been to Kentucky since losing his shoe after seeing an Indian near Boonesborough, wrote that the problem was poor leadership, including the rash actions of McGary. He went on to criticize the other officers, saying that Todd and Trigg lacked experience, and that Boone, Harlin, and Lindsay, though they had experience, were "defective in capacity." He was most critical, however, of Benjamin Logan, whom he felt was a "dull, narrow body, from whom nothing clever need be expected." General Clark he called a "sot [or] perhaps something worse."[26] No doubt Campbell was still unhappy with everyone in Kentucky, as he had been in 1775, when, using the pseudonymn of Philo Ohio, he sent out letters criticizing Floyd and Preston.

Many settlers in Lincoln and Fayette Counties blamed General Clark for the defeat. Clark countered by blaming the affair on the conduct of their officers. Governor Harrison seemed to agree with the men of Lincoln and Fayette Counties, telling them that he had personally ordered Clark to build two forts along the Ohio River and to garrison each with sixty to eighty soldiers. Rarely mentioned is the then universally known fact that Todd and Logan refused to send their militia away to help build these forts and that Clark had too few regulars to spare for the job. Clark reasoned that sending forty to fifty men out to build forts in isolated positions would invite attacks by superior enemy forces. Clark also pointed out that when the Indians surprised the Fayette County settlers, it was Todd's fault since Todd's militia had been excused from performing all duties except furnishing scouts to patrol along the Ohio River to search for any invaders.

Daniel Boone never censured the conduct of either Todd, Trigg, or McGary but later told his son that he believed the two leaders were disabled at the first fire, or else they acted cowardly. Those blaming McGary for the defeat rarely mentioned that after the officers' conference, the Kentucky companies crossed the deep river at a narrow ford, then traveled nearly a mile farther prior to forming for battle, all of which would have taken about fifteen minutes. This gave Col. John Todd ample time to assume command again, presuming that he had lost it to McGary at the conference. In retrospect, it would almost appear that Todd was more eager to fight the Indians than the hot-headed major from Lincoln County.

Some historians have reported that the battle of Blue Licks was the last battle of the American Revolutionary War, a ridiculous contention. The power and practice of the Northern Indians to launch attacks in Kentucky did not effectively end until General "Mad" Anthony Wayne's victory at the battle of Fallen Timbers in 1794.

On August 31, less than two weeks after the defeat at Blue Lick, the settlers in Jefferson County became aware that a war party was in their neighborhood. Scouts were sent out and reported that the enemy had passed near the abandoned station at Painted Stone. The next day someone reported spotting a party of Indians at Mud Garrison near Bullitts Salt Lick. While the militiamen were still attempting to locate the position of this force, the Indians staged a night attack on Kincheloe Station, overrunning it on the evening of September 2, killing or capturing thirty-seven people. William Kincheloe, the leader at the station, who had served as a lieutenant in the Eastern campaigns circa 1777, was absent during the attack.[27] Only a few settlers escaped in the darkness, fleeing to Cox's Station about seven miles away. This party of about 150 warriors then retreated northward, pausing on a ridge beyond Brashears Creek, along Harrod's old trace near Jeptha's Knob, as if inviting the Jefferson County militia to attack them. Floyd, who had only sixty-five militia fit for action, wrote, "it is truly mortifying to think they should miss it, yet I am sensible of the Evill [*sic*] consequences that might attend our engaging them to a disadvantage."[28] Consequently, the Indians and their prisoners retreated across the Ohio without being molested.

Sometime during the summer, probably after the fall of Kincheloe's, a large party of Indians briskly attacked the settlers at the lower McAfee's Station, killing several people.[29] Soon after, the survivors decided their station was too exposed and decided to move to a safer location.

This turn of events was too much for General Clark. He immediately started plans for an invasion of the Indian territory. By mobilizing the militia of three Kentucky counties, he thought he could collect 950 men, including the 100 regular Virginia troops he could spare. On September 16 he wrote General Irvine that he planned to march north with this army on September 21 with fifty days of provisions. He hoped General Irvine would cooperate by marching west with his troops. Together, he believed they could seriously defeat the British and their Indian allies, at the same impairing their ability to invade the string of settlements to the south. Governor Harrison instructed the county lieutenants of nine of the Western counties to mobilize 1,700 militia and have them ready to march to Pittsburgh, expecting a major attack there by the British and Indians.

But Clark's plan for a September invasion was too optimistic. His efforts to get support from the officers in Lincoln and Fayette received only a half-hearted response. On October 10 Gov. Benjamin Harrison wrote county officers that he had authorized General Clark to call up the militia. On the eighteenth he wrote Clark that he was also authorized to call up the militia of the "eastern counties," though not to exceed 200 men per county. By this time there were five counties east of the Kanawha River. Col. William Christian offered to raise 500 volunteers from Augusta, Rockbridge, Greenbrier, Botetourt, Montgomery, and Washington Counties "to hasten out on horseback," but nothing came of the offer.[30]

Clark also received word that on September 10 the Indians had unsuccessfully attacked Fort Henry. During this siege, the enemy managed to capture a passing boat laden with cannonballs. Remembering Squire Boone's log cannon used at Boonesborough, the warriors improvised their own. As might be expected, the improvised log cannon failed. When it was fired, it exploded, killing several of the Indians manning the wooden gun.

The defenders of Fort Henry by this time were forced to contend with their own troubles. Gunpowder was running low, and not a man could be spared for a hazardous dash to the nearby fortified Zane house, which had a large supply of ammunition. At this time, according to one of the most persistent legends of the Western Virginia frontier, Betty Zane, the sister of Ebenezer, became a heroine of the Revolution. Under fire, she rushed to the Zane house, obtained the gunpowder, and then ran back to the fort. After three days of failure, the Indians gave up the siege. About 100 of the warriors then traveled twenty-three miles north to attack Rice's Fort on Buffalo Creek at present-day Bethany. The little stockade had only six defenders, one of whom was killed soon after the Indians attacked. Nevertheless, the remaining five men held out during a twelve-hour attack, killing several Indians and wounding numerous others.

At the same time that the Virginians were planning to strike the Northern Indians, Gen. Andrew Pickens of South Carolina organized a campaign against the Cherokee. When Governor Harrison of Virginia was asked to participate, he refused. Nevertheless, the presence of Carolina troops in their country prompted the Cherokee to sue for peace.

Although not interested in a Southern offensive, Governor Harrison appeared to support George Rogers Clark's proposed campaign, but he also discredited him by insisting that had Clark built the forts on the Ohio River, as he had ordered, the mishap at Blue Licks would never have occurred. In addition, the governor wrote William Fleming that he had heard Clark had a drinking problem: "A report much to his prejudice prevails here of his being so addicted to liquor as to be incapable of Attending to his Duty."[31] There is some indication that Harrison favored treaties with the Indians, measures that would lead to future consolidation.

Despite Harrison's misgivings, George Rogers Clark succeeded in collecting an army of 1,128 men by calling up thirty-nine militia companies. Jefferson County furnished eleven companies, Fayette five or six, the remainder apparently being from Lincoln county.[32] From the surviving documents, it appears that Gen. George Rogers Clark personally financed this campaign by selling 3,500 acres of land for the delivery of 70,000 pounds of flour.[33] By November 1, 1782, the various companies took to the road, marching northward to their rendezvous at the mouth of Licking River. The men from the various counties were commanded by their respective leaders. Benjamin Logan was in charge of two Lincoln County battalions; Daniel Boone of Fayette County and John Floyd of Jefferson each commanded a battalion. The latter also escorted artillery that had been brought from Vincennes. There were also some regulars in service under Maj. George Walls. General Clark commanded this patchwork army, one of the largest assembled in the Western country during the war. The troops crossed the Ohio on November 4 and proceeded parallel to the Miami River, marching in five columns, with Floyd's men on the right and Logan's men on the left, the artillery and baggage in the rear. The first objective was the Shawnee town of New Chillicothe, or Standing Stone, on the Miami River.

Upon reaching the "principal" Shawnee towns on the evening of the tenth, General Clark dispatched his battalions to attack, at the same time sending Colonel Logan with 150 mounted men to capture the British trading post at the portage near the head of the river. When the Indians became aware of the advance, they abandoned their villages rather than fight the invaders. Clark later reported that "in a few Hours two thirds of their Towns was laid in ashes and everything they ware [sic] possess'd or destroy'd except such articles most usefull to the Troop."[34]

The Virginians then regrouped and waited for the British and Indians to mount an expected counterattack. Though they lingered about the Indian towns for four days, the enemy did not appear. During this time General Clark was still under the impression that General Irvine was conducting a campaign against the Sandusky area. Fearing that the weather might change for the worse, on November 15 Clark departed with his army, returning them to their homes on the south side of the Ohio. Most of the various militia companies were mustered out between November 21 and 25. The average pay to a private for his service during this campaign was two pounds and eight shillings. Samuel Wells Jr., who had given his horse to John Floyd at the Long Run defeat, served as an ensign in Capt. James Asturgus's company of light horse for thirty-four days and received only two pounds, seven shillings. At this time Virginia was selling Western land at one pound, twelve shillings per acre.

Gen. William Irvine had failed to launch a campaign against the Indians. His attempt to recruit men from the Pennsylvania frontier in October had failed because only half the men he expected showed up. Then, in the latter part of the month, the secretary of war cancelled the expedition "as General Washington had been assured by the British General, that all the Savages were called in from the frontiers, and were not to commit any farther depredation upon the inhabitants."[35]

In spite of the fact that the British had allegedly called in the Indians, Governor Harrison and many other Virginians were still clamoring for forts along the Ohio to protect the settlers. Clark continued to explain that even if he could get the forts built and manned, he could not keep them supplied with food since nothing could be purchased in Kentucky or Illinois with the worthless Virginia money at hand. He explained that he still had some of the flour left over from the campaign stored at the Falls, but if this were divided between three or four new posts, the amount would be "but trifling." Instead of building forts, he felt that launching a campaign against the Wabash in the spring of 1783 would be a more effective way to protect Kentucky.

In December Clark also informed Governor Harrison that he had sent Captain George to attempt to arrange a peace treaty with the Chickasaw and suggested that while he was dealing with this tribe he hoped Captain George would also be able to purchase some of their land for Virginia, a task he hoped could be accomplished for a small sum. The governor replied that he thought that this was a splendid idea and wanted Clark to keep him informed of the progress of such a treaty.

CHAPTER 9

1783
Who Owns What?

VIRGINIA'S FRONTIER SETTLERS WERE AT A LOSS TO UNDERSTAND WHAT was happening in Congress. Who owned what? They knew, or thought they knew, that Virginia's boundary had always extended all the way to the South Sea, encompassing all the territory north of the 36.5 parallel except what had been granted to the other colonies. Of course, most of the land to the South Seas was unobtainable, being occupied by the Spaniards and under their control. Many were also aware that New York had a very vague (and illegal) claim on all the land north of the Ohio River, a claim based upon the cession of this country by the Iroquois. Because New York had already ceded its claim on this territory to Congress, the issue was moot. In 1781 Virginia had also offered to cede its territory north of the Ohio to Congress (except for a small tract opposite the Falls reserved for Clark's soldiers). But the members of Congress had refused the offer. Obviously, many of the leaders in the Northeast did not want the Western land included as part of their new nation, believing that a Western boundary along the old Proclamation line of 1763 would be the most agreeable boundary with England.[1]

Other members of Congress objected to Virginia's condition for the cession of the Northwest Territory; they wanted the cession of all Western land, including Kentucky. This faction was led by members who had connections with the old land companies, particularly the Indiana and Vandalia Companies. They feared that if Congress accepted the land north of the Ohio River and confirmed Virginia's claim to land on the south side, this act would invalidate the proposed land company claims.

Fortunately, those congressmen who felt that it was in the interest of the new nation to extend its border to the Mississippi were in a majority. Yet many of them were jealous of Virginia and hoped to limit the state's boundary to the Appalachian Mountains. Some claimed that Virginia was already too large. Excluding the western counties, Virginia would still contain about 65,000 square miles, compared to 8,260 square miles for Massachusetts and 10,460 square miles for Maryland. Including the Kentucky district, Virginia's total was more than 100,000 square miles.

Furthermore, it was pointed out, the Western land was valuable, and Virginia was even then selling it to anyone for the price of one pound, twelve shillings per acre, the equivalent of about sixty pounds of tobacco. States such as Maryland had very little vacant land to sell. They reasoned that if Virginia were allowed to keep her Western land, the Virginians would all become rich while many other states struggled to pay off their war debts. James Monroe wrote that Congress wishes "to wrest that country from us & we further know that if they can do it they will & that without making us a recompensation of the immense expense we have been at [defending it]."[2]

The New York legislature came up with a unique plan to invalidate Virginia's Western claim. They brazenly asserted that they had unquestionable title to the whole great Western domain from the Great Lakes to Florida and promised to transfer all the land to Congress. The New York claim was based upon the theory that the West was owned by the Iroquois, inhabitants of New York, who had ceded their Western land to the colony at the treaty of Fort Stanwick. The leaders of Northern colonies that had no Western land claims were led to believe that cession by New York would lawfully give their states a valid title to a share of this vast country.

During the preliminary peace talks in Paris, American negotiators discovered that Spain was still interested in holding the land east of the Mississippi. The French supported Spain's claim to Florida and the territory between the Great Lakes and the Appalachians, a claim that would have put part of Kentucky, Tennessee, and Alabama under their control. They proposed a zigzag boundary line from the west end of Lake Erie to the Cumberland River and from the mouth of Cumberland River to the eastern boundary of West Florida. This territory would become an Indian reservation under Spanish protection. Another proposal was for the area

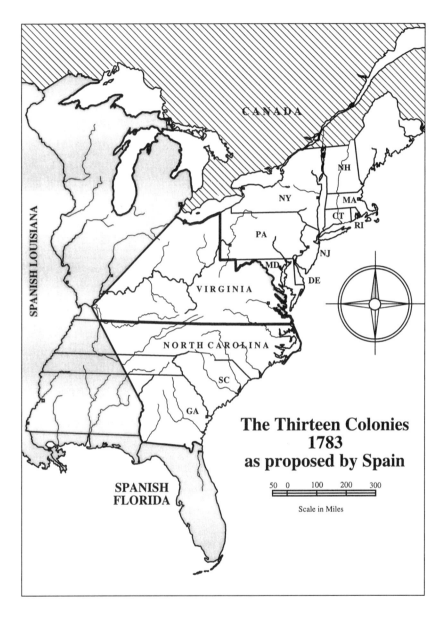

The thirteen colonies, 1783, as proposed by Spain.

north of the Ohio River to remain under British control, but the American diplomats never conceded this territory.

The settlers on the frontier had a more militant opinion about the future of the Western land. Above all, they were mindful that they might be completely abandoned by Congress and left to fend for themselves, a condition they had in some degree already experienced. Some Western citizens, including George Rogers Clark and Daniel Boone, signed a petition stating that they were alarmed by being removed from Virginia, particularly since so many had already paid Virginia for Western land. If Congress were to take over the West, they feared that their claims might become worthless. Furthermore, the petitioners maintained that

> . if the country they possess does not of right belong to Virginia, the property of course must be vested in themselves, and that Congress has no right to any part thereof; and when [we] make a request to Congress for a new state and to be received into the Union, they are then, and not before, subjects of another state.

The most important factor restraining Congress from taking all of Virginia's and North Carolina's Western land was probably the fear that Virginia and the other Southern states would walk out of Congress and form another country.[3] In any event, the Northern states did not support any further military actions in the West, even the taking and securing of the British fort at Niagara, which was within the alleged boundary of New York.

What all of the colonies shared were large war debts and little income. Virginia's debt was estimated at over £4 million, about the same as that of Pennsylvania and of Connecticut. The war debts in New York, Massachusetts, and several other states were smaller, but each still exceeded £1 million. Unlike many of the other colonies, Virginia made a determined and successful effort to pay its war debt by taxing and selling land. Eventually, it was able to call in its paper money at 1,000 to 1, thereby wiping out its debt. The next biggest item of debt was the vast number of military certificates issued to pay for supplies, such as those issued by George Rogers Clark and his officers. Beginning in 1782, holders of such certificates were allowed to exchange them for Western land certificates called treasury warrants. This policy did not afford the opportunity for serious speculation of Virginia money.[4]

Photograph of Mulberry Hill, where George Rogers Clark lived for many years after retirement. Once owned by General Clark's father, the house previously stood in present-day Louisville, but has since been torn down. THE FILSON HISTORICAL SOCIETY, LOUISVILLE, KENTUCKY

Some of the other colonies had serious problems in paying their debts. Massachusetts, for example, had a debt of about £11 million in paper money. It provided for liquidation of this debt by a scale of depreciation that was a gift to speculators, allowing them an exchange for new money at face value. If Massachusetts had funded her debt as Virginia did, it would have been only £627,000. Thus it ended the war with an extraordinarily large debt, so that high taxes were required. The mercantile group, creditors who had a firm grip on the government, shifted most of the tax burden to the farmers, causing much dissatisfaction. When the farmers could not earn enough to pay their taxes, the price of land plummeted as they started migrating to other states.

People in Kentucky had hoped that when fighting ended in the East federal troops would be sent west to protect them from the Indians. But none were forthcoming. Although Congress had hoped that it could maintain the army until ratification of the peace treaty, it was not able to raise money to pay the soldiers. Without pay, many of the soldiers demanded that they be released from duty. On May 26, Gen. George Washington was instructed to grant furloughs to those enlisted for the duration of the war. Finally, on June 13, 1783, most of the soldiers and many of the officers left for home without any farewell. In a single day the Continental army disappeared as a major force in politics and war.

The Virginia government was still in favor of building forts along the Ohio for protection, assuming that Clark would soon have one under construction. He had been instructed to put an outpost at the mouth of the Kentucky River, even while Thomas Marshall and William Christian were both lobbying for the fort to be built at Limestone. In January Clark sent official word to Richmond that he had not received the cannons for the proposed blockhouse, and even worse, "not a ration is to be got on the Credit of the state," so he was having difficulty feeding his unpaid soldiers.[5]

Even Governor Harrison by this time was doubtful that forts along the Ohio River would deter further attacks from the North. On January 13, 1783, he wrote George Rogers Clark: "[T]he British had call'd in all their scalping parties, and intended no more to carry on that kind of war against our back Settlements, whether they really mean as they say, Time will discover. It has ever been my Opinion th[at] attacking them in their own Country was the only way to keep them quiet and save expense."[6]

In the meantime, General Clark was writing to Richmond, pleading for the government to give his troops at least partial pay. By then, there was very little hope that many soldiers would reenlist when their time was up; only seven or eight found the bounty money, then £11.7, tempting enough to do so. Virginia at least made an attempt to keep an army in the field, even after the U.S. Congress had abandoned theirs.

In January William Fleming visited Fort Nelson at Louisville and found the garrison had barely enough provisions for subsistence, mostly consisting of bad flour and beef. There was, however, an abundance of whiskey in town, which sold for about £1 per gallon. On the day that Fleming visited the fort, three boats from Pittsburgh arrived at Louisville with 2,000 gallons of whiskey.

By February Fort Nelson was also a forsaken outpost. Six officers stationed there signed their names to a report, saying:

> [T]here is not above one third of the men necessary for its defence, and in a short time the unavoidable casualties will reduce the number to not more than twenty or thirty men. That there is

not more than three months Flower [*sic*] in store, not one pound of meat, and no possibility of procuring a sufficiency by the usual methods of hunting. That there is not a sufficiency of lead to defend the Garrison twenty four hours in case of an assault. Some parts of the Fortifications going to wreck, and not men to make necessary repairs. Also that the men appear to be on the Verge of Mutiny in consequence of having served so long without receiving pay & other necessaries, and no prospect of an alteration for the better.[7]

One of the soldiers, Stephen Shelton, said that when his company returned from Vincennes, the Indians nearly "starved out the garrison for want of water." To permit the men to reach the nearby Ohio safely, Clark had the troops construct a double wall from the fort to the river, with defensive portholes on each side. The Indians, however, were still hiding around the fort in order to attack careless stragglers. One of the garrison, Joe Kaumanaugh, decided to supplement his diet and went fishing in the Ohio River next to the wall. No sooner had he left the wall's protection than he was shot down and scalped.[8]

By March, things were worse. The Wabash Indians declared war on America, and it was feared that many of the other tribes might join them in an attack on Kentucky. The Wabash Indians had been the only tribe that was neutral when Clark invaded Illinois in 1778. They had remained friendly during the time the Americans had been at war with the Shawnee, Huron, Cherokee, Chickasaw, and others. General Clark warned the governor that the Illinois settlements, occupied by loyal Frenchmen, would be an easy target, should the British and the Indians decide to capture them. About the same time, William Fleming and the other commissioners sent word to the governor that Fort Nelson would certainly fall if attacked.

These commissioners had been appointed the year before by the Virginia legislature to settle all claims and war debts against the state. The members were William Fleming, Thomas Marshall, Samuel McDowell, and Caleb Wallace. Fleming acknowledged the receipt of $150 specie to cover the cost of this mission, but complained that it was "by no means adequate to the purposes."[9] They held their first meeting at Harrodsburg on November 1, 1782, and continued this work until July 1, 1783. The commissioners determined that George Rogers Clark had drawn $146,400 on Virginia credit for the Illinois campaign. Other drafts had brought the cost of the campaign up to $533,839 plus £583,036. In addition to the expense of the Virginia line troops, the militia also expected to be paid whenever they served outside the state boundary.

Clark was criticized for spending too much money and for allowing his officers to sign for supplies purchased on the credit of Virginia. There was a big question whether Colonel Montgomery and other officers had used a rate of exchange based upon species or the inflated paper currency. It would appear that initially they did not know the difference. Later they were forced to pay inflated amounts for food and other necessities or see their troops starve. Of course, there were some abuses. One officer, Lt. John Craig, informed General Clark that he purchased twenty-five gallons of whiskey on state credit for his company, "for which I have made Bold to Draw an Order on you and your Honouring it will Infinitely Oblige me."[10]

On April 8, while the commissioners were calculating the cost of the war in the West, the Indians ambushed and mortally wounded Col. John Floyd. Floyd was riding along the trail to Bullitts Lick. After being shot, he was carried to safety by his brother Charles but died two days later at the cabin of James Francis Moore at the Fishpools.[11] His wife brought his body back to his beloved Woodstock, and he was buried in the small cemetery overlooking Beargrass Creek. Floyd was the second and last of the four 1774 Fincastle County surveyors to be killed by Indians. He was also the second and last of the county lieutenants to be killed by Indians, his friend John Todd being the first. Not long afterwards, his widow married Alexander Breckinridge, and the couple continued to live at Floyd's Station.

Farther north, the Indians were also raiding in the Virginia counties of Washington and Ohio, pushing many inhabitants to the interior settlements. Even as far east as Westmoreland County, Pennsylvania, people were preparing to move back across the mountains. There was a likelihood that Wheeling would be abandoned. During the spring about forty people were killed in these counties and on the adjacent Pennsylvania frontier. Farther south, Indians attacked settlements on the Clinch River, at Blue Stone, and along Walker's Creek.

In Kentucky, the Indians captured slaves as well as whites, but for them, this was anything but freedom. In most cases the slaves in captivity never lived long enough to reach the Ohio River. A slave couple owned by William Pope was abducted, but the woman was soon tomahawked when she did not walk as fast as the warriors. Her husband reached the Indian village and was put to work in the fields.[12] Another incident was reported by Dr. William Fleming in April. Near Whitley's Station, six Indians ran up to the house of Michael Woods and one going in, the door was shut. Old Will Woods, a young woman [Hannah Woods] & Negro being in the house, that the Negro knocked the Indian down, whilst the young woman got an Ax, they got him dispatched. The Old woman kept the door shut, that before the Indians without could break the door open, a man run up & firing on them wounded one, on which they ran off.[13]

During the time that the Indians were causing havoc on the frontier, Governor Harrison kept insisting that Detroit and Niagara would soon be evacuated by the British and garrisoned with Continental troops. When General Clark received this report, he proposed to raise 1,500 men in Kentucky and take them north to the headwaters of the Wabash River. Coordinated with the advancing federal troops, their combined force could end the Indians' offensive. Rather than supporting such a campaign, Governor Harrison wrote General Clark that it would be more economical not to conduct such an "offencive war," and since there would be no campaign, Clark could "easily perceive [this] will render the Services of a General Officer in that quarter unnecessary, and will therefore consider yourself as out of Command." In other words, because state government decided there would be no offensive against the Indians, Clark was to be fired. The official discharge was effective June 26, 1783.

The Indians would have rejoiced had they been informed of General Clark's dismissal. He had always been a proven leader who had defeated the British and whatever Indians had backed them. But by 1783 most of the Indians realized that their major problem was the British defeat in the East and that, as a result, they would be forced to deal with the victors. They were also aware that the western counties of Virginia, Pennsylvania, and North Carolina were gaining population. Some of their leaders realized that with growing numbers of enemies their chance of winning the war in the West was becoming remote.

A few Indian leaders sought to strengthen their position by unifying the tribes in a common effort. By organizing the various tribes politically, they could present a united front in dealing with the United States. Given the diversity of the tribes themselves, this was a formidable task. It was made more difficult because of centuries of fighting among themselves. Consequently, some decided to continue the war even when other tribes were committed to peace. Splinter groups from peaceful tribes continued to raid the frontier settlements, adding to the confusion. Significantly, after 1782, when the British decided to act neutral, there were no large Indian armies crossing the Ohio.

Although the Cherokee leaders had asked Virginia for peace, a few warring factions of the Southern Indians were also a problem. Gov. Benjamin Harrison then did his best to promote good relations between the state governments and these nations. In forwarding the Cherokee entreaties to Gov. Alexander Martin of North Carolina, Harrison offered a defense of Indian rights, a rarity indeed among Americans:

> Indians have their rights and our Justice is called on to support them. Whilst we are nobly contending for liberty, will it not be an eternal blot on our National character if we deprive others of it who ought to be as free as ourselves.[14]

The North Carolina governor ignored Harrison's philosophizing. To be sure, he commented, peace was necessary on "some permanent Principles, that the cruelties and Horrors of Indian wars, intolerable among civilized nations may in future be prevented."[15] Martin did promise his fellow executive that no military action would be taken against the Cherokee and that the matter of delineating the boundary would be presented to the legislature.

In the fall of 1783 John Donelson, representing Virginia, met with the Chickasaw leaders at French Lick, Tennessee, and praised them for their peace overtures. A chief called Red King reaffirmed that they wanted peace, then laid down a complaint. The Chickasaw had allowed some white men to hunt on their land. They later discovered that these men were not hunters but surveyors searching for choice sites. In spite of this trespass, the parties agreed to keep the peace and to establish a mutual boundary. This ended the unofficial state of war that had existed between the Chickasaw and Virginia.

Not surprisingly, the frontier raids continued even after some Indian leaders pledged their tribes to peace. The raids were very annoying to the settlers, but they were not the type experienced in earlier times when forts were taken and militia forces destroyed. They were milder, less frequent, smaller in scale. In retrospect, these raids are what the Indians did best. A small party of warriors would come into a small community without being observed, wait for unsuspecting victims to come within pistol shot of their hiding place, and then make an attack. Afterwards, they would leave with the horse, clothing, and scalp of the victim. Occasionally the Indians would attack weakly-defended pioneer stations if they felt there was a reasonable chance of success.

In the fall of 1783, John Filson arrived in Kentucky. A native of Pennsylvania, he, like so many others, was interested in acquiring land on the frontier. But in other respects, he was very different from the average newcomer to the West. In addition to teaching school for a living, he had studied the history of the region and interviewed some of the first inhabitants, such as Daniel Boone. Without wasting any time, he wrote the history and description of Kentucky, the first of its kind relating to the country west of the Appalachians. His manuscript included a reasonable map of the area showing over sixty stations, seats, and mills. It was not the first map made of the area, but it was certainly the most detailed. In the small area now covered by Jefferson County, this map shows no less than the town of Louisville, the Falls, five stations, one mill, two "seats" or houses, two roads, five creeks, several islands, and the then-famous "fish ponds." Other areas received similar attention.

In 1782, another frontiersman, Robert Johnson, had produced a reasonably good manuscript map of central Kentucky, "Drew near 10 miles to the inch," but it was never published. Filson's book and map were printed in 1784, soon followed by another good map of western Virginia, published by John Fitch. As previously mentioned, Fitch had been captured in Kentucky but had been released from captivity by the British and had returned to Pennsylvania. He composed and engraved the map in the workshop of a friend. The job was completed by the summer of 1785, and several hundred copies were printed on, of all things, a cider press.[16] Of course, John Fitch is better known as the inventor of the steamboat than as a mapmaker. When he originally conceived his famous invention, he attempted to use the proceeds from the sale of his map to finance his new venture.[17] By 1787, several of his boats were in operation on the Delaware River. These vessels would probably have been more useful on the Ohio, especially if armed with swivel guns.

It was becoming obvious that the Ohio River was to become the new highway in the West. While Congress was engrossing the Northwest Territory of Virginia, the state government made plans to survey land on the north side of the Ohio River, opposite Louisville, to use as payment for General Clark's soldiers. In December 1783, George Rogers Clark was appointed the surveyor for this project. He and his assistants proceeded to lay off tracts in a one-mile-square pattern, running parallel to the river above the Falls. The Ohio at this location flowed about forty degrees from the cardinal compass points, so all the surveys ran in the same direction. The tract started at Silver Creek and ran about eighteen miles up the Ohio River. The western boundary is now called Grant Line Road. Interestingly, this is one of the few places in the United States where section lines do not run north and south.

More significantly, this was one of the first official acts where Indian land north of the Ohio was confiscated without going through the formality of a treaty. The area was so small (about 150,000 acres) that it may have been ignored by the owners, whoever they were. Of course, Fort Laurens was well inside Indian country, but it was a military establishment, not a place intended to be settled and farmed. The newfound and uneasy peace reinvigorated an era of expansion and settlement, signaling the next phase of a major migration of westering peoples that would occupy the nation's attention for the next 100 years.

CHAPTER 10

1784–86
Virginia's Last Campaigns

THE FIRST YEAR OF PEACE BEGAN WITH VIRGINIA CEDING THE NORTHWEST Territory, except for Clark's grant, to the Congress. This area comprised approximately a quarter million square miles of habitable land and included most of what is now Ohio, Indiana, Michigan, Illinois, Wisconsin, and Minnesota. The official deed was signed by Gov. Thomas Jefferson on March 1, 1784. The very day that Congress received this land, it discharged all the Continental troops in the West except for twenty-six men assigned to garrison the fort at Pittsburgh. The western counties of Virginia were left to defend themselves, but, ironically, their inhabitants were instructed to stay on "their side" of the Ohio River. Since Virginia no longer owned or controlled the Northwest country, their leading citizens decided they no longer wanted the expense of defending or policing it. The only white people in the area were the French villagers, who for a time were completely neglected by Congress, and a few British soldiers still holding their lake outposts.

Actually, it was the British who still controlled the Northwest Territory. The instrument of their policies was their Indian allies on whom they still exercised great influence. Gen. Frederick Haldiman, the British commander in Canada, actively began to conspire for the retention of British military bases, especially Detroit and Niagara. Should the new U.S. government fail, Great Britain, having retained possession of these posts, would own the Northwest Territory by default. If Britain could control the Northern Indians, it could also protect the profitable fur trade against the intrusion of the Americans. In order to promote these policies, Indian war parties continued to be sent south.

On October 2, 1784, American commissioners arrived at Fort Stanwix to discuss peace terms with the Indians. Those present, consisting of some Iroquois and a few Shawnee, were informed that the United States had absolute sovereignty over the Northwest Territory and "would seek peace upon such terms as the United States shall think just and reasonable." The Americans, it was clear, would decide what land the various tribes should occupy. If the tribes did not accede to these terms, they would be punished. They further informed the Indians that all former British land belonged to the U.S. Congress by right of conquest, but the Americans would take only a small part of the land formerly reserved for the Indian nations. Stunned and thoroughly intimidated, the Indian chiefs who were present finally signed this historic document on October 22.

Many other Indians, displeased that their countrymen had submitted to the Americans, boycotted this treaty and refused to cooperate. Another treaty, scheduled at Fort McIntosh in December, finally got under way on January 8, 1785. Again the Wyandot and Delaware chiefs who were present agreed to be confined to reservations in Ohio. After the document was signed, liquor, kettles, blankets, paint, lead, and gunpowder were distributed to seal the agreement. George Washington confided that he "did not expect such a [large] cession of territory." Congress was pleased and passed the land ordinance of 1785, providing for the surveying of ranges and the sale of much of the ceded Indian land.

In spite of these peace overtures, the Indians continued to harass travelers on the "Wilderness Road" to Kentucky. One party, which included the McClure family, was attacked just before dawn at their camp on Skaggs' Creek. Six of the travelers, including the three McClure children, were killed instantly. McClure made his escape, but Mrs. McClure and a Negro woman were captured. When the news reached Whitley's Station, a party of twenty-two men led by John Logan and William Whitley went in pursuit. The savages were overtaken, two of them killed, the two prisoners rescued, and a large quantity of plunder was recovered. Ten days later, another company of travelers led by a man named Moore was attacked near Raccoon Creek with the loss of nine of their number. Again Whitley led the pursuit. After killing three of the Indians, he recovered eight scalps and all of the horses and other loot.

By 1784 many of those who claimed Kentucky land had received their official titles, or patents as they were then called. Of course many of these people were old residents, but others had hesitated in making a permanent move until they felt their land claim was secure. Some of the grants, such as the 2,000-acre military surveys for John Ashby on Beargrass and Elkhorn Creeks, were issued as early as November 1779. John Carter Littlepage, heir of Colonel Byrd, received his military grant in 1780, as did Zachary Taylor, Patrick Henry, and many others. By 1782 the early settlers were being awarded patents; these included Benjamin Logan at St. Asaph, James Harrod at Boiling Springs, Squire Boone at Painted Stone, and Abraham Chaplin on Shawnee Run. Daniel Boone's settlement grant was issued in 1785 and Isaac Hite's tract at Fountainbleau in 1786. In the same year Cuthbert Bullitt, the heir of Capt. Thomas Bullitt, received 2,800 acres on the Ohio River just south of Louisville.

John Bowman, the ranking officer in the original Kentucky County militia, probably did not live to see a Kentucky land grant. His first deed was signed by the governor in Richmond on April 19 and he died of natural causes at his station a few weeks later, on May 4, 1785.

Some of the more wealthy landowners with large tracts near the Falls and in the Bluegrass began sending out their grown sons accompanied by slaves to start plantations. For example, William Russell (whose oldest son had been killed alongside Daniel Boone's son, when on their way to Kentucky in 1773) obtained his patent in 1781 and soon after sent another son to Kentucky to take charge of the property. William Hickman, for whom Daniel Boone had located land on a military warrant in 1775, sent out two sons with slaves to develop his 2,000 acres between Lexington and Boonesborough. James Nourse, who had come to Kentucky in the same canoe as George Rogers Clark, sent his two sons and a slave west to secure the land he had claimed in 1775.

Many of the large, sparsely occupied military tracts were sold when patents were obtained from Virginia. In 1786 near Louisville the 1,000-acre Oxmore tract, east of Floyd's Station, was purchased by Judge Benjamin Sebastian for £800, and in 1787 Sebastian sold the tract to Alexander Scott Bullitt for $8,000. The 6,000-acre Southall and Charlton grant along Beargrass Creek was sliced up, with the Spring Station tract purchased by Samuel Beall and much of the remainder going to William Pope and James Speed.[1] In 1789 Richard C. Anderson obtained half of the Linn Station tract, where he built his home called "Soldiers Retreat." Maj. William Croghan, George Rogers Clark's brother-in-law, purchased parts of two old military surveys overlooking the Ohio River, where he built his "seat" called Locust Grove. Richard Taylor, the heir of surveyor Hancock Taylor, sold his 1,000-acre military survey on the Ohio River and Beargrass Creek near Louisville and acquired another tract five miles farther up the river.[2]

Land claims around Lexington.

The old military surveys awarded for service in the French and Indian War amounted to nearly a half million acres (750 square miles), much of it located on the best land in central Kentucky. No historian has investigated how many of the large grants were eventually sold, but upper-class Virginia leaders, including John Brown and John Breckinridge, acquired some of these old military surveys, which were developed into profitable plantations.

Settlers were also selling land. In 1786 Squire Boone sold Painted Stone, which by then included a mill and distillery, to Nicholas Mereweather. Daniel Boone's settlement claim was transferred to an in-law. Benjamin Logan disposed of his claim at St. Asaph and purchased land on Bullskin Creek near Shelbyville.

Much of this activity was due to migration. People were moving west, many of them hoping to find cheap land. Some of the old frontiersmen who had obtained settlement and preemption tracts, which were from 1,000 to 1,400 acres, sold parts of their large, mostly undeveloped estates, for ready cash. Many large grants were also divided when the old settlers died so that their children would get an equal share.[3] Such transactions tended to reduce the size of Kentucky farms.

By 1784 the population of Kentucky was estimated at 56,000.[4] Many of the newcomers were unable to purchase land and became tenants. In some instances tenants eventually became landowners by clearing land for the original owners. Some new arrivals were blacksmiths, carpenters, masons, coopers, and other tradesmen who thought there would be a need for their services on the frontier.

In July 1784, Col. William Christian, a well-known Revolutionary frontier leader from Fincastle, decided to move his family west to settle on his 2,000-acre military survey on Beargrass Creek. Christian, a former member of the Virginia council, was a brother-in-law of Patrick Henry and William Fleming. He had served as a civil and military leader in Fincastle and Montgomery Counties. Colonel Christian had led the reserve force to Point Pleasant after the battle in 1774. Originally appointed as the county lieutenant of Jefferson County, he had declined in favor of John Floyd. For over a month his party had been delayed at the North Fork of the Holston River, waiting for enough settlers to gather to insure a safe passage through the wilderness. But on August 17, Christian reported that he had reached his farm on Beargrass and was settled in Asturgus Station. He moved his family into a double cabin and built a third as "a lodging room for strangers & neighbours. Company we are at no loss for."[5]

William and Ann Christian soon discovered the hazards associated with living on the frontier. To his brother-in-law, William Fleming, he wrote:

> Your Goose Creek Land joining mine is unsafe at present for a House. The Indians have taken Horses twice from there & between that and the No[rth] fork since I came out, and they shot a Cow with arrows at Hites. My Family however is quite safe, but we release the Cows with caution. I see nothing here at present desirable for Farmers who have Improvements elsewhere. Money there is none & everybody is waiting to get a little from new Emigrants. . . . I sow twenty or thirty acres now with wheat & rye. My corn will produce this year about 30 Bushels to the acre & that appears to be the general appearance in Jefferson. This country is not at present possessed of any Money. The stores get what little the Lawyers leave & I guess both are often disappointed.[6]

Ann Christian confirmed some of her husband's misgivings:

> All the time we lived on Beargrass we have been all exposed to the Savages every time we were out of Sight of this Station, the Indians have been Continually in this Country & have kill'd people all round us, but that mercifull [sic] God who had protected us all our days has preserv'd us in Safety till now.[7]

Despite their concern for safety, there was time for romance. Before the year was over, the colonel's daughter, Priscilla Christian, married Alexander Scott Bullitt, the nephew of Thomas Bullitt, who had originally surveyed the site of Louisville. Young Bullitt had moved to Jefferson County about 1784 after an attempt to settle in Shelby County. During this period he probably resided in one of the Beargrass stations. Eight years later he was elected the first lieutenant governor of Kentucky.

By November 1784, as Colonel Christian notes, conditions had not improved:

> The People at the old Stations about here are chiefly going away, five or six Families are gone to Fayette. The Burks at the mo[uth] of Goose Creek are middling strong—I can stay if they don't move to Cumberland by water. Coleman lives at Home & has a station. Hite & Edm[un]d Taylor are yet at Home but their stay is doubtful as they both have safe Places on the other side of me. Hite at Fern Creek & Taylor at Hoglin's [sic]. I have long tried to fix a station on my land where it joins yours at the Bank of Goose Creek which would make me safe, & offered 5 years clear of rent but none can be had. If any Emigrants come down the River I shall continue to try to get a Station there, but I have no hopes of it. Currys Station upon Floyd fork, four miles above the Ford as you go to Squire Boones, have broken up. They had 7 Families, two of the men have been killed in three weeks past. Their widows & Children & the others are moved down, some to Linns & some to Sullivans old Station near Bob Daniels. Nobody in this Country are doing much. The Stores have poor Encouragement & the farmers none. Not a Family has moved to this country this Fall but mine. Some few have gone to Fayette of the few that has come through the wilderness, but more to Cumberland.[8]

Jefferson County, as usual, seemed to suffer the most from Indian raids because it was the county in closest proximity to the Wabash towns. People were still being killed, however, traveling along the Kentucky Road or coming down the Ohio River. Indian incursions increased in the fall of the year when rivers and creeks were usually low and could be crossed with ease on horseback.

In Fayette County, Col. Daniel Boone was also concerned about safety of the inhabitants, as well as the assistance that the legislature might provide for them. In a letter to Col. William Christian he explained this situation:

Yesterday I received an express from the inhabitants of Limestone which obliges me to address your honor thus: No doubt the murder done to Colonel Lewis and company has reached your ears by this time. Likewise a boat and family [were] lately taken and killed [and] two late murders done at Squire Boones Station and a deal of sign seen in different places, in particular at Limestone. In short, an Indian War is expected. We are creditably informed that three Nations from the Wabash are united against us and whatever may be the case, unless an actual invasion [occurs] it is out of the power of any officer of the Militia to give the frontier any assistance.

Know Sir, I hope to receive such instructions from your Honor as will enable me to force our scouts, spies or to do monthly tours at some of the frontier stations, at least at Limestone and the Blue Lick that the salt works may still go on. Your Honor was kind enough to give me orders to receive one thousand weight of lead at Fort Chiswell, which I never sent for as yet; powder is as much wanting as lead as we have no brimstone here. Pray Sir, give me instructions as you think proper by my express. I am willing to take any trouble on myself only let me know how the expenses of getting those articles here is to be paid. In my opinion by the way of Fort Pit and Limestone will be the safest and best way they can come.

One hundred stands of arms are wanting at Limestone as I am informed by the express. [As] there are a number of persons without any arms I should think it necessary [that] a small garrison should be built at Limestone and a few men stationed at that place for the protection and receiving families when they arrive at that place as it is become a very great landing place.

I hope our petitioning for a new State will be no barrier against any assistance government might give us, as it is entirely against the voice of the people at large. A few individuals who expect to be statesmen have put this afoot. Some petitions will be sent down in opposition to the new State [during] this assembly.[9]

The next and perhaps the last council for some time between representatives of the United States and the Indians was held at the future site of Cincinnati on January 14, 1786. It was attended by 318 Shawnee. Upon hearing the terms offered by the Americans, the Shawnee signaled their disapproval. The U.S. commissioner, Richard Butler, then took the Shawnee's string of wampun and dashed it on the table. Not to be outdone, George Rogers Clark pushed it off the table with his cane and walked over it as he left the council. Later, the Shawnee who were present finally capitulated to the American terms. But there were still a great many Indians under other leaders who favored war with the United States.

In April 1786, only eight months after he had moved his family to Kentucky, Col. William Christian met the same fate as John Floyd. After a party of Indians had raided his station, he gathered eight or ten men and started in pursuit. The chase continued across the Ohio River and about a mile farther north, where the Indians were forced to make a stand. In the ensuing battle Colonel Christian was killed leading the charge. A few minutes later Capt. Isaac Kellar, a veteran who had fought with General Clark, was killed by an Indian who was believed to be dead.[10]

On the heels of this episode, Col. William Pope, the leading officer in Jefferson County, sent messengers to the adjacent county officials pleading for aid. He pointed out that Jefferson County was a barrier to invasion from the north and that if this county did not receive aid, he would be forced to evacuate the town of Louisville, leaving the adjacent counties exposed on the frontier.

On April 11, another distinguished citizen, Col. John Donelson, was killed in Lincoln County. Colonel Christian had written to a friend that "Lincoln is safe, but the other three counties rather exposed. Hence go pretty fast from Fayette & Jefferson."[11] But the degree of safety on the frontier was relative. Benjamin Logan reported Donelson's death to Gov. Patrick Henry and expressed the opinion that the Northern and Southern Indians had combined to destroy the Kentucky district. He also hinted that George Rogers Clark, who was still in Kentucky, would be able to organize men for "our safey."

Judge Samuel McDowell also wrote the governor, urging a campaign against the Indians. Clark had estimated that 1,500 warriors along the Wabash were being encouraged by British agents to go against Virginia. In his opinion, the only way to protect the settlements was to organize an immediate volunteer campaign.

Governor Henry was no doubt influenced by the death of his brother-in-law, the late Colonel Christian. He immediately reported to Congress that to protect themselves the frontier settlers must attack the towns of the hostile Indians, even though these villages were no longer in Virginia territory. Congress did nothing. It was loath to incur any expense to restrain the Indians, even if this was necessary to protect lives and property in Virginia. The truth was that most of its members were far more interested in the sale and disposition of their newly acquired public lands in the West than in defending Virginia's frontier.

So the raids continued and even the more populated areas in Virginia were not free of Indian intrusions. In March 1784, several young boys were captured near Louisville. One was William Wells, the fourteen-year-old son of Samuel Wells Sr., killed at Floyd's defeat on Long Run; two others were Ansel and William Lynn, orphaned sons of William Lynn, the founder of Lynn Station. The Lynn brothers managed to escape from the Indian town, but William Wells was adopted by the Miami chief, Little Turtle, and afterwards married a young Indian woman. His brother, Samuel Wells Jr., eventually located him and brought him back to Kentucky, but he was not happy living the life of a white man.

William Wells was luckier than the stepson of James Harrod. By 1787 a Latin school had been established at his Boiling Springs station. Malcomb Worly, a Latin teacher, was hired, and children from nearby towns were enrolled and boarded at Harrod's farm. In November, however, after the school had been in operation for several months, young James McDaniel, the son of Ann Harrod, was captured by Indians after he left the school, and it was soon discovered that he had been burned at the stake. James Harrod disbanded the school and sent the pupils home.

During the war the Virginia government, using certificates, had purchased military supplies from citizens. Corn and cattle collected at the beginning of a campaign were appraised, and the state promised to repay the owners. By 1779 these debts could be redeemed with treasury warrants, which in turn could be used to acquire land in the public domain. But vacant tracts had to be located by the owners of the warrants or their agents. This presented a problem because most of the better land was already surveyed and deeded to those with old French and Indian military warrants or by settlement and preemption claims of early Kentucky inhabitants. John Floyd and company, acting as surveyors of Fincastle County, had surveyed all the land around Louisville and over 100,000 acres around Lexington in 1774, the year before any permanent settlement was made in Kentucky. Early settlers had claimed what was left of the good land in central Kentucky.

Another problem was the expense of making and entering surveys when many of the warrant holders were short on cash. A survey that Daniel Boone made for John Overton cost over £26, including over £7 to register the tract in the surveyor's office and £10 for the chainmen and their provisions. Boone wrote Overton to request payment for the job.[12] Some historians wonder how successful he was in collecting his fees.

Land locators were soon required to travel farther from the settlements, often entering their tracts in places not considered very valuable. Whereas almost all of the early settlement claims were entered in central Kentucky, land entered with large treasury warrants was often in the Appalachian plateau or in the lower wetlands of western Kentucky. Many of the men claiming land with these treasury warrants were eager to sell the land they had entered. For example, Samuel Beall wrote his partner, John May:

> I am much pleased with the Sale you have made of the Lands you mention; pray go on to sell it is the best plan you can pursue. With the abundance of Land we claim, if the Titles are confirmed to us, the Taxes, surveying, Pattenting [sic] &c will ruin us. I prefer much a Sale [than] to hold the Lands, except a few Valuable tracts.[13]

Virginia had put a tax on land, initially amounting to about a shilling per hundred acres. Taxes could be paid with tobacco and even hemp or flour, but many landowners neglected to make any payments. Finally, in May 1784, the legislature suspended the land tax for six months. In October another act reduced the tax by one-half for that year because the tax could not be collected without distressing the citizens of the Commonwealth.

Since the Indian raids continued on the frontier, the governor wrote Benjamin Logan authorizing him to call a meeting of the militia commanders of all counties in the district of Kentucky. The purpose was to adopt measures for defense. Logan and other militia officers interpreted this message to authorize the use of troops as the military situation required. Logan then called for a meeting at Harrodsburg.

Some of the officers worried about the legality of a campaign beyond Virginia's borders, debating what the objective of a military campaign should be and who should lead it. Abraham Chaplin, an early settler and militia officer, warned George Rogers Clark, who was being suggested as

Growing tobacco.

the commander, that no one in the district had the authority to order militiamen to go beyond the borders of the state of Virginia without their consent. Clark was disappointed about the change of plans from a volunteer campaign to a militia campaign. In the former, which he advocated, each man would furnish his own equipment and provisions. In the latter, men were mobilized against their will and supplies might have to he obtained by impressment.

No one doubted that the most hostile Indian tribes were then living along the upper Wabash. The raids usually came from that direction. Even the French settlers at Vincennes had suffered several attacks and had appealed to Clark and the Kentuckians for aid. As mentioned, after Virginia had ceded the Northwest Territory, the French settlers had become neglected orphans of the U.S. Congress. No federal troops or any kind of government agents were stationed at Vincennes, Kaskaskia, or other villages in the Northwest Territory after Virginia had relinquished it.

There was little controversy when the officers of the western Virginia militia chose a commander for the campaign against the Indians. Clark had lost his brigadier general's commission in 1783, but in the minds of most Kentuckians he remained the outstanding military man in the western district. His enemies continued to circulate rumors about his drinking, but few frontiersmen were bothered by such stories. "I have been with him frequently," wrote one of the governor's correspondents, "and find him as capable of Business as ever, and should an Expedition be carried against the Indians I think his name alone would be worth Half a regiment of men." Benjamin Logan, to whom the writer showed this letter, agreed and asked that his own recommendation of Clark be conveyed to Governor Henry.[14]

Even before Governor Henry sent the county lieutenants authority to form an expedition, the militia officers had been organizing an army composed of volunteers who would bring their own horses, provisions, guns, and ammunition for a campaign across the Ohio. For the most part these volunteers were willing and efficient soldiers, and they picked General Clark to command them. But after the governor authorized an expedition, this army of volunteers was abandoned. On August 2 a meeting of the county lieutenants and a majority of the field officers of the seven western Virginia counties was held at Harrodsburg. Most agreed that an expedition against the Wabash Indians was necessary. They further agreed that half of the militia, except in the region east of the Licking River, should be mobilized for that purpose and that Clark would be asked to take command. If he should refuse, that duty would fall to Benjamin Logan, the ranking military officer in the district.

Soon the various Western militia companies were mustered with a large percentage of the new landless migrants selected for active duty. Many of the drafted men expressed the opinion that they would rather stay at home. General Clark said he would not consent to command such a force. Not only were the drafted men likely to be unfit and sulking soldiers, but under the militia law they could not be lawfully moved out of the state without their own consent. If taken across the Ohio into the enemy's country, they could obey or disobey orders from their commander as they chose. In any case, they could not be legally punished for disobedience, desertion, or any other offense.

Uncertain about their power to impress supplies, the militia officers sought the opinions of the attorney general and the judges of the district court. These officials replied that it was their belief that the military powers of the Virginia Executive under the state's militia laws and under the Articles of Confederation had been delegated to the field officers of the district by the Order in Council of May 15, 1786. Under the terms of these documents, they were authorized to take the necessary steps for defense. Consequently, in their opinion impressment was legal.

The militia officers decided that their county lieutenants should collect enough provisions and ammunition for fifty days and a packhorse for every four men. If these things had to be obtained by impressment, they were to be appraised and receipts given to the owners. John May was named as commissary for the expedition, and Christopher Greenup was to act as quartermaster. Some of the needed supplies were offered willingly, but at times impressment was required. Many of the frontier families realized that their livestock and grain were worth more than the paper money they would receive for the products. But even when impressment was necessary, there was surprisingly little resentment. An officer of the Continental army who had just arrived in Kentucky recorded in his diary, "The people take it middling kindly."

Not wishing to lead this army, General Clark refused to take command. Nevertheless, on September 10, 1786, the militia companies crossed the Ohio to rendezvous opposite the Falls at the new town of Clarksville. Twenty-five hundred men were expected, but so many of the new draftees were missing during the mobilization that only about 1,200 appeared. From the beginning, discord and sulking prevailed to such a degree that many of the officers wanted to abandon the expedition.

Convinced that this was the last chance to punish the tribes on the Wabash, Gen. George Rogers Clark reluctantly consented to lead the disgruntled militia. Politically, he decided to ask for the advice of the field officers. On September 13, they met in council and recommended that Clark proceed to Vincennes with the men at hand. In the meantime, one officer from each county would return home to collect all delinquents and deserters from the first draft. To further increase their numbers, he would call up one-half of the remaining militia men. Colonel Logan, as second in command, was to lead this force in an attack against the Shawnee towns on the Miami River. It was Clark's opinion that most of the Shawnee warriors would have gone to the Wabash to help in blocking his expected thrust in that direction. Their villages would be virtually undefended, thus providing a favorable opportunity to destroy them.

But Col. Benjamin Logan had additional problems organizing this second expedition because the settlements had already been combed for provisions. Nevertheless, by September 29 his men had gathered sufficient provisions and began assembling at Limestone on the Ohio River.

From Clarksville, Gen. George Rogers Clark immediately marched against the Indians, who were assembled about 150 miles northwest near the Wabash River. The officers of the Lincoln troops, under command of Colonel Barret, insisted that the army take the road to Vincennes in order to get extra provisions, which could be sent there by water on the Ohio and Wabash Rivers. This detour via Vincennes was about forty miles farther than a more direct path. Some historians believe the detour ultimately caused the campaign's failure. Historian Temple Bodley pointed out that the supply of food on hand was ample for a direct march against the enemy, since it was adequate to feed the army during a sluggish, seven-day march to Vincennes, 100 miles away, during eight more days there awaiting the boats, and during two more days after leaving that place. Some said that the Lincoln County draftees did not want to carry provisions on their backs in hot September weather or ever to engage the enemy. About half the army was made up of disgruntled men from Lincoln County. Located a considerable distance from the Ohio River, it had not been invaded by the Northern Indians as often as the closer counties.

After camping in Vincennes, the army finally started northward and crossed to the west side of the Wabash River. On the third day out, the Lincoln County men began yelling, "Who's for home? Who's for home?" and a short time later, most of them, or about half of the army, marched away under the leadership of an ensign. The remainder of the troops formed a large circle to hold a general council. Some proposed forcing the Lincoln County militia to return, and others advocated attacking the Indian towns with the men who were left. The officers attempted to persuade the retreating troops to return, but to no avail. Finally, the entire army headed back to Vincennes.

To the people of Vincennes this disgraceful retreat of the army was appalling. Their fort had recently withstood three days of siege by several hundred Indians. Now they watched the Virginians leaving for Louisville in groups of six, ten, or a dozen. It appeared that they would soon be left alone again to face the warring tribes.

When General Clark again called the officers to council to determine what should be done, they unanimously resolved to enlist men to garrison the town. To feed them, however, was a serious problem. The inhabitants were dreadfully poor and hardly able to support themselves. To impress their scant supplies for the garrison seemed cruel; yet without the troops the town would probably be taken by Indians within a few weeks. This desperate condition was relieved, fortunately, by the arrival of a Spanish trader with a cargo of supplies from New Orleans. The supplies were impressed to support the volunteers at the fort.

The Indians, aware that the troops had returned to Vincennes, patiently waited for the army to leave for home. Because some of the volunteer troops were still at the fort several weeks later, they delayed their planned offensive against Kentucky. The Indians were naturally reluctant to leave their own towns with an enemy close by. They were also averse to attacking the fort at Vincennes. Their delay saved the straggling mutineers who were returning to Kentucky while the remaining soldiers protected the people of Vincennes.

General Clark and the leading citizen of the town, Colonel Le Gras, took prompt advantage of the situation. With bold action on Clark's part and an ingenious and deceptive speech by Le Gras, the Indians were led to believe that Clark was still formidable and that he had only consented to abandon his march against them and had returned to Vincennes because of the earnest appeals of their French friends. Le Gras, warning the savages that they would find peace better than war, sent them a bold speech from Clark offering them the choice.

The result was a request for peace. A truce was then agreed and a treaty meeting scheduled for the following April. Thus, the disgraceful mutiny had turned out favorably, and one of the most formidable Indian invasions to threaten Kentucky came to naught.

Meanwhile, some Indians had been harassing settlers around Limestone. At Lee's Station, four miles southeast of Limestone, two sons of Moses Phillips were killed and three Negroes captured. At Clark's Station, six miles south of Limestone, Robert Clark, son of the station's founder, George Clark, was taken along with two more Negroes. A detachment from the gathering army followed the Indians to a point about six miles above Limestone where they had recrossed the Ohio. The captives were taken to Piqua. Clark was treated well but not so the Negroes. At the village Clark noticed a horse that had been stolen from Simon Kenton. He was determined to escape from the Indian town with this horse but had problems finding the right opportunity. The Negroes decided they could not wait longer and left on their own. They were quickly intercepted and the Shawnee war party returned with their scalps to intimidate the other prisoners.[15]

In Kentucky, the pursuing force under the command of Benjamin Logan consisted of about 800 men formed in two regiments. One was under Logan's brother John Logan, the other under Col. Robert Patterson of Fayette County. Although he served in the campaign, Daniel Boone was no longer the ranking officer in Fayette, having moved to Limestone in the spring of the year. His place would have been with the militia contingent of newly formed Bourbon County, Virginia.

The army crossed the Ohio during the day and evening of September 30, 1786. Logan explained afterward that "a barrel of rum was impressed at Limestone, and [there] being much rain it was given freely to the soldiers, & in consequence of its effect, the army was somewhat delayed in crossing . . . the river."[16] The pursuit had also taken the time to kill and dress about twenty head of cattle. Apparently, the Lincoln County men were much more willing to march with their own leader against the Shawnee than with Clark against the more distant and formidable Wabash Indians.

North of the Ohio each regiment marched in three columns, with John Logan's Lincoln County men composing the right wing and Patterson's Fayette County men the left. Maj. John Hinkston led a rear guard of thirty-five officers and men. The advance guard consisted of three officers and fifty-three men led by Benjamin Logan himself. The troops marched up Eagle Creek to the pass where this stream breaks through the hills north of the Ohio, afterward called Logan's Gap. By October 5, the army was within fifty miles of its destination, the Shawnee villages on the upper reaches of the Big Miami.

Logan's orders for the day directed his officers to have their men march as quietly as possible. They were not to take any plunder until specific permission was granted. The orders also specified that "in case any person, under any description or any color, attempts to come to the army, all persons are forewarned to receive them in a friendly manner." He believed that the approach of his army had been discovered by the Indians who committed the murders. They had taken the prisoners in the vicinity of Limestone, and when he and his men reached the Shawnee villages emissaries might come out to sue for peace. Even if this did not occur, prisoners attempting to escape to the white army might be mistaken for Indians. George Clark, whose son had been captured only a few days before, and Robert Maffet, who also had a son with the Indians, accompanied Logan's army. This order, Logan afterward declared, was issued for the protection of such persons as these and "not in favor of any Indian on earth."[17]

On October 5, the army marched northward. The following day, about one o'clock in the afternoon, the troops halted a short distance from the first Indian villages. No peace emissaries appeared and there were no signs to indicate that any Indians had tried to escape. Logan began to fear that his orders might prevent his men from fighting as vigorously as would be required. Some might lose their lives in trying to make prisoners of Indians who could have been killed at long range with less risk. Accordingly, he rode through the lines and verbally modified his original instructions. His soldiers were told to be careful to spare white persons but were to do as they pleased with Indians.

Then the army was divided so that several villages could be attacked simultaneously. As had been expected, many of the Shawnee warriors had gone to the Wabash, where General Clark's army was headed. When Logan's men advanced, they discovered the defense to be almost nonexistent. By the end of the day, Mackacheck, Wappatomica, New Piqua, Will's Town, McKee's Town, Blue Jacket's Town, and Moluntha's Town—seven towns in all—had been destroyed. Nathan Boone describes an incident involving his father:

> On arriving at the Indian town, the Indians fled. Some dogs were seen running and father said if they would follow these dogs they would find the Indians. He and his party pursued on horseback and soon discovered several Indians running off, and as they gained on them, one of the Indians looking back over his shoulder. Father was mounted on a pony somewhat in the rear of the pursuers, and recognized the Indian by his remarkable physiognomy.

He called out to those with him, "Mind that fellow—I know him—it's Big Jim, who killed my son in Powell's Valley." Two or three dismounted and Big Jim, apparently hearing what father said, whirled about and fired at one of the men on horseback who fell off dead. Big Jim almost at the same moment fell wounded in the tall grass. While the white men were gathering around the dead man who had fallen from his horse, Big Jim reloaded his gun, and as some of the men approached him he killed or wounded another. Then some of the men rushed up and shot him.[18]

The Kentucky casualties in the several brief encounters had been light. One man was killed outright, two mortally wounded, and two slightly wounded. More than 200 cabins had been burned along with an estimated 15,000 bushels of corn. Plunder valued at nearly 1,000 pounds was taken, and a number of hogs, considered too slow to drive back to Kentucky, were slaughtered. Ten warriors were killed and thirty-two prisoners were taken, most of them women and children.

One of the prisoners was the old chief Moluntha, also called the Shawnee King, the same man who had headed the delegation that had signed the treaty with the United States earlier in the year. He and his followers had agreed to accept the sovereignty of the United States and to live at peace with the white man. For this reason he had taken refuge under an American flag erected in his village, surrendering himself and some women and children who were with him. While talking with his captors, Hugh McGary, now a lieutenant colonel in the Mercer County militia, walked up and asked Moluntha if he had been at Blue Licks. When the chief answered yes, McGary took a small ax and sank the blade in Moluntha's head.

Those present were shocked at McGary's conduct, especially James Trotter, a lieutenant colonel in the militia of Fayette County. A heated argument ensued, during which time McGary stated, with considerable profanity, that he would chop down Colonel Trotter or anyone else who tried to keep him from killing Indians whenever he liked. Some of the officers wanted an immediate court-martial for McGary, but Logan, believing that he could not get a fair trial while feelings were so high, refused to order it. The order was given for the army to retire.

Logan's men were only one day's march south of the ruined villages when they discovered that some Indians were following the army, hoping to capture those who fell behind. To discourage further skirmishes, Logan left a message in a conspicuous place stating that if any of his men were killed the prisoners would be executed. This turned the pursuers back. Upon reaching the Ohio River, horses, cattle, and other plunder were sold at auction as was the custom.

The Indian captives were possibly assigned to Daniel Boone to house and feed for a short time when the army reached Limestone, since he was reimbursed £3 for furnishing nineteen gallons of whiskey.[19] They were then marched to Danville, put in jail, and finally turned over to John Crow, who was responsible to feed and house them.[20] Logan assumed that by holding these Indians hostage, he could arrange an exchange of prisoners. After several months of negotiations with the Shawnee leaders, with the preliminary affairs being handled by Daniel Boone, the two sides met in August 1787 near Limestone, with Boone furnishing the provisions for the informal treaty. This time thirty gallons of whiskey was consumed, for which he was paid £9. The Indians who were present said that they desired to live in peace, but that some members of the tribe who still favored war with Virginia had moved north and settled on the Wabash. Finally, all but ten of the Indians were exchanged, and the meeting ended with both sides skeptical of the other's intentions.

Gov. Edmund Randolph spoke favorably of Clark and Logan's campaign against the Indians, saying that it had been necessary for the protection of the citizens of Virginia. He even asked Congress to pay the expenses involved in the campaign, since the operation was then outside the limits of the state. Congress was not impressed; the senators declined to pay for a campaign that they had not authorized.

This was to be the last large-scale campaign sponsored by the Virginia government against the Indians. There would be skirmishes between the various county militias and Indian raiding parties, but these were small affairs, involving only a few men. John Logan, the brother of Benjamin Logan, was censured for leading some Lincoln County militia into North Carolina (now Tennessee) in the pursuit of some raiders. Seven Indians were overtaken and killed, several more injured, and several stolen horses were recovered. The Cherokee registered a complaint that was forwarded to Governor Randolph; he reprimanded Logan, but no prosecution was attempted.

Arthur St. Clair, the governor of the new Northwest Territory, attempted to schedule a treaty with the Indians in May 1788, but it was postponed after several American soldiers were killed while preparing the meeting place. Afterwards, St. Clair could not come to terms with the Indians. In Kentucky the Indian raids continued.

To counter the threat from the Indians, it was decided that Jefferson, Lincoln, Fayette, Nelson, Bourbon, and Madison Counties should each keep six to twelve militia rangers on active duty to scout and repel the raiders. But even this measure failed to prevent settlers from being killed by small parties of Indians. The greatest difficulty of keeping the militia rangers on patrol was the inability of the officers to obtain provisions. The state paid only six pence per ration, and no one would furnish food for this amount. Eighteen thousand people, however, are said to have moved to these frontier counties during the last nine months of 1787; in the first six months of 1788 over 6,000 came down the Ohio River, and thousands of others used the trail through the Cumberland Gap. Thus the few casualties suffered by the Virginians had no real bearing on the outcome of the war.

The Canadian governor wrote that the Indians were on the warpath. In March 1789, a number of people were killed by the Indians while traveling down the Ohio. Among them was John May, the well-known Kentucky land jobber and the brother of George May, the former surveyor of Kentucky and Jefferson Counties. The May brothers had acquired over 765,000 acres in Virginia, much of which they sold soon after receiving the patent. John May, who had spent months in the woods as the frontier's most successful land locator, was shot between the eyes when he attempted to surrender; all others in the flatboat were either killed or captured. Such travelers were afforded virtually no protection. At the time there were fewer then 800 regular soldiers in the entire American army, only a few of whom were posted on the Western frontier.

The final independent militia affair to occur north of the Ohio River was in August 1789 when Maj. John Hardin, a Revolutionary war veteran, led a party to the Wabash region to interdict Indian warriors who had been successful in raiding Kentucky settlements. One company, made up of men from around the Painted Stone Station under Capt. Bland Ballard, included Isaiah Boone, the son of Squire Boone, and Dr. John Knight. Knight had been captured with Col. William Crawford in 1782 and was forced to watch his commander being burned at the stake. He later wrote an account of Crawford's torture and burning. Accusing Simon Girty of refusing to aid Crawford in his suffering, Knight did much to give Girty his dark reputation.

Hardin's force, consisting of 220 mounted militia, headed for the Wea towns. On route he attacked a small Shawnee camp, killing three warriors, three squaws, and two children. Hardin's men then stopped at Vincennes to report on their victory.[21] The federal authorities were not pleased with this little expedition, as they had been trying to make peace with the tribe.

This was the last military campaign waged solely by Virginia. This colony had acted independently against the Indians since Lord Dunmore's War in 1774. Without stint, it had continued to protect her interests in the West during the Revolution. Eventually the Congress of the United States appointed commissioners to determine the amount to reimburse Virginia for expenses incurred while securing the Northwest Territory. In 1788 they decided that $500,000 would be ample compensation for their efforts.[22]

The Virginia leaders considered themselves Englishmen, and the majority, as property owners, were taught it was their born duty to serve the state. Individual as well as collective or state property rights were part of their freedom.

Once the Indian nations had relinquished what is now Kentucky, the vast area became public domain, that is, the property of Virginia. When the governor and, later, the legislature decided that the land could be acquired by Virginia citizens, those citizens, who moved onto it, fought for it. Their property rights were important to them. In fact, in keeping with John Locke's influential *Two Treatises on Government,* most of the Western settlers regarded property rights as more important than freedom of speech, freedom of press, or freedom of religion. Of course, they all agreed that they must have the right to bear arms against their ever-present enemies.

Virginia settlers moved west, then built or used captured outposts to defend these settlements. Overall, this proved to be successful even though the professional military organization was forsaken by the government owing to the lack of funds. In the end, it was the militia, reinforced by new arrivals from the East, that made the final difference in the outcome of this war.

In retrospect, it is clear that the West was won almost entirely by the efforts of the citizens of Virginia, both native born and those who migrated from other colonies, especially Pennsylvania and North Carolina. Had it not been for the efforts of Virginia, the original United States would likely have been confined to the area between the Atlantic Ocean and the Appalachian Mountains. The Mississippi valley would have most likely been under the control of the Spanish. How this scenario would have affected history is highly speculative. Unfortunately, American historians usually neglect this important aspect of the country's early history.

EPILOGUE

The Federal Government
Takes Command

GEORGE WASHINGTON, DRESSED IN HIS NEW BROWN SUIT, WAS INAUGU-
rated as the first president of the United States on Thursday, April 30,
1789. He expected to face an ocean of difficulties, one being the failure of
Arthur St. Clair, the governor of the Northwest Territory, to make anything that even remotely resembled a peace treaty with the Northern Indians. In fact, St. Clair, like many other Western leaders, had already
concluded that since the federal government intended to sell land north of
the Ohio River to settlers, there was no way to avoid an Indian war. It was
well known that Congress was counting upon the money from the sale of
the Western lands to pay federal loans and war debts. Eventually, selling
Western land was to make the United States one of the richest countries in
the world; for over a century Western expansion, sold to new emigrants
who arrived from Europe, created opportunity that was never equaled before or after. But that was later.

The first public land offered to the citizens of the United States did
little to discourage migrants from moving to Kentucky or Tennessee and
purchasing land at the going price from speculators. Land in the Northwest Territory was offered only in tracts that were one mile square, at
$1,280, at a time when not many people had $1,280. It wasn't until 1800
that Rep. William Henry Harrison was able to pass his "land reform bill"
allowing settlers to purchase as little as 320 acres for $640. The bill was
sharply attacked by Rep. Harry Lee of Virginia, son of the man responsible for Harrison's army commission, as well as by other Eastern Federalists

who believed that the land should be retained in the hands of "responsible parties" if not by the government.[1]

There were then two places in the West that particularly concerned the president and his secretary of war—the Northwest Territory and the Southwest or Mississippi Territory. The latter included a large tract of land, reaching to the Mississippi River, which was claimed by both Georgia and Spain. Although they had never recognized the independence of the United States nor given up their claim to the land east of the Mississippi, the Spanish were becoming troubled by both the American expansion westward and the British influence over the Indian nations. To keep control of the West, Spain arbitrarily closed the vital Mississippi River to American trade. This caused enormous pressure on the inhabitants of Kentucky and Tennessee, whose only easy exports were down that river.

The area claimed by Georgia and Spain was also claimed by the Creek nation, at the time dominated by a notorious Tory fur trader, Alexander McGillivray. Because his grandmother was an Indian, McGillivray was accepted as a member of the tribe. The federal government negotiated with the Creek for several years, and most of the land was finally ceded to the United States in the summer of 1790, after McGillivray was awarded a large pension and trading concessions by Congress.[2]

The negotiations in the Northwest Territory were not so easy. In 1788 the American government operated under the assumption that the Indians had relinquished their rights to land in eastern Ohio by the treaty of Fort McIntosh in 1784 and the treaty at the mouth of the Great Miami in 1786. Not long afterward surveyors began plotting the one-mile-square sections in the seven ranges on the west side of the upper Ohio. Congress in 1787 also approved the purchase of 1.5 million acres by the Ohio Company, located north of the Ohio and southwest of the seven ranges. By July 1788 the town of Marietta was established by the Ohio Company, which was then recruiting settlers to occupy its new purchase.

The government decided to occupy Vincennes and sent Brig. Joseph Harmar north with a few soldiers. When Harmar arrived on July 11, 1787, he found Fort Patrick Henry so dilapidated that he started another fort about a mile up the Wabash, at the foot of Buntin Street. By then the town consisted of about 400 houses, mostly log, and a population of 1,300—900 French and 400 Americans. While the construction was under way, Harmar traveled to Cahokia and also St. Louis. Later he passed the ruins of Fort St. Charles; the rear of the fort had been destroyed by erosion of the shifting Mississippi River, but the 400-foot-long front wall remained. It had been constructed of stone and plastered and was as good as ever. Harmar noted that Kaskaskia had fewer than 200 people, and there were 239 people at Cahokia. The Spanish at St. Louis had told the French inhabitants on the east side of the river to cross over and settle there, tempting them with free land grants. Colonel Hamtramck assumed command of Vincennes and wrote that it was a hardship post because of the high prices. Flour was $7 per hundred pounds, corn $2 per bushel, whiskey $8 per gallon, eggs $1 per dozen, and sugar $1.50 per pound.

The Virginians who lived in the frontier counties of Jefferson, Mason, Kanawha, Ohio, and Harrison continued to suffer from Indian raids. Harry Innes wrote James Knox, the secretary of war, that in the Kentucky district alone, 1,500 people had been killed or captured, and more than 20,000 horses stolen since the end of 1783. In the Virginia counties along the Ohio, land surveyors were usually accompanied by armed guards. On a trip to Kentucky, Col. William Fleming, while visiting his niece at Oxmore near Louisville, wrote:

> I was in Jefferson—numbers of Persons Kild [sic] & horses stolen by the Indians. Mr Fountains horse & another was taken out of Colo Bullets pasture close by the house; mine was hobled [sic] & a bell on [but] escaped with his. In Fayette there are parties of Indians but I will not dwell on these disagreeable thing[s].[3]

In 1788, two young men were captured by Indians but managed to escape. When they reached Vincennes they told Colonel Hamtramck that their captors had boasted that they were little interested in a peace treaty, "that they prefered [sic] war to peace as they got much more by it."

St. Clair wrote that the Kentuckians could not be expected patiently to submit to the "cruelties and depredations of those savages; they are in the habit of retaliations." But even so, the raid of John Hardin in August 1787 was the last expedition by organized Virginia militia to cross over into the Northwest Territory, despite the fact that small bands of Indians from various tribes continued to raid their settlements, kill civilians, and steal horses. From then on, the Virginia militia would only initiate attacks when invited to do so by the federal government.

In July 1789, Colonel Hamtramck lost some men in a skirmish with the Indians. He had sent Lt. William Peters out with thirty-six men to travel down the Wabash to meet a boat with provisions for Vincennes. On July 27, when they were only two miles from the Ohio, they were attacked by fifty Indians. Ten men were lost and eight more wounded, and the Indians were able to make off with a great deal of loot.

The 1784 U.S. Congress had authorized an army of 799 men, but the ranks were never filled because of the low pay. In the summer of 1789 there were only 672 regulars under arms. In January 1790, Governor St. Clair decided to move west and take personal command of the army. He traveled down the Ohio and soon reached the little town of Losantiville, a name meaning "city opposite the mouth of the Licking River." He renamed it Cincinnati. By then Bvt. Brig. Gen. Joseph Harmar was commander at the newly constructed Fort Harmar in Marietta and Colonel Hamtramck was appointed the commander at Vincennes. There were five federal posts inside the Northwest Territory: Fort McIntosh, located near the present Midland, Pennsylvania; Fort Harmar, near Marietta, Ohio; Forts Washington and Fenney, near the present Cincinnati, Ohio; Fort Steubin, across the river from Louisville in the present Jeffersonville, Indiana; and Fort Knox, in Vincennes, Indiana. Fort Steubin was also originally named Fort Fenney, after Maj. Walter Fenney, the army officer who oversaw the construction, but the name was soon changed to avoid confusion with its upriver twin. Unfortunately, these army outposts did not stop the Indians from crossing the Ohio. Most of the forts contained only a few soldiers, and those present were neither trained nor equipped to intercept the raiders.

In the spring General Harmar decided to punish the Indians who had been murdering Virginia settlers; he organized an expedition consisting of 120 regular troops and 200 Virginia militia commanded by Brig. Gen. Charles Scott. In April Harmar's regulars rowed down the river to Limestone, where they met Scott's militia. Then the combined infantry force marched northward to Paint Creek and came back by following the Scioto River southward to the Ohio. They returned on April 27. This short letter by Harry Innes describes this campaign:

> The Indians still continue troublesome; A party of Volunteers under the command of General Scott crossed the Ohio at Limestone, were joined by 100 regulars under Gen'l Harmar, proceeded up the Scioto to Paint Cr., saw a number of old Imcampments [sic]—were prevented from crossing the River by high water, they marched to the mouth of the Scioto but the provision of the Volunteers being eshausted [sic] they could proceed no farther—soon after the Troops marched from Limestone they fell in upon the Trail of 4 or 5 Indians, Gen'l Scott detached a party in pursuit of

them, who overtook the Indians on Eagle Creek about 20 miles from Limestone & kil[l]ed 4—one was kil[l]ed by our acquaintance George Madison, who overtook the fellow in the creek, grapled [*sic*] with him & kil[l]ed him with his knife.[4]

On June 7, Secretary Knox instructed Harmar to go on the offensive again and conduct a raid against some of the Indian towns. This move had political as well as military advantages, in that it would be popular with the frontier settlers in both Pennsylvania and Virginia. Harmar was authorized to call up 1,500 militia to augment his smaller force of U.S. army regulars. He ordered the militia to assemble at Forts Steubin and Washington in September 1790. But the militia from the Kentucky district were found to be mostly young men without military experience, interested only in seeing the country. Then, only 300 of the authorized Pennsylvania militia arrived, and they were inferior to even the Kentucky militia, consisting of poorly armed old men and boys. Cols. James Trotter and John Hardin headed the Kentuckians, and Col. Christopher Trudy led the Pennsylvanians.

This army finally started north on September 26, 1790, and traveled past Piqua and then on to the St. Mary River. In the meantime, on September 30, Colonel Hamtramck led another force, consisting of 50 regulars and about 280 Virginia militia under William Whitley, from Vincennes to the Vermilion village. He arrived there on October 10 and found the village empty. The soldiers returned to Vincennes and were back in their barracks at Fort Knox on October 26. These militia companies then disbanded and headed home.

The Indians were aware of Harmar's advance so they evacuated the Miami towns of Kekionga and Chillicothe; the women and children were sent to other villages. The warriors then decided to destroy the towns to prevent their use by the Americans, and on October 15 both villages were burned. A troop of militia cavalry under Colonel Hardin, scouting ahead of the main army, rode into Kekionga the same afternoon. Harman's infantry arrived two days later, and the men amused themselves searching for hidden Indian treasure. The following morning Colonel Trotter was selected to search for the enemy along the trail leading to the Kickapoo towns. About forty cavalry led the way, and around midday they encountered a few Indians. One trooper reported seeing fifty mounted Indians, but later they disappeared. The men returned to Kekionga that evening and reported this information to General Harmar.

Harmar decided to send 180 men back on the trail used by Trotter, but this force was to be under the command of Colonel Hardin, the highest-ranking militia officer. The next morning about 180 men marched off with Hardin, a force of 150 militia and 30 regular troops. Hardin's men traveled only a few miles before they were ambushed and fled to the rear, leaving the outnumbered regulars to hold off the Indians. This small force fought bravely but were nearly annihilated, while most of the militia were able to escape.

After this setback, the army destroyed the crops around the Indian towns, and on October 21 the army began its march back to Cincinnati. They had traveled only a few miles when scouts reported that 120 of the Indians had returned to their village. General Harmar then ordered about 400 men back to engage these Indians, anticipating an easy victory. But it was not to be. The Indians managed to ambush the militia cavalry crossing the river. Others warriors, hidden in a cornfield, surprised some of the infantry before finally being driven off. Harmar's soldiers sustained numerous casualties, sixty-eight killed and twenty-eight wounded. The U.S. army then resumed their march to Cincinnati, which was made without incident.

General Harmar claimed a great victory, but there were too many private soldiers and junior officers who told a different story. Harmar was transferred and resigned. The war went on.

On January 2, 1791, a small settlement called Big Bottom, located about thirty miles up the Muskingum River from Marietta, was attacked by a large party of Indians. The settlers were completely surprised, and about a dozen (including women) were immediately killed and several taken prisoner. Only two men managed to escape.

Eight days later a party of Indians attacked settlers and surveyors at Dunlap Station, a small outpost located about seventeen miles north of Cincinnati. A surveying party was caught outside the walls and one of the four men was instantly killed. Another man was captured and later executed in front of the fort gate. At the time, the stockade included a squad of U.S. soldiers. Together with a few settlers, they managed to hold out until relief arrived from Fort Washington.

On January 22, 1791, Secretary Knox informed Congress that an active war was already under way in the Old Northwest and that another campaign should be made against the Wabash Indians. He proposed an offensive to establish a strong American post at the Miami village of Kekionga and requested 3,000 troops for this expedition. Gen. Arthur St.

Clair, governor of the Northwest Territory, was instructed to march most of this enlarged American army northward to establish this base. Congress allowed the regular army to be expanded from 1,216 men to 2,128 men so that the army would not have to rely upon the "unreliable" militia for the majority of its troops.

While St. Clair was getting organized, he sent Brigadier General Scott with the Virginia militia on a raid to the Indian village of Ociatanon on the Wabash River. His army of 750 cavalry crossed the Ohio River at the mouth of the Kentucky River on March 9, 1791, and rode northward through the flat countryside. The Indians were aware of this raid and expected Scott's force to attack the Miami towns. Instead, after going about forty miles, Scott turned westward toward the Wabash. They found the village of Ociatanon nearly deserted. The warriors had left to reinforce the Miami towns against the expected attack. The Americans arrived on June 1 and easily captured some women and children to use for exchange of prisoners. General Scott informed the Indians that if they wished to recover these prisoners, they would have to bury the hatchet and smoke the pipe of peace. By June 15 he and his men were back in Fort Steuben across the river from Louisville.

One newcomer to Kentucky who quickly became prominent was James Wilkinson. Born in 1753 in Maryland and educated as a physician, he rose from captain to the rank of brigader during the Revolutionary War, serving as the aide-de-camp of General Gates. He moved to Kentucky in 1784. He obtained property in Frankfort adjacent to the Honorable John Brown, where he built an impressive mansion on what was to become Wilkinson Street. Wilkinson became a trader and gained prestige as a man with connections because of his success in trading goods with the Spanish in New Orleans. After dealing with the Spanish governor, he gained an exclusive right as the sole American trader at that port city. What was not known is that he was also a secret agent for the Spanish with orders to separate Kentucky from the United States as an independent state under Spanish protection.

He also became involved in the state militia and was appointed lieutenant colonel under Brig. Gen. Charles Scott, but he and Scott were never on friendly terms.

After Scott's raid on the Indian towns, James Wilkinson, not to be outdone, led a similar raid. He left Fort Washington with 523 mounted volunteer militia on August 1, 1791. His cavalry also advanced northward toward the Miami towns, but turned westward to attack L'Anguille on the

Wabash River. His raiders arrived on August 5, took thirty-four prisoners, mostly women and children, then returned to Kentucky.

St. Clair had hoped to lead the regulars northward at the same time as Wilkinson's raid, but he was plagued with trouble organizing his army. During this period he managed to construct another fort, Fort Hamilton, on the Miami, about twenty miles north of Cincinnati. Nevertheless, Harry Innes reported some problems:

> I fear the Grand Military Operation will not move this fall— the pack horses for the quartermaster's department are purchased in Pennsylvania and not yet come to hand—the pack saddles have been made at little York & there paded [sic] with hay, then waggoned [sic] to Fort Pitt & since condemned being too large for the poneys [sic] purchased by the quartermaster, & the reason assigned for this measure, is that he was afraid the People of Kentucky would Jew him.[5]

St. Clair's army of about 2,000 regulars, trailed by 200 female camp followers, finally marched out for Fort Hamilton on October 14, 1791, after being reinforced by 300 Virginia militia under Col. William Oldham. They traveled north, building a road as they moved. After advancing forty-five miles, they stopped and constructed another stockade, Fort Jefferson. When this wilderness base was supplied and reinforced, General St. Clair resumed his campaign on October 24. The progress of this large army was slow, but it managed to reach the headwaters of the Wabash River, twenty miles north of Fort Jefferson, on November 3, 1791.[6] St. Clair formed his regulars, then numbering about 1,200 men, in a rectangle at a bend in the river and made camp, but sent the milita ahead to camp on the far side of the stream.

At dawn the next day, the Indians attacked St. Clair's camp and quickly defeated the U.S. troops. The initial advance routed the 250 militia, who were camped across the river and several hundred yards in front of the regulars. Colonel Oldham and most of his men who survived this assault waded across the Wabash to take shelter behind the regulars. Then the main attack began. The Indians quickly surrounded the main camp, which had been formed in a square. By 9:30 A.M. it was all over. The Indians easily overwhelmed the poorly organized defenders, including the artillery emplacements. Within a half hour the Indians had broken through the lines and were inside the camp. General St. Clair and a few survivors barely managed to break out of the trap to escape. The retreat soon turned into a rout.

This defeat cost the Americans 52 percent of their army killed or missing. They had 630 men and officers killed, many of them tomahawked as they lay wounded, and of the 200 women in camp, 56 were slain. A total of 66 percent of the U.S. force was killed, wounded, or missing. The survivors, including several hundred who were walking wounded, managed to flee and to hold Fort Jefferson only because the victorious warriors were more interested in the plunder than following the beaten U.S. army. On the battlefield the Indians recovered 1,200 muskets and eight cannons, There were fewer than 100 Indian casualties. The losses by the American army were greater than those suffered by General Braddock near Pittsburgh during the French and Indian War.[7] St. Clair's defeat was one of the worst disasters ever to befall the American army.

After receiving an account of this embarrassing defeat, President Washington and his cabinet decided that a major revision in the U.S. military establishment was needed. Harmar had been defeated leading an army consisting of a core of regulars reinforced with a large number of militia. This fiasco was blamed on the inexperienced militia. Most of St. Clair's army consisted of newly recruited but poorly paid regulars, but they experienced an even more disastrous defeat. The United States was a new country, and a new approach was needed. President Washington's solution was to appoint a new general and give him more men.

The selection of a new general presented some problems. Washington considered the first four ranking officers—Weedon, Scott, Hand, and Huntington—without enterprise and thought that Weedon and Scott were too fond of the bottle. He passed on Hand and Huntington without giving a reason. He considered Daniel Morgan unfit for the job because he was dishonest, intemperate, and illiterate. The other ranking general, Anthony Wayne, he believed to be more prone to action than judicious and cautious, vain, and apt to be drawn into scrapes. Nevertheless, he considered Major General Wayne the least unpromising, so the president offered him the job.

The first order of business was to increase the size of the U.S. army to 5,000 men, including a regiment of riflemen at a cost of over a million dollars. Mounted militia would still be used for scouting and protection against flank attacks. When this military buildup was discussed in Congress, some of the representatives objected, complaining that it was the U.S. forces invading Indian country that caused the problems, not vice versa. Many New Englanders felt we had lost the battle because we were the aggressors. But the Virginia congressmen settled the debate by pointing out that an Indian war was already under way and it was too late to stop it.

Nevertheless, the government continued to deal with the Indians, and was prepared to offer them peace while preparing for war. During the spring and early summer of 1792 two separate U.S. peace envoys were sent north from the Ohio River outposts to confer with the Indians, but everyone in both parties was killed or captured. That ended the government's attempt at peace talks.

In 1792 one of Kentucky's early pioneers vanished without a trace. According to his wife, in February James Harrod decided to go up the Kentucky River on a hunting trip, but on the way he was killed by James Bridges, against whom he was scheduled to be a witness in a land trial. James Bridges had come to Kentucky with Daniel Boone early in 1775 and was later to be one of the first men to demand money from Boone for an alleged loss when Boone received his Missouri grant from the U.S. government.

In June 1792 Kentucky became a separate state, a factor that greatly reduced Virginia's part in the Indian war. The border of this new state, being along territory occupied by hostile Indian tribes, became the object of their raids. Nevertheless, the Old Dominion still had three counties with borders on the Ohio River, and so her citizens still experienced Indian raids. In Ohio, Harrison, and, especially, Kanawha Counties, men rarely tended their crops without an armed guard.

In March 1792, a federal detachment that included a new nineteen-year-old lieutenant, William Henry Harrison, constructed another fort, called Fort St. Clair, approximately midway between Forts Hamilton and Jefferson. This location was designed to give overnight protection to the packhorse convoys going along St. Clair's "Wilderness Road" to supply Fort Jefferson. Not long after it was finished, St. Clair was formally dismissed, and Gen. Anthony Wayne was appointed in his place. His efforts to establish an effective military force, trained in Pittsburgh, were initially hampered by a budding insurrection of the "whiskey boys"—a disorderly mob of Scotch-Irish farmers who violently resented a federal tax on distilled spirits.

About this time the new British minister, George Hammond, arrived in the United States and alleged that American violations of the peace treaty were so numerous that the British were justified in not relinquishing their Western outposts. Obviously the official position was then to ignore the American claim to the Northwest Territory and support the Indians in their war against Virginia.

Holmes House in Frankfort. It became the temporary statehouse when Kentucky was admitted to the Union in 1792.

But by and large the summer of 1792 was peaceful. The Indians' only offensive movement against the U.S. outposts occurred on June 25 when a party of warriors ambushed and killed some soldiers cutting hay outside the walls of Fort Jefferson. The failure of the Indians to launch a major campaign was fortunate for the U.S. army, as there were only 700 soldiers in the six forts in the Northwest Territory.

In November 1792 a large group of Shawnee attacked a company of Kentucky militia under the command of Maj. John Adair, camped outside the walls of Fort St. Clair. These militiamen had been escorting 200 pack-horses that were returning after supplying Fort Jefferson. During this skir-mish six men were killed and five wounded, but most of the militia were able safely to take shelter inside the fort. The Indians, however, took most of the valuable packhorses.

In April 1793 General Wayne led his new "Legion of the United States" westward and then moved his army down the Ohio River to Fort

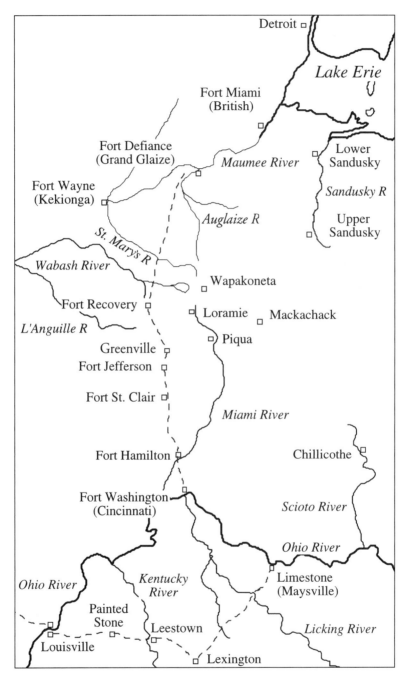

The Northwest Territory.

Washington. By May 9 most of them had arrived in Cincinnati and were welcomed as heroes. On orders from Secretary Knox, however, the troops did not immediately march northward since peace negotiations with the Indians were scheduled for the summer months. Finally, in October the U.S. regulars started for Fort Jefferson, which Wayne had designated as a major supply base for upcoming operations.

On October 17, Wayne's army suffered its first setback. One convoy consisting of 120 men, taking corn and supplies to Fort Jefferson, was ambushed on the road and defeated. Wayne took the defeat well, calling it "a little check to one of our convoys."

The new American strategy was to establish a strong military base in the area where the troublesome tribes lived on the Maumee River. The secret to success in this operation would be their ability to supply such a base. Provisions would have to be obtained in Kentucky or brought down the Ohio to Cincinnati, then shipped nearly 200 miles overland on St. Clair's road to this new fort. The logistics were staggering. This strategy required protecting the road, so General Wayne established another outpost six miles north of Fort Jefferson, which he named Greenville.

On October 6, Wayne had 2,600 troops, but a month later sickness and expired enlistments had reduced the size of his legion. Nevertheless, he felt his force was large enough to meet any threat from the Indians.

On December 23, 1792, General Wayne led a detachment of eight companies of infantry and one company of artillery men to the site of St. Clair's defeat on the Wabash River. There they constructed another log fort, which he named Fort Recovery. At that site the soldiers were able to recover three of the cannons previously captured and hidden by the Indians, incorporating them into the fort's defenses. The new fort was completed on December 28, and the majority of soldiers marched twenty-three miles back to Greenville, leaving only two companies to man the new outpost.

The construction of Fort Recovery did not go unnoticed by the British. On February 10, 1794, Sir Guy Carleton (also known as Lord Dorchester), the British governor general of Canada, ordered a fort to be built on the Maumee River to replace a post demolished after the peace of 1783. This fort was constructed near the Miami rapids on the west side of the river. As would be expected, the Americans considered the erection of this fort an act of aggression.

General Wayne had hoped to begin a campaign against the Northern Indians in early summer, but the lack of provisions delayed his offensive. Then on June 30, 1794, a large party of Indians decided to go on the offense and started for Fort Recovery. This small outpost had just been reinforced by fifty dragoons and ninety riflemen, who were guarding a supply train. The provisions had been delivered, and the men were camped outside the walls. In the morning the Indians advanced and fired on the packhorse herders. The dragoons mounted and rode to the rescue only to be shot down by the numerous enemy. The survivors retreated through the infantrymen, who then were forced to meet a sustained attack by the Indians. Soon the infantry was also driven back, but most were able to reach the fort. Once inside the walls, the U.S. soldiers were able to pick off many of the Indians. With casualties mounting and having an inferior field position, the Indians lifted the siege and retreated the following day.

In the meantime the Whiskey Rebellion had become so widespread that the governor of Pennsylvania was unable to control the western part of the state. President George Washington was finally forced to call up several thousand militia from Virginia, Maryland, New Jersey, and Pennsylvania. Washington took charge of the latter two contingents in Carlisle on October 4, 1794, then traveled to Cumberland where the Virginia and Maryland troops had collected. The army then marched to Bedford without opposition; Washington then left for the capital, leaving the policing to the militia officers. When this military force moved against the Scotch-Irish rebels, the tax evaders were brought to a "perfect sense of their misconduct without spilling a drop of blood."[8]

Near the end of July, Anthony Wayne was reinforced by 760 Kentucky militia under Gen. Charles Scott, so he started his legion north on the attack. The militia from Shelby County, under Maj. Aquilla Whitaker, included Bland Ballard's company, which had five of the young Boones in one mess. The army marched about twelve miles a day, and each night the men were positioned for defense against an Indian attack. On July 29 the army passed Fort Recovery and soon reached St. Mary's River.

On August 1 the column halted to build another fortification, with log blockhouses at the corners. It was called Fort John Adams. Even before it was completed, most of the army marched off to the northeast, and on the eighth they reached an Indian village known as the Grand Glaize, located near the confluence of the Maumee and Auglaize Rivers. There the men found cornfields and others crops; several trading houses were burning, which meant that the occupants had recently made a hasty retreat. From some Indians captured nearby, the Americans learned that 700 warriors had collected at McKee's storehouse, and another 600 were expected soon to join them there for an attack on the advancing Americans.

At this Indian village of Grand Glaize, General Wayne constructed still another fort, which he called Fort Defiance. On August 15, he felt that the structure was secure enough to shelter his army during an emergency, so he crossed to the north side of the river and ordered the army to march down the river, toward the British fort. On August 19 mounted scouts ranging ahead of the army discovered the Indians and reported their presence to the general.

The following morning Wayne's army, then numbering about 850 men, marched out in close order, expecting a battle. In the lead were Maj. William Price's mounted Kentucky militia, followed by a small detachment of regulars acting as a reserve under Capt. John Cook. Then came the main army in two columns, one led by Col. John Hamtramck on the left and the other by Brig. Gen. James Wilkinson on the right, marching along the river. General Wayne and his staff, accompanied by some artillery, were in the center between the infantry columns. One of the scouts for the army was William Wells, adopted son of Chief Little Turtle and the brother of Samuel Wells, the man who had given his horse to John Floyd at the Long Run battle.

Wayne's army marched northeast through mostly wooded terrain. Upon encountering an area covered with old fallen timber, the advanced scouts were suddenly shot down, and a few seconds later the concealed Indians fired a volley into the mounted Kentuckians. Many were wounded, and the entire 150-man cavalry unit wheeled and retreated as fast as possible. Cook ordered his regulars to fire at any militia who retreated, a measure that temporarily stopped the rout. As the retreating cavalrymen mixed with the regulars, however, the combined force fell into disorder, and they all began to retreat. Before long, the attacking Indians pushed them out of the fallen timber and into the center of their comrades, then forming up for action. General Wayne gave an account of what followed:

> After advancing about five miles, Major Price's corps received so severe a fire from the enemy, who were secreted in the woods and high grass, as to compel them to retreat. The Legion was immediately formed in two lines, principally in a close thick wood, which extended for miles on our left, and for a very considerable distance in front; the ground being covered with old fallen timber, probably occasioned by a tornado, which rendered it impracticable for the cavalry to act with effect, and afforded the enemy the most favorable covert for their mode of warfare. The savages were

formed in three lines, within supporting distance of each other, and extending for near two miles at right angles with the river. I soon discovered, from the weight of the fire and extent of their lines, that the enemy were in full force in front, in possession of their favorite ground, and endeavoring to turn our left flank. I therefore gave orders for the second line to advance and support the first; and directed Major General Scott to gain and turn the right flank of the savages, with the whole of the mounted volunteers, by a circuitous route; at the same time I ordered the front line to advance and charge with trailed arms, and rouse the Indians from their coverts at the point of the bayonet, and when [*sic*] up to deliver a close and well directed fire on their backs, followed by a brisk charge, so as not to give them time to load again.[9]

The warriors who had led the attack were about 500 Ottawa and Patawatomi. By advancing, they became separated from a force of Canadian militia under Col. William Caldwell on their right flank as well as from the Shawnee under Blue Jacket. This advancing force came up to within sixty yards of Wayne's line.

During the confusion of battle, Lt. William Henry Harrison asked the general what to do. "Charge the damned rascals with the bayonet!" he answered, "then shoot in their backs as they retreat to keep them moving." The lieutenant passed these orders on to Wilkinson and Hamtramck.

At about the same time, Capt. Robert Campbell, leading his company of dragoons, charged the Indians. The captain and many of his men were shot down, but as the infantry advanced to support them, the Indians began to run, and as they did, they received a volley directed at their backs. The soldiers pursued with fixed bayonets, but the Indians offered little resistance. The Canadians, opposite Hamtramck's battalion, laid down a heavy fire for a while, but they too were forced to join the retreat when Robert Todd's militiamen fell on their flank. Among those retreating were Simon Girty and Alexander McKee. As the soldiers moved on, they also encountered and routed the Shawnee, Wyandot, and Delaware. The battle lasted only fifteen minutes, but the chase lasted over an hour. The American losses were 35 killed and about 100 wounded. Bland Ballard's company, containing the five young Boone boys, was on the flank and did not get into the heat of the fight.

The beaten Indians retreated to the British fort, followed by the victorious Americans, but, almost unbelievably, they were not allowed to enter the stockade. They then scattered, and most headed back to their respective villages. General Wayne assembled his troops in front of the fort but did not attack. The Americans and British were not at war with each other, and also the U.S. troops were running low on provisions. But so that there would be no question who was victorious, General Wayne burned the Indian villages and crops within sight of the fort, along with the storehouse of Alexander McKee. Within a few days he marched his army back to Greenville.

General Wayne decided to establish a base at the forks of the Maumee, at the old Miami town, Kekionga, where Harmar's troops had engaged the Indians in 1790. He planned to make this a base from which American traders could exchange goods with the Indians, thus weaning them away from the British. This post became Fort Wayne, Indiana. The following August, at the treaty conducted at Greenville, the Indians agreed to a new boundary with the Americans, for which they were to receive $20,000 in trade goods and an additional sum of $9,500 annually. This new boundary line ran down the Cuyahoga River to Fort Laurens, then west to Fort Recovery, and then south to the Ohio at the mouth of the Kentucky River.

When the smoke cleared from the battle of Fallen Timber, Wayne quietly gathered evidence of Wilkinson's criminal activities, apparently planning the court-martial, the cashiering, and perhaps his execution for treason. From a returning deserter he had obtained certain information implicating Wilkinson in treasonous correspondence with the British. Beyond this initial testimony, there were tantalizingly damning fragments of evidence linking Wilkinson to a Spanish pension and a conspiracy to divide the Union. Yet Wayne was unable to obtain positive proof that would stand up in a court of law. In mid-November 1796, he sailed to Presque Isle, where on December 15, he died following an acute attack of the gout and an intestinal disorder. He was not yet fifty-two years of age. In one of his last letters to the secretary of war, he had proclaimed further knowledge of his disloyal subordinate's treachery. Instead of being shot for treason, James Wilkinson was appointed commander of the U.S. army while still serving as Spanish secret agent number thirteen; he was destined for a checkered career and later received praise from President Thomas Jefferson as well as $11,000 in "expenses" for the betrayal of Aaron Burr. He was probably America's most disreputable soldier, Benedict Arnold not excepted.

Many who were prominent during the conflict for the Old Northwest were plagued by ill health or misfortune. Both Lord Dorchester and John G. Simcoe were recalled or reassigned by the home office in 1796. Dorchester survived a major shipwreck on Quebec's Anticosti Island during his

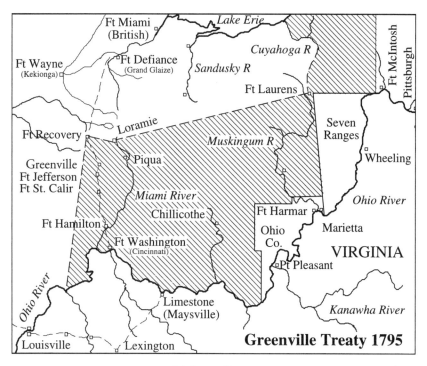

The Greenville treaty.

voyage home. Simcoe, although appointed overall commander in India during 1806, died after taking sick on his journey to that post. Alexander McKee, whom Anthony Wayne had referred to as the "principal stimulator of the war," suddenly died on January 14, 1799, of a high fever. Simon Girty, half blind and prone to drunken stupors, was regarded "incapable of anything." The memory of his defiance of the U.S. occupation of Detroit in 1796, when Girty allegedly swam his horse across the river shouting invectives and gesturing with his fist, was but a shadow in 1813. Then the aged Girty was compelled to flee his farm in the face of an American invasion and was unable to return until the War of 1812 ended.

The part of the West that was Kentucky County, Virginia, in 1776 grew rapidly and become the fifteenth state of the Union in 1792. Isaac Shelby, a young lieutenant during the battle of Point Pleasant in 1774, became Kentucky's first governor. He settled on his land near Danville, which he called "Traveler's Rest." Later, when war with Great Britain became imminent, he ran for governor again and defeated Gabriel Slaughter, 29,285 to 11,936 votes, largely on the strength of his military experience. While in office Shelby insisted that Gen. William Henry Harrison be given top command in the Western theater and prepared Kentucky for war. In 1813, at the age of sixty-two, Shelby raised 3,500 troops, double the number requested. With the permission of the General Assembly, he personally led the troops to join Harrison's army. The old soldier/governor was active at the battle of the Thames on October 5, 1813, where the British and the Indians were decisively defeated. After a second retirement to his farm, he assisted Andrew Jackson in negotiating with the Chickasaw Indians for the purchase of land on the west side of the Tennessee River, the part of Kentucky that became known as the Jackson Purchase. He died at Traveler's Rest on July 18, 1826.

Unlike Isaac Shelby, many of the first settlers were dead or had moved away by the time Kentucky became a state. James Harrod, the man who had attempted to establish a town in 1774, disappeared in February 1792, and was presumably murdered by a companion over a land dispute. Of his company, Abraham Chaplin was perhaps the most successful. He served as an officer under George Rogers Clark and, after some litigation, became the sole owner of his 1,400-acre settlement and preemption tract near Harrodsburg, where he lived and died.

For a time, the old Long Hunter, Daniel Boone, made a good living as a surveyor and owner of a trading post in Maysville; but in 1790, he moved to Kanawha County, Virginia, from where he served in the legislature. He lived there for five years, but returned and settled on Bushy Forks (near Cynthiana). Daniel speculated in Kentucky land but was unsuccessful in holding the thousands of acres he claimed. In September 1799, Daniel Boone left for Missouri, where he was made magistrate of the Femme Osage District. Daniel Boone died at the home of his son Nathan in 1820 and was buried in Defiance, Missouri, next to his wife, Rebecca. Twenty-five years later his remains and those of his wife (or, as a rumor would later claim, the remains of Rebecca and a slave, whose grave was supposedly mistaken for Daniel's) were removed to Frankfort, Kentucky, and reinterred on a high bluff overlooking the Kentucky River, which was so often associated with his experiences and the early settlement of the Kentucky country.

Daniel's brother and early hunting companion, Squire Boone, also had land problems in Kentucky. Although he had acquired several large tracts in Shelby County, he fell upon hard times and was forced to sell his land, including the station at Painted Stone, which by then included a mill and distillery. Afterward he moved to Wells Station on Bullskin Creek, where he stayed for several years. This station had been established by Samuel Wells, who had given Floyd a horse to escape from the Indians. Squire Boone then moved to Vicksburg, Mississippi, then to New Orleans, where he opened a gun shop. When he heard his brother was moving to Missouri, Squire moved there also but only stayed about a year. In 1806 he moved to Boone Township in Indiana. He died there in August 1815 and was buried in a cave near Corydon.

Benjamin Logan, who fought in many campaigns and eventually became the ranking military officer in Kentucky, also purchased property on Bullskin Creek near Boone, where he lived from 1793 until his death in 1802. If he and Squire Boone spent any time together reminiscing, there is no record of it. Col. James Knox, who had guided James Harrod on his way home from Kentucky in 1774, received a claim on Beargrass Creek, but sold it to Nicholas Merewether, the same man who purchased Squire Boone's Painted Stone property. When Benjamin Logan died, Knox married his widow, and they continued to reside on Bullskin Creek until his death in December 1822. Logan and Knox were buried within ten feet of each other in a small family cemetery overlooking Bullskin Creek.

There were five McAfee brothers from Botetourt County who came to Kentucky. James, Robert, and George were the first three. They explored Kentucky in 1773 with James McCoun Jr. and Samuel Adams. They came down the Ohio with Capt. Thomas Bullitt's party and had surveys made for them by Hancock Taylor. In 1775 several of the brothers returned to Kentucky with indentured servants and further improved the property they claimed in the vicinity of Harrodsburg. Accompanied by brothers William and Samuel, they permanently moved to Kentucky in 1779. James built a station north of Harrodsburg. William McAfee received a mortal wound during General Clark's expedition against the Shawnee in 1780. James McAfee died on his farm, as did his brothers George and Samuel. Robert was killed on a trip to New Orleans in 1795.

Another famous frontiersman, Simon Kenton, alias Butler, became well known because of his many exploits. Born in 1755 in Fauquier County, Virginia, he mistakenly thought he had killed a man during a fistfight and, fearing the authorities, changed his name and moved West. By the time he was twenty, he was an experienced woodsman and scout in Kentucky. On one occasion he carried his wounded captain, Daniel Boone, back to the fort in Boonesborough during an Indian attack. He served under George Rogers Clark in Illinois and was later captured by the Shawnee while stealing horses. He escaped and settled near Harrodsburg.

His original land claim near Lexington was in litigation for many years. In 1787 he married Martha Dowden, and they moved to Washington, Kentucky, on the old buffalo road between Lexington and Maysville. In 1796 his wife died when their house burned, and the following year he married Elizabeth Jarboe. Like several other early pioneers, he hoped to get rich speculating in land, but instead ended up in debt. In 1798 he moved to Ohio, where he spent his later years, often in poverty but still a traveler. He made four trips to the new state of Missouri where he bought more land, visited his old friend Daniel Boone, and even considered relocating. Kenton died on April 29, 1836, near Zanesville, Ohio, where he was buried.

Of the Fincastle surveyors, only James Douglas and Isaac Hite lived to an old age. Hite was active in land speculation for the remainder of his life and acquired a great deal of property before he died. His cousin, John Bowman, the ranking military leader in Kentucky County, settled at his station near Dick's River, east of Harrodsburg. He recruited people to tap the maple trees on his property and made a profit selling the sugar. Subsequently, John Bowman became ill and died at home in May 1784.

A frequent guest of Colonel Bowman was William Fleming, the land commissioner from Botetourt County, who had been badly wounded at the battle of Point Pleasant. Fleming was often in Kentucky on business and was the chairman of the first Kentucky Convention. Though he owned land on the Ohio River and Goose Creek, he (or his wife) decided not to move to Kentucky because his in-laws, Stephen Trigg and William Christian, had been killed by Indians soon after moving there. Fleming died in 1794 of natural causes while traveling to South Carolina. When his brother-in-law William Christian was killed near Louisville, his widow, Ann, moved to Viney Grove, near Harrodsburg, with her widowed sister Mary Trigg. Mary soon found a new husband, and Ann Christian moved to nearby Myers plantation, which she considered safer.

Anne Christian's daughter Priscilla married Alexander Scott Bullitt, who purchased Oxmore, and his wife inherited the part of her father's estate that included Asturgus Station. When Colonel Fleming died, his heirs sold his tract of land on the Ohio River to Zachary Taylor, nephew of the Fincastle surveyor Hancock Taylor. This land was only a mile from land purchased by George Croghan, who had married the sister of George Rogers Clark. Croghan built a fine house on the tract, called Locust Grove, where Clark died at the age of sixty-five.

After General Clark's commission was revoked by Virginia, the French agent, Citizen Genet, offered him a military commission to attack Spanish-held New Orleans. He was given the title major general in the armies of France and commander in chief of the French Revolutionary Legions on the Mississippi River. In June 1798 Clark was informed by the U.S. government that he had to resign this position or be arrested.

In 1803 George Rogers Clark moved to Clark's Point in Clarksville, which overlooks the Falls of the Ohio. In 1804 he proposed that a canal be dug to circumvent the Falls as well as facilitate trade and commerce. But by 1805 Clark was described as frail and helpless. In 1809 he fell unconscious in front of his fireplace, burning one of his legs so badly that it had to be amputated. Some contend he was drunk, while others say the accident was caused by a stroke. He was then moved to Locust Grove, the home of his younger sister, Lucy (Clark) Croghan, up the Ohio from Louisville, where he remained for nine years. In 1813 a stroke left him paralyzed. On February 13, 1818, Clark suffered another stroke that took his life. Clark was initially buried in the Croghan family cemetery at Locust Grove, but in 1869, when, like Boone, he was finally recognized as a hero, his remains were exhumed and buried in Louisville's Cave Hill Cemetery.

The British-allied Indian leaders also endured hardships. Joseph Brant, disillusioned with the rival Six Nations factions led by Red Jacket and Cornplanter and plagued by the intrigues of McKee's replacement, William Claus, at one point seriously considered moving under the protection of the United States. Following the death of his son Isaac by his own hand, Brant was periodically burdened by debilitating sickness in his family as well as the recurring political intrigues among the Iroquois tribes. After a lengthy illness Brant died on November 24, 1807, at age sixty-four, at his spacious Lake Ontario residence. His unyielding spirit was evident to the end.

Despite his former New Lebanon, Connecticut, education, the Mohawk chieftain had once written, to an unidentified correspondent, a sarcastic reflection on the white men's way of life, citing the American penal system as an example of the "dreadful contrast" between the native and white societies. Brant wrote that protracted incarceration of wrongdoers was beyond the natives' conception.

> Perhaps it is [best] that incorrigible offenders should sometimes be cut off [from society]. Let it be done in a way that is not degrading to human nature. . . . Liberty to a rational creature, as much exceeds property as the light of the sun does that of the most twinkling star. But you put them on a level—to the everlasting disgrace of civilization. I seriously declare I had rather die by

the most severe tortures ever inflicted on this continent, than lan-
guish in one of your prisons for a single year.

Does then the religion of Him whom you call your Saviour in-
spire this spirit and lead to such practices? Surely no. It is recorded
of Him a bruised reed he never broke. Cease then to call your-
selves Christians, lest you publish to the world your hypocrisy.
Cease, too, to call other nations savage, when you are tenfold
more the children of cruelty than they.[10]

Brant's outrage foreshadowed the profound sadness of the century to
come, during which the Indian peoples struggled to adopt to the alien
white civilization.[11]

Little Turtle, whom even his former enemies acknowledged to be a re-
markable man, perhaps best reflected the somber dignity of the lost cause.
Residing near Fort Wayne, he remained loyal to the United States, despite
the provocations of the years before the War of 1812, and worked tirelessly
in the cause of temperance among his people. During a visit to Philadelphia in 1797, the Miami chief expounded on the unhappy plight of the
red race, perceptively speaking of the inability of his people to adopt to
urban life:

> Here I am deaf and dumb, When I walk through the streets I
> see every person in his shop employed about something. One
> makes shoes, another hats, a third sells cloth, and everyone lives by
> his labor. I say to myself, which of all these things can you do?
> Not one. I can make a bow or an arrow, catch fish, kill game, and
> go to war, but none of these is of any use here. . . . I should be a
> piece of furniture, useless to my nation, useless to the whites, and
> useless to myself.[12]

Inevitably, the future required adaptation and a new kind of education
from succeeding generations of Indians. Yet assimilation under adverse cir-
cumstances was to be a tediously painful process. One historian of the period wrote that the Indian civilization was like a rock, which could not be
changed in form without destroying it. This immutability was to be fully
evident after the advent of widespread development and settlement in the
Old Northwest lands. Little Turtle was one of the Indian leaders who fore-
saw the tragic consequences of the many nuances associated with the
American lifestyle. Particularly distressing was the Indians' affinity for, and

inability to tolerate, strong liquor. He had warned, in vain, that it would perhaps be better to be at war with the white people than submit to the degradation of alcoholism.

"This liquor that they introduce into our country is more to be feared than the gun and tomahawk," he said around the turn of the eighteenth century. "More of us have died since the Treaty of Greeneville than we lost by the years of war before, and it is all owing to the introduction of liquor among us."[13]

Granted a yearly annuity, which was all too frequently misspent, his Miami tribesmen continued to degenerate, so that by 1814 William Henry Harrison reflected that they were "merely a poor drunken set, diminishing every year." An estimated 500 deaths occurred among the Miami tribe alone from drink-related murders and accidents between 1813 and 1830. Devastated by smallpox and other diseases of European origin, the Miami, once one of the largest and most powerful tribes of North America, had dwindled to a mere 300 to 500 souls by the early 1900s.

Throughout his life Little Turtle refused to compromise his dignity, and while younger, when more radical leaders such as Tecumseh urged open defiance of the Americans, he advocated accommodation with the white civilization, which he knew the Indians could not withstand. It was characteristic of the aged Miami chieftain that, shortly before hostilities began in 1812, he wrote to Indiana territorial governor William Henry Harrison professing his strong commitment to peace.

Only a few months later Little Turtle was dead. Afflicted with the gout, he had pitched his camp on the property of William Wells, who since 1795 had been his son-in-law. There he died on July 14, 1812, following treatment by an army surgeon. Although he was buried with appropriate honors in an old orchard on the Saint Joseph River, even a century later his body was not to escape desecration by white men.

In July, 1911, two brothers, while excavating a cellar for their house near Fort Wayne, uncovered Little Turtle's remains. Appropriated by the laborers were many of the chief's prized belongings, including a pistol presented by Kościuszko and his sword, a gift of President Washington in 1797. Eternal peace obviously did not extend to Indian grave sites.

Of Little Turtle's contemporaries there were few who found enduring happiness. Blue Jacket, regarded with enmity by Little Turtle for his political liaison with the Americans, failed to survive long in the limelight. A heavy drinker, this former Shawnee war chief had become so demoralized by August 1800 that he conveyed intelligence to the British on confidential

American plans at the risk of his yearly pension. Although his name appeared on the treaty of Fort Industry, Ohio, in 1804, there are few references to Blue Jacket in the histories of the succeeding years, and his own obscurity was accentuated by the rise to prominence of his two sons. Blue Jacket, christened Maraduke Van Swearingen, himself had been a white captive who had been adopted and taken readily to life as an Indian.

The Shawnee leader Tecumseh did not attend this treaty, and continued to lead his Indians followers in their war against the United States until his death during the War of 1812.

To the others, time brought varying fortunes and controversy. Buckongahelas, the Delaware, died in 1804 amid rumors that he was poisoned by a rival. Tarhe (the Crane) perhaps personified the American interpretation of a "good Indian." First to sign at Greenville, he remained dedicated to a U.S. alliance despite alienation by many of his Wyandot tribesmen. In 1813, during the unpropitious War of 1812, Tarhe, who was then about seventy, led a contingent of Indian scouts under William Henry Harrison into Canada to confront his former allies and tribesmen.

It was during that conflict that another contemporary, William Wells, was slain while attempting to rescue the garrison of Fort Dearborn (Chicago) in August 1812. The War of 1812, in fact, witnessed the last great Indian insurrection east of the Mississippi River. The insurrection was as anticlimactic as it was futile.

John Murray Dunmore, fourth earl of Dunmore, viscount of Fincastle, baron of Blair, Monlin, and Tillimet (1732–1809), who was responsible for mobilizing the Virginia militia against the Indians in 1774, also lived to see the end of Virginia's Western war. After being defeated at Norfolk in 1776 by Gen. Andrew Lewis, he retired to Great Britain and in 1787 was appointed by the king as the governor of the Bahamas. He served as governor until 1797 and died on March 5, 1809.

ENDNOTE ABBREVIATIONS

AWL: Thomas Perkins Abernethy, *Western Land and the American Revolution* (New York: D. Appleton-Century, 1937).

Belue, *Boone:* Lyman C. Draper, *The Life of Daniel Boone,* ed. Ted Franklin Belue (Mechanicsburg, Pa.: Stackpole Books, 1998).

Bowman: George Rogers Clark, *Sketches of His Campain in the Illinois in 1778–9, with an Introduction by Hon. Henry Pirth of Louisville and an Appendix Containing the Public and Private Instructions to Col. Clark and Major Bowman's Journal of the Taking of Post St. Vincents* (Cincinnati: Clarke, 1869).

BS *VaSur:* Joan E. Brookes-Smith, *Master Index: Virginia Surveys and Grants, 1774–1791* (Frankfort: Kentucky Historical Society, 1976).

CCR: Circuit Court Records (county, state). The court records in Kentucky were originally inspected at the courthouse of the various counties, but most of these records have now been taken to Kentucky Archives, Frankfort, Kentucky.

CCRF: Circuit Court Records, Fayette County Complete Books, inspected at the courthouse in Lexington. For a printed version, see Michael L. Cook and Bettie A. Cummings Cook, *Fayette County Kentucky Records,* 2 vols. (Evansville: Cook, 1985).

Clark: Draper MSS 49J, Clark's Memoir, Illinois Historical Collections, 8; also quoted in Temple Bodley, *Our First Great West* (Louisville: Morton, 1938).

Clark's Diary: Diary of George Rogers Clark, December 25, 1776 to March 30, 1777, quoted in Temple Bodley, *History of Kentucky,* 2 vols. (Chicago: Clarke, 1928).

Collins: Lewis Collins, *History of Kentucky,* ed. and rev. Richard H. Collins (Louisville: Richard H. Collins, 1877).

Cowan: Draper MSS 4CC30, John Cowan's Journal, 1777.

CRP: Published court records by Bibb, Hardin, Hughes, Littell, or Marshall, commonly called Kentucky Reports. See bibliography for detailed information on these publications.

CRWA: Court Records of the District of West Augusta, Ohio, and Yohogania Counties, Virginia, 1775 to 1780 from Boyd Crumrine, *Virginia Court Records in Southwestern Pennsylvania* (Baltimore: Genealogical, 1974). These are mostly taken from the minute books of the various courts.

CVSP: William P. Palmer et al., eds., *Calendar of Virginia State Papers and Other Manuscripts Preserved in the Capitol at Richmond, 1652–1869,* 11 vols. (Richmond: R. F. Walker, superintendent of printing, 1875–1893).

DM: Draper MSS, State Historical Society of Wisconsin, Madison.

EJCV: Benjamin J. Hillman, ed., *Executive Journals of the Council of Colonial Virginia, June 20, 1754–May 31, 1775* (Richmond: Virginia State Library, 1966).

EKLR: Neal O. Hammon, *Early Kentucky Land Records, 1773–1780* (Louisville: Filson Club, 1992).

FCHQ: *Filson Club History Quarterly,* Louisville, Kentucky.

Filson, *Kentucke:* John Filson, "Appendix: The Adventures of Col. Daniel Boon; Containing a Narrative of the Wars of Kentucky," the alleged autobiography of Daniel Boone in *The Discovery, Settlement, and Present State of Kentucke* (Wilmington, Del.: Adams, 1784), 68–86.

Hanson: Draper MSS 14J58–84, *Journal of Thomas Hanson, 1774.*

Henderson: Draper MSS 3B195–213, *Journal of Richard Henderson, 1775.*

MilRec: Margery Heberling Harding, ed., *George Rogers Clark and His Men: Military Records, 1778–1784* (Frankfort: Kentucky Historical Society, 1981).

Ranck, *Boonesborough:* George W. Ranck, *Boonesborough* (Louisville: Morton, 1901).

RKHS: *Register of the Kentucky Historical Society* Frankfort, Kentucky.

SVa: William W. Henning, *The Statutes at Large of Virginia,* 13 vols. (Richmond: 1810–1823; reprint, New York: AMS Press, 1970).

Talbert, *Logan:* Charles Gano Talbert, *Benjamin Logan: Kentucky Frontiersman* (Lexington: University of Kentucky Press, 1962).

TB*HK:* Temple Bodley, *History of Kentucky,* Vol. 1 (Chicago: Clarke, 1928).

VAHS: Virginia Historical Society.

WF: Draper MSS 2ZZ, *The Journal of Colonel William Fleming.* Page numbers from version published by the Kentucky Historical Society, *Travels in the American Colonies.*

WFP: William Fleming, Papers, Special Collections, Leyburn Library, Washington and Lee University, Lexington, Virginia.

WW: "William Whitley Narrative," *Register of the Kentucky Historical Society,* July 1938.

Young, *Trabue:* Chester Raymond Young, ed., *Westward into Kentucky: The Narrative of Daniel Trabue* (Lexington: University Press of Kentucky, 1981).

ENDNOTES

INTRODUCTION

1. *EJCV*, 6: 552–54.
2. Hanson, entry of April 20.
3. Ibid., entry of May 14.
4. CCR, Mercer County, Kentucky; *Robertson heirs v. George Corn,* deposition of James Green, September 26, 1807.
5. Data based upon the various directions of roads that were later established along survey boundaries in the Georgetown-Midway, Kentucky, area, specifically Ironworks Pike, Lible Road, U.S. Highway 62, Etter Lane, and Lemons Mill Road.
6. CCR, Shelby County, Kentucky; Complete Book, 103, deposition of Jacob Hubbs, January 13, 1804.
7. There has never been any doubt that some of the surveyors visited Harrodsburg about this time; see DM 4CC33–36. Hanson's journal precludes the possibility that Floyd's men were the early visitors, so the Fincastle surveyors who reached Harrodsburg must have been the men with Taylor. Obviously, it is not practical to lay out half-acre and ten-acre lots without surveying equipment. Some historians have suggested that Isaac Hite visited Harrodsburg while Harrod was there, but Hanson's journal proves otherwise.
8. Taylor's next two surveys, for Charles Lewis and Hugh Mercer near the forks of the Elkhorn, were dated June 28, 1774. Possibly Willis Lee, who returned these surveys after Taylor's death, misread the date

on Zachary Taylor's survey notes and mistakenly entered 17 instead of 27 in the entry book.

9. Hanson, entry of June 25.

10. Ibid., entry of July 8.

11. CCRF and Filson, *Kentucke*. Although the so-called Boone autobiography by Filson gives the date as June 6, Daniel Boone corrected the departure date in his deposition given for the case of the *Boofman heirs v. James Hickman,* Fayette County Complete Record Book A, June 27, 1804.

12. DM 3QQ84, Russell to Preston, August 28, 1774. Taylor's group consisted of his cousin, Willis Lee; his old traveling companion, Abraham Haptonstall; James Strother; John Green; John Willis; and one unknown person, possibly John Bell or John Ashby, since five men returned with Daniel Boone. Haptonstall was of either Dutch or Danish heritage; he was born in New York and was raised on the Virginia frontier, possibly near Greenbrier.

13. American Archives, Ser. 4, Vol. 1, 707. William Preston to Governor Dunmore, July 1774. Historians usually say that Jarred Cowan was killed, which is incorrect.

14. CCRF, Fayette County Complete Book C, 320, deposition of James Sodowski.

15. CCR, Jefferson County Circuit Court, Case no. 2107; *Bate v. Zachary Taylor,* deposition of Jacob Sandwoky [Sodowski or Sandusky], November 29, 1830, on file in Kentucky Archives.

16. Hanson, entry of July 24.

17. DM 6S85–6, Nathan Boone interview.

18. CCRF, Fayette County Complete Book A, 604–42: *Boofman heirs v. James Hickman,* deposition of Daniel Boone.

19. Albert B. Faust, *The German Element in the United States* (Boston: Houghton Mifflin, 1909), 1: 79.

20. Charles Arthur Hopping, *The Washington Ancestry and Records of the McClain, Johnson, and Forty Other Colonial American Families,* Three Volumes (Greenfield, Ohio: Privately Published, 1932), 1: 436.

21. Marshall Wingfield, *A History of Caroline County, Virginia, from Its Formation in 1727 to 1925* (Richmond: Trevvet Christian, 1924).

CHAPTER 1

1775: THE FOURTEENTH COLONY

1. Ranck, *Boonesborough,* 151. The original deed says, "in consideration of the sum of two thousand pounds of lawful money of Great Britain, to them in hand." Some historians have suggested other amounts, sometimes in dollar equivalents.

2. *CVSP,* 1: 283.

3. Ibid., 1: 284.

4. Ibid.

5. DM 6C188; Lyman Draper and other historians insist upon claiming that Boone was present at the signing even though the deed from the Cherokee was dated and signed on March 17, 1775, a week after Boone departed from Long Island for Kentucky.

6. Both groups had been attacked by Indians in July 1774, and several men were killed, including Hancock Taylor, a deputy surveyor of Fincastle County.

7. Belue, *Boone,* 74–76. Joseph Martin had started construction on this station in April 1769. White Rocks is a long cliff, void of trees, that is seen from the valley. It is now owned by the National Park Service.

8. The branch, called Far Fork by some of the early pioneers, was later called Roundstone or Roundstone Lick Creek.

9. Ranck, *Boonesborough,* 163; Felix Walker's narrative.

10. Blue Lick, or Boones Blue Lick, is northeast of the present town of Berea. For a detailed description of Boone's trace in this area, see Neal O. Hammon, "The First Trip to Boonesborough," *FCHQ* 45 (July 1971): 249–63.

11. DM 17CC165, from the "true copy" of the letter, quoted in the letter by John Floyd to William Preston, April 15, 775.

12. Henderson, entry of April 7, 1775.

13. According to modern measurements, this fort site was on or near the existing public toilet building in the state park.

14. *CVSP,* 1: 308.

15. DM 4QQ19, William Russell to William Fleming, June 12, 1775. The Pics or Picks were a division of the Shawnee who lived near modern Piqua, Ohio.

16. DM 4QQ7, William Preston to Lord Dunmore, March 10, 1775.

17. After Todd's death in 1782, May attempted to obtain the land that Todd had claimed for him, but Mrs. Todd insisted that her husband had paid May for the property, a tract now within Lexington.

18. Henderson, entry of May 8, 1775.
19. *CVSP,* 1: 309.
20. The promise never went beyond this conversation, and the matter was later settled by a lawsuit between Hickman and the Boofman heirs.
21. DM 4QQ29, Thomas Lewis to William Preston, August 19, 1775.
22. CRWA, 31, 43.
23. No cabins were constructed at Bryan Station until the following spring.
24. The only members so far identified are Matthew Rust and Lawrence Thompson.
25. Sgt. Zachary Taylor's grandson, also named Zachary Taylor, became the twelfth president of the United States.
26. CCR, Clark County, Kentucky; Deposition Book, 238–40 and 325–37. There is no information on the type of warrants Clark used that would authorize a 15,360-acre survey, but the tract may have been for the Ohio Company; in 1780 he entered several tracts on the Licking River with treasury warrants. No single survey of this size between the two creeks was ever entered by Clark in Fincastle or Kentucky Counties.
27. Entry of June 10, 1775, *The Journal of Nicholas Cresswell, 1774–1777* (New York: Dial, 1924).
28. James H. O'Donnell III, *Southern Indians in the American Revolution* (Knoxville: University of Tennessee Press, 1937), 22.
29. DM 45J101, Henry Hamiliton to Gen. Guy Carleton, November 30 1775.
30. DM 7C76.
31. This name is spelled both Harlin and Harlen in the Kentucky land records but never Harlan.
32. DM 4B62–63; the old fort was exactly one block north of the existing reproduction. The fort site was later used for a quarry and is now a parking lot.
33. *Early Kentucky Settlers: Records of Jefferson County, Kentucky,* from *FCHQ* (Baltimore: Genealogical, 1988), copied for publication by Alvin L. Prichard, 22–23. Apparently their beds and other furniture were handmade and of so little value they were not mentioned in the inventory.
34. CRP, 49–51.
35. WW; William Whitley was born in Augusta County in 1749.

36. Ibid., 190; Whitley also stated that when he was traveling to Kentucky, he passed Henderson at Yellow Creek going in with about forty men.
37. DM 33S290–1.
38. Ranck, *Boonesborough*, 237; report of John Williams to the Transylvania proprietors, January 3, 1776.

CHAPTER 2
1776: THE WAR STARTS IN THE WEST
1. The area included Kentucky and Northwest Territory, of which part was claimed by other colonies.
2. Ranck, *Boonesborough*, 237; report of John Williams to the Transylvania proprietors, January 3, 1776.
3. CRWA, 119. After Samuel Wells returned to Augusta County, he was accused of ill treating and "wounding" his wife.
4. DM 33S291–2, John Floyd to William Preston, May 1, 1776. It is not clear if Floyd was referring to John or Levi Todd. By the summer of 1776, brothers John, Levi, and Robert Todd were all in Kentucky.
5. AWL, 154, 188.
6. DM 33S296–8, John Floyd to William Preston, May 27, 1776.
7. Ibid.
8. Ibid.
9. *EKLR*, 18.
10. DM 4B66, John Todd to William Preston, June 22, 1776. Conocheague was a place in Pennsylvania inhabited mostly by Scotch-Irish. The community began when Scotch-Irish became squatters on Conestoga Manor, a tract of 15,000 acres that the Penns had reserved for themselves. When the squatters were told to move on, they replied that this would be contrary to the laws of God and nature and that so much land should not be idle while so many Christians wanted to work there to raise their bread. And they stayed. See John A. Caruso, *Appalachian Frontier* (Indianapolis: Bobbs-Merrill, 1959), 38. Waller was a noted Virginia lawyer.
11. This unusual custom, also used by some of James Harrod's original company, appears to have originated in Pennsylvania.
12. TB*HK;* quote from the Illinois Historical Collection, 1: 209–10, George Rogers Clark to Jonathan Clark.
13. Carl E. Kramer, *Capital on the Kentucky* (Frankfort: Thomson-Shore, 1986), 14.

14. DM 1U580, unsigned letter from Detroit, dated April 2, 1776.
15. Robert Middlkauff, *The Glorious Cause* (Oxford: Oxford University Press, 1982), 607–9. This source gives additional information on the Virginia constitution and government.
16. Francis W. Hirst, *Life and Letters of Thomas Jefferson* (New York: Macmillan, 1926), 135. George Washington, although not so vocal on this subject, did free all his slaves upon his death, something Jefferson failed to do.
17. TB*HK,* 118, quotation from "delegate Huntington."
18. Christopher Ward, *The War of the Revolution* (New York: Macmillan, 1952), 2: 934, quotation from Captain Graydon, in his *Memoirs,* 148.
19. Faust, *German Element,* 1: 135.
20. DM 7C33.
21. DM 3ZZ1, John Stuart to William Fleming, August 2, 1776.
22. DM 4QQ64, William Preston to the Committee of Safety, August 2, 1776. The lead was usually shipped to the militia in bars, then molded into bullets.
23. Most historians claim this occurred at Drennons Lick, but John Floyd (DM 33S300–5 and 4C20) wrote "they killed a man whose name I do not know at your salt spring on Licking Creek," so perhaps he was killed at the Lower Blue Lick instead.
24. DM 4B100–3.
25. DM 4B102–4. According to Lyman Draper, the fort at McClelland's "appears to have been promptly prosecuted to completion," while those at Harrodsburg and Boonesborough "dragged along slowly, if not entirely abandoned," as the people's alarm subsided. Boone's original fort lacked two or three days' work to make it safe when Captain Cocke arrived there in April 1775, but it remained unfinished in June. When the Callaway and Poage families arrived in September, there was yet no picketing. So Fort Boone could never have consisted of more than a line of cabins, which two or three days' work could have connected with palisades, rendering it reasonably secure.
26. DM 4B105–6, Daniel Boone to Col. William Preston, September 7, 1776.
27. DM 4C20 and 33S300–5, John Floyd to William Preston, July 21, 1776.
28. Ibid. According to DM 4B100, only a few men had been left to guard Boonesborough while men went after the captive Boone and Call-

away girls. The fourteen Cherokee (those mentioned as loitering in Kentucky) were only able to burn the cabin of David and Nathaniel Hart, located between a quarter and half a mile distant from Boonesborough; they completed their mischief by cutting down a garden and a nursery belonging to the settlers.

29. DM 2ZZ78, Matthew Arbuckle to William Fleming, August 15, 1776.
30. DM 4B105.
31. DM 4B104–5; Lyman Draper gives the date as August 7, but most historians use August 6.
32. DM 4B106; Moccasin Gap is just north of Kingsport, Tennessee.
33. *EJCV,* 6: 552–54.
34. AWL, 191; *EKLR,* 1.
35. DM 4B104.
36. DM 13S190–1, Dorsey Penticost to Gov. Patrick Henry, November 5, 1776. The two men killed were James Wernock and Joseph McNutt.
37. DM 3ZZ7, John Cook to Andrew Hamilton, October 2, 1776. Chief Pluggy was even then reported to be the leader of the "company" that started for Kentucky.
38. This cabin was seventeen miles from the Blue Licks and forty miles from where the men had come ashore. Ruddle Station was built at this same site in 1779, on the east bank of Licking River, about five miles south of the present city of Cynthiana, Kentucky.
39. Clark, 214–15. Clark noted in his diary that Joseph Rogers, William Graden, and Josiah Dixon were also killed.

CHAPTER 3
1777: THE WAR CONTINUES

1. CCR, Mason County, Kentucky; *John Williams v. John Kenchival,* deposition of Simon Kenton, dated November 24, 1815: "In the year 1776 [*sic*] a number of Early adventures [*sic*] went to the Islands in the Ohio for some powder deposited there—at the Blue Lick the Company separated—some went the upper road [and] the rest went the road leading to the head of Lawrences creek & the road was then well known to the Company by that name." The document was obviously stolen from the Mason County Court's old legal records. It was sent to the Filson Club on April 2, 1968, by a company in Massachusetts, offering it for sale for $400. The draft of the original was made by Neal O. Hammon.

2. Ward, *War of the Revolution* (New York: Macmillian Company, 1952), 1: 321–22.

3. DM 3NN128–30 and 1SS 43, 55; the invasion force was to consist of 300 militia under Capt. David Shepherd of Ohio County.

4. Talbert, *Logan,* 31–35; WW, 190. The exact date when this fort was first occupied is not known, but William Whitley indicated that he moved to Logan's in March.

5. DM 4B115–6, quotation by Lyman Draper.

6. DM 4B116–7; John Floyd previously mentioned that they started working on the fort in the summer of 1776.

7. Cowan, entry of March 7, 1777.

8. Ibid., entry of March 18, 1777.

9. Ibid.

10. DM 7B 89; John Gass, the nephew of David Gass, aided in the defense of Boonesborough during the big siege of September 1778. He settled in Clark County, Kentucky, where he died about 1825 at the age of about seventy-seven.

11. Clark's Diary, entry of March 8, 1777; also found in DM 48J12.

12. Cowan, entry of March 18, 1777.

13. DM 4B117.

14. Cowan, entry of May 1, 1777, which includes census.

15. DM 48J10.

16. Clark's Diary, 140–44; also found in DM 48J12. Cowan said that the men had come from "Ozark," so apparently they had left the powder boat on the Mississippi River and traveled eastward overland to Kentucky.

17. Cowan, entry of March 28, 1777.

18. For a detailed description of this skirmish, see Belue, *Boone,* 440.

19. Cowan, entry of April 25, 1777.

20. Reuben Gold Thwaites and Louise Phelps Kellogg, *The Revolution on the Upper Ohio, 1775–1777* (Madison: Wisconsin Historical Society, 1908; reprint, Port Washington, N.Y.: Kennikat Press, 1970), 250, 254, quoted from an article in the *Maryland Journal,* May 20, 1777. The Muchmore plantation was a well-known landmark on the east side of the Ohio River below Pittsburgh near present Weirton, West Virginia.

21. Cowan, entry of May 12, 1777. In an often-quoted paragraph from Collins, Jared Cowan is said to have been killed at Fountainbleau in 1774, but this is incorrect; contemporary records prove the man killed was James Cowan.

22. Clark's Diary, entry of May 23, 1777. Apparently, during this attack the Indians burned down the original Fort Boone, which was then abandoned; it was located about 300 yards downstream from the main fort.

23. There is some confusion as to the date when Logan Station was under siege. Talbot says the party left the fort on "the morning of May 30, twelve days after the Indians had first arrived," thus implying that they arrived on the eighteenth. Cowan's journal says "the Indians attacked that place last Friday [May 30 was Friday], and killed William Hudson."

24. Cowan, entry of June 25, 1777.

25. Ibid. The man with Harrod was identified as "Elliott," probably Robert Elliot, who received settlement claim for being in Kentucky in 1775. For mileage from St. Asaph's to Long Island see Neal O. Hammon, "Early Roads into Kentucky," *RKHS* (April 1970), and modern road maps. Logan was most likely on horseback, and assuming he spent two days at Long Island of the Holston, he would have averaged 28.7 miles per day.

26. Cowan, entry of June 20, 1777.

27. Ibid., entry of July 16, 1777.

28. Ibid., entry of July 28, 1777. This journal says "Andrew Gressom," but the man's name was actually Ambrose Grayson. Clark also reported the incident in his diary entry of August 25, 1777.

29. Clark Diary, entry of August 1, 1777.

30. Isaac Riddle (or Ruddle) applied for and was awarded a settlement and preemption on Flat Run of the Licking River in January 1780. Subsequently he obtained an additional 3,500 acres of land nearby. John Duncan (or Dunkin) obtained some land for making a settlement preemption, but this may have been a different person.

31. CRWA, 116/110.

32. WFP, MSS PP4.

CHAPTER 4
1778: WINNING THE WEST

1. Filson, *Kentucke,* 63. Also see William Dodd Brown, "The Capture of Daniel Boone's Saltmakers: Fresh Perspectives from Primary Sources," *RKHS* 83 (winter 1985): 1–18; Ted Franklin Belue, "Terror in the Canelands: The Fate of Daniel Boone's Salt Boilers," *FCHQ* (January 1994): 3–34; and Neal O. Hammon, *My Father: Daniel Boone* (Lexington: University Press of Kentucky, 1999), 53–55.

2. The Indian War Road passed by the Upper Blue Lick, then went to a crossing of the Ohio at the mouth of Cabin Creek. The Lower Blue Lick was on a large buffalo road that led from the future site of Lexington toward Limestone, later Maysville. For a map showing these trails, see Neal O. Hammon, "Pioneeer Routes in Central Kentucky," *FCHQ* (spring 2000): 132.

3. DM 6S103–4.

4. Filson, *Kentucke,* 63; Henry Hamilton in Detroit wrote that the Indians captured twenty-six men that were then making salt with Boone.

5. DM 6S114, interview of Nathan Boone.

6. Filson, *Kentucke,* 64, quote from Daniel Boone.

7. Ibid., 63, quote from Daniel Boone.

8. DM 5B81 and 4NN46; CRWA, 145. The exact date of his death is not known. This name was spelled Hamon in the twelfth and thirteenth centuries, but by 1778 Hammon or Hammond was the usual and arbitrary spelling. In contemporary records one will most often find Nathan Hammond and Philip Hammon.

9. DM 6S115.

10. DM 4C78, letter of Arthur Campbell to William Fleming, July 31, 1778; WW, 19.

11. Hammon, *My Father: Daniel Boone,* 58.

12. DM 6S116.

13. Clark, 7: 222; also DM 49J. The location of Corn Island is shown on many of the early maps of Louisville. Later, when the dam was constructed at the Falls, what remained of the island was flooded.

14. DM 4B172. Some thought this attention was because Boone was a Tory and would like to have seen Kentucky under English rule.

15. Clark, 7: 222.

16. Mann Butler, *Valley of the Ohio,* ed. G. Glenn Clift and Hambleton Tapp (Frankfort: Kentucky Historical Society, 1971), 111–12.

17. BS *VaSur;* see grant for Kentucky survey no. 2743.

18. Filson, *Kentucke,* 66.

19. Temple Bodley, *Our First Great West* (Louisville: Morton, 1938), 93. Clark's overland route was thought to be more or less along highways U.S. 45 and Illinois 30 to the Carbondale-Murphyboro area, then northwest.

20. Ibid., 80 n. 15. The ensuing events are in two narrative letters of Clark commonly called "Mason Letter" and "Memoir" 22 and in the journal of Capt. Joseph Bowman.

21. AWL, 189, 202. Abernethy claimed the invasion of Illinois was due to the influence of merchants, traders, and Gov. Patrick Henry. He says, "The idea of the campaign is generally supposed to have originated with Clark, but the Spanish agent Miralles thought that Bentley and Henry were the prime movers," and "the idea of the conquest of the Illinois by Virginia appears to have originated with Thomas Bentley at Kaskaskia and William Murry in New Orleans and in view of the close cooperation between Clark and the Illinois merchants who were friends and associates of Murry, it seems clear that it was the collaboration of the interests supporting the [Wabash and Illinois] land companies and the Henry administration in Virginia which made the result possible."

22. The well-used term "Wabash Indians" is a misnomer in that the reference is to an area. There were several tribes, including the Mascoutin, Kickapoo, and various divisions of the Miami, living on the upper Wabash River.

23. William Poage had served as a lieutenant under Capt. Daniel Boone at Castlewood, Virginia, during the fall of 1774, and had apparently moved to Kentucky with him in 1775. Daniel Boone later established a land claim for him on Floyds Fork because, as Boone explained in a deposition, Poage was no woodsman.

24. Presuming that the repairs started the day after Boone returned, they would have been completed about June 27.

25. DM 7C69–71.

26. DM 4B203.

27. The exact date that Boone set off is uncertain. Boone's account, according to Filson, *Kentucke,* says the men left on August 1 but suggests that they were out for only seven days. In Belue, *Boone,* Draper gives the date as the latter part of August, which is probably correct.

28. Filson, *Kentucke,* 69.

29. The identity of "Rollins" could not be positively determined. Possibly Anthony Rollings, but most likely Pemberton Rowlings. The Rolling Fork of Salt River appears to have been named for one of these men.

30. Ranck, *Boonesborough,* 35. In DM 19C12, Squire Boone's son, Moses, said the fort contained an acre and was one-third longer than wide; thus it would be 180 by 240 feet. Michael Bedinger said the dimensions were 125 by 250 feet; also see Ann Crabb, *And the Battle Began Like a Clap of Thunder: The Siege of Boonesboro—1778, As Told by the Pioneers* (Richmond: n.p., 1998), 4.

31. Based upon the map of the town in the Madison County court records (reprinted in Ranck, *Boonesborough,* 111). The assumption is that the fort walls were oriented parallel with the river and the boundary of the town common; however, during an excavation at the site, Nancy O'Malley discovered a cabin foundation that was only 12 degrees from north, so there is a possibility that the fort was not oriented parallel to the river.

32. DM 19C12; a plan of the fort drawn by Moses Boone. He stated that in July 1778 the fort wall was extended to the east (southeast?), so the middle buildings were probably originally along the southeast wall.

33. As is frequently the case in historical accounts, there are many conflicting stories about the siege of Boonesborough. According to Ranck, *Boonesborough,* 103 n, the proper spelling of the French leader is Dagniaux DeQuindre; he was born in Montreal in 1743, lived in Detroit, and died in 1784. The name of the French leader is sometimes spelled Duquesne, according to Crabb, *And the Battle Began Like a Clap of Thunder,* 11. Also the sketch map drawn by John Gass, DM 24C89, indicates that the Indians marched in on the trail from the future ferry crossing rather than along Boone's Trace, as stated in most accounts.

34. DM 48J42, John Bowman letter.

35. Ibid and Filson, Kentucke, 69–70. Daniel Boone says nine men went outside to confer with the Indians, and Daniel Trabue says "about 15." All agree that the conformation took place at the Salt Lick, but the distance from the lick to the front gate is also disputed, varying from fifty to eighty yards.

36. DM 1A19.

37. Filson, *Kentucke,* 69.

38. DM 4B232–3.

39. DM 21S253, interview of Samuel Millard.

40. Young, *Trabue,* 58–59. Trabue reported the cannon was made by Col. Richard Callaway, but DM 4B240 (and others) give the credit to Squire Boone, who was a gunsmith.

41. Filson, *Kentucke,* 70.

42. DM 19C11.

43. Ted Franklin Belue, "Did Daniel Boone Kill Pompey, the Black Shawnee, at the 1778 Siege of Boonesborough?" *FCHQ* 69 (January 1993): 5–22.

44. DM 4B236.
45. DM 14S18, letter from Henderson to the assembly, November 21, 1778.
46. DM 4B237.
47. DM 4B241–2.
48. Young, *Trabue,* 60.
49. DM 4B252.
50. *CVSP,* 1: 272.

CHAPTER 5

1779: THE COUNTERATTACKS

1. TB*HK,* 182, quote from Illinois Historical Collection, 8: 138–39.
2. *MilRec;* John Rogers is shown on the February 1779 payroll as a captain of state cavalry.
3. TB*HK,* 182, quote from Illinois Historical Collection, 8: 138–39.
4. *Bowman,* 99–100. Clark said he had "eighty troops in garrison," but with the militia his force numbered "a little upward of two hundred." The pay records show that about sixty men with French names, presumably militia, served under McCarty and Charlaville. Thus Clark would have had about seventy of his regulars with him, the remaining ten regulars on the boat with Rogers.
5. Ibid., 100. At this point it is difficult to determine Clark's position. The two rivers are about seven miles from each other near present Greyville, Illinois, but here Clark would have been about forty-five miles southwest of Vincennes. Taking a more direct route, they would have reached the Little Wabash about ten miles west or southwest of Olney, Illinois, but here they would have been about thirty to forty miles from Vincennes and over twenty miles from the main Wabash. Most historians believe that the route at this time was near present highway U.S. 50; thus the reference to the two rivers would refer to the two forks of the Little Wabash River.
6. TB*HK,* 191, quotation from Illinois Historical Collection, 7: 275–76.
7. Ibid., 193, quotation from Illinois Historical Collection, 7: 275–76.
8. Collins, 19. This author dates these two stations, but the date cannot be verified by any other source. Harlin's Station was said to be seven miles south of Harrodsburg and Irvine's Station on Otter Creek. Of course, Harrod's and Hart's Stations were occupied earlier, then abandoned, then reoccupied, but these would not be considered new set-

tlements. Many stations started as only two or three cabins without stockades.

9. BSVaSur, old Virginia land survey no. 662. By plotting the surveys of William Whitley and his neighbors, it can be established that this station was approximately two miles west of the Whitley State Park. The Whitley house on the park property was built later.

10. DM 19C87.

11. DM 19C26.

12. The name is usually spelled Riddle before 1780 and Ruddle after 1780 in the Virginia records. Both names are frequently found in England.

13. AWL, 225.

14. Talbert, *Logan,* 75.

15. TB*HK,* 202.

16. Talbert, *Logan,* 77

17. TB*HK,* 202.

18. This is according to two participants, George Michael Bedinger and William Whitley. Bowman did not mention the incident in either of the two accounts he wrote upon his return from the expedition. He explained his order to retreat in terms of the strong position held by the enemy and the very satisfactory amount of damage that already had been done to the village of Chillicothe.

19. TB*HK,* 202; quotation from DM 49J89, Lt. James Patton's report of battle.

20. Illinois Historical Collection, 8: 300.

21. J. Stoddard Johnson, ed., *Memorial History of Louisville* (Chicago: American Biographical, 1896), 1: 37–45.

22. During his lifetime William Fleming's home, called "Bellmont," was in several counties.

23. John Todd obtained a settlement and preemption near Lexington as assignee of John May, who had raised a crop of corn in the country "at his expense" in 1775. For more information on this family, see Ben H. Coke, *John May, Jr., of Virginia, His Descendants, and Their Land* (Baltimore: Gateway, 1975).

24. DM 17CC184 and 33S314, Floyd to Preston, October 30, 1779.

25. CRP, James Hughes, *A Report of the Causes Determined by the Late Supreme Court for the District of Kentucky and by the Court of Appeals, 1786–1801* (Cincinnati: Anderson, 1909), 251 (hereafter cited as Hughes), October term of court, 1799. The best-known lawsuit of this type was between Simon Kenton and Alexander McConnell.

26. Ibid., 372.

27. CRP, George M. Bibbs, *Reports of Cases at Common Law and in Chancery Argued and Decided in the Court of Appeals of the Commonwealth of Kentucky,* 3rd ed. (Cincinnati: Clarke and Russel, 1909), 1: 522–53 (hereafter cited as Bibbs), *Clay v. Smith et al.,* fall term, 1809.

28. CRP, Alexander K. Marshall, *Kentucky Reports* (Louisville: Fetter, 1899), 1: 140, appeal from Mercer Circuit Court, *Samuel Moore et al. v. John Dodd et al.,* November 25, 1817. Moore was deceased at the time the land transaction was made and the suit was brought by the heirs.

29. Beall-Booth Family Papers, manuscript department, the Filson Club, letter from John May to Samuel Beall, December 18, 1779.

CHAPTER 6
1780: THE LAND RUSH

1. Henry Lee, *Memoirs of the War in the Southern Department of the United States,* new edition with revisions and biography by Robert E. Lee (New York: University, 1780). Lieutenant Colonel Lee (in his biography) blamed the success of the night attack conducted by Tarleton's cavalry and Ferguson's riflemen on General Lincoln for his failure to reinforce Monk's Corner with 700 Virginia soldiers then available.

2. WF, 628; Fleming reported that about 3,000 people came to Kentucky while the commissioners were there, and they eventually heard over 1,300 claims.

3. Ibid., 630.

4. Ibid., 634. He refers to the person killed with Colonel Callaway as Pemberton Rawlings. It is spelled Rowling in the land records before he was killed and Rawlings afterward.

5. DM 33S315–6 and 17CC185, letter from John Floyd to William Preston, November 26, 1779.

6. Beall-Booth Family Papers, John May to Samuel Beall, April 15, 1780.

7. WF; DM 2ZZ654–5.

8. DM 17CC185 and 33S315, letter from John Floyd to William Preston, November 26, 1779. The only exception was when the administrator of the estate of James Terry, deceased, was allowed a claim at the mouth of Harrods Creek on land previously surveyed for Col.

William Byrd. Possibly the commissioners were not aware of the location of this survey made by Hancock Taylor.

9. DM 33S317–8, letter from John Floyd to William Preston, February 20, 1780.

10. Neal O. Hammon, "Early Louisville and the Beargrass Stations," *FCHQ* 52 (April 1978) 147–165; Vincent Akers, "The Low Dutch Company: A History of the Holland Dutch Settlements of the Kentucky Frontier," part 4, *de Halve Maen* (spring 1980). These stations were Floyd's, Dutch, and Hogland's on Floyd's property, Asturgus on Colonel Christian's property, Spring on the Southall and Charlton tract, and Linn's on the John Ware land. Many of the inhabitants were Dutch pioneers who had migrated from Pennsylvania.

11. CCR, Shelby County, Kentucky, Complete Book, 159–60, deposition of George Yount, n.d., circa 1811.

12. After Fitch's release he published a map of western Virginia and used the profit from the map to finance his steamboat. He eventually settled and died in Kentucky.

13. Kenneth C. Carstens, "George Rogers Clark's Fort Jefferson, 1780–1781" *FCHQ* 71 (July 1997): 259–84. His research revealed that forty-three civilian families resided at this town during its existence.

14. *CVSP,* 3: 448, quoted by TB*KH,* and Temple Bodley, *George Rogers Clark: His Life and Public Service* (Boston: Houghton, Mifflin Co., 1926), 161.

15. John Bakeless, *Background to Glory* (Philadelphia: Lippincott, 1957), 248.

16. DM 17CC124–7, John Floyd to William Preston, May 5, 1780.

17. DM 17CC 128, John Floyd to William Preston, May 30, 1780.

18. WF, entry of May 5, 1780. His tally is in slight variance with the land records; see *EKLR,* 283. For a complete list of entries in Kentucky County, Virginia, see *EKLR,* 47–104.

19. DM 17CC128, John Floyd to William Preston, May 30, 1780.

20. John Campbell, then held captive in Detroit, had an interest in this land, which he recovered later. Campbell was a Tory spy according to Abernethy. The authors believe he was more likely a double agent, whose main interest was looking after his own skin.

21. Transylvania College is still in existence. It is the oldest college west of the Appalachian Mountains and one of the oldest in the United States.

22. CCR, Grant County, Kentucky, Order Book A, 453, deposition of John Zinn, May 12, 1834.

23. CCR, Bourbon County, Kentucky, Court Case 481, *Halbert v. Haws,* deposition of Col. James Garrard, May 23, 1818. The attack in May is described in WF, 647.

24. *MilRec.* These pay records list sixteen companies of militia numbering 557 men and 242 regulars, about 200 fewer than the 1,000 men Clark said were on the campaign.

25. WW, 196. The bore size was slightly larger than the famous German 88s used in World War II. Several old prints show British cannons attached to two wheel limbers, which was the practice in most armies. Cannons, however, could also be pulled without limbers by attaching a "leading bar" to the "trail." It is not known if the cannon pulled to the Indian villages by Clark had a limber, but it probably did; otherwise it would have been very difficult to manage. Without a limber someone would have to walk ahead and guide the horses—not too practical with a six-horse team. For nonmilitary operations, these cannons were often pulled by oxen.

26. Neal O. Hammon, "Clark and the Land Office," *FCHQ* 70 (July 1996): 317–25.

27. The Indian side refers to the north side of the Ohio. See Neal O. Hammon and Nelson Dawson, *The Letters of James John Floyd, 1774–1783,* unpublished manuscript, 57–58.

28. DM 8J136–7.

29. Some historians contend (without supporting evidence) that the American force was mostly made up of men of Scotch-Irish ancestry, but actual studies of the nationalities of these frontiersmen would seem to disprove this idea. See Forrest McDonald and Helen McDonald, "The Ethnic Origins of the American People, 1790," *William and Mary Quarterly* 37 (1980): 179–87, and John B. Sanderlin, "Ethnic Origins of Early Kentucky Land Grantees," *RKHS* 85 (spring 1987): 103–10. Ferguson was also said to be Scotch-Irish.

30. Patrick Ferguson had invented a breech-loading rifle in 1776 that was superior to any used during this period. The British army, however, refused to use them. See Matthew C. Switlik, "Shooting the Famous Ferguson Rifle," and Maj. Reginald Hargreaves, "The Fabulous Ferguson Rifle and Its Brief Combat Career," *American Rifleman* (August 1971): 33–41.

31. Clark Collection, Missouri Historical Society, St. Louis, Missouri, memo from Robert George to George Rogers Clark, September 2, 1780.

32. DM 6S129–151. The account by Nathan Boone is slightly different.
33. DM 7C82, Mercer County, deposition of James Ray, October 24, 1817.
34. *CVSP,* 1: 434–37, letter from Arthur Campbell to Thomas Jefferson, January 15, 1781.
35. Not all of these counties were on the frontier; in 1792 Virginia had 93 counties.

CHAPTER 7
1781: A QUICK END TO THE WAR IN THE EAST
1. DM 51J39.
2. BSV*aSur,* survey no. 2743. This land was sold to William Oldham.
3. Otis K. Rice, *The Allegheny Frontier* (Lexington: University Press of Kentucky, 1970), 112–14.
4. *CVSP,* 2: 529–31, John Floyd to Gov. Thomas Nelson, October 6, 1781.
5. DM 51J89, John Floyd to George Rogers Clark, September 14, 1781.
6. DM 51J85, Field Officers to Clark, September 6, 1781. All of the officers agreed that an expedition to the Indian towns on the Wabash was not practical.
7. For date, see DM 51J89, John Floyd to G. R. Clark, and DM 19C29, Moses Boone interview. In DM 17CC137–8, John Floyd to William Preston, September 30, 1781, Floyd says the defeat was on the sixteenth.
8. DM 17CC34.
9. DM 15C94.
10. Vince Akers, *The American Revolution in Kentucky, 1781,* manuscript, Columbus, Ind., 1982.
11. The total number of men that surrendered was 7,247 soldiers and 840 seamen; they had 482 casualties during the siege.
12. Dale Van Every, *A Company of Heroes* (New York: Morrow, 1962), 283.
13. Executive Papers, 1891, Virginia State Archives. This letter is printed in part in Calendar of Virginia State Papers, 2: 651, letter from Robert Todd to Thomas Nelson, December 11, 1781.

CHAPTER 8
1782: CORNWALLIS SURRENDERS BUT THE WAR GOES ON
1. *CVSP,* 3: 89–90.
2. WW, 197.
3. DM 52J12, letter from William Davies to Clark, April 6, 1782. Davies stated that due to the inattention of the state assembly, the tobacco fund, previously used for credit, was abolished, and so the state treasury would be without funds until November 1782.
4. *CVSP,* 3: 133.
5. Four of the enlisted men killed were Adam Carpenter, John Coltfoote, Jonathan McMullen, and James McNeely.
6. DM 52J18. John Neville in a letter to Clark blamed the act on "a set of rascals as was in this part of the country, I mean the leading men of Washington and Westmoreland Counties [Pennsylvania], who did every thing in their power to prevent your campaign."
7. Virginia State Archives, quoted in James Alton James, *George Rogers Clark Papers, 1781–1784* (Springfield: Illinois State Historical Library, 1924), 59, John Todd to Governor Harrison, April 15, 1782.
8. DM 52J9.
9. These calibers are equivalent to 93, 81, and 64 mm.
10. A similar but smaller galley was later authorized by Congress. For a description and illustration, see Howard I. Chapelle, *The History of the American Sailing Navy* (New York: Bonanza, 1959): 151–52.
11. DM 52J25, Robert George to John Todd, May 19, 1782. *MilRec,* 130, shows that on this occasion Capt. Robert Patterson had forty-one men in his company, including Israel Boone, the son of Daniel Boone.
12. Canadian Archives; Colonial Office Records, Ser. 2, Vol. 20, 288, report from Alexander McKee to Major DePeyster, August 28, 1782.
13. Haldimand Papers, Ser. B, Vol. 123, 297, report of Capt. William Caldwell to Major DePeyster, August 26, 1782. There is some controversy about the date, as various old accounts give different dates. Most modern historians, however, believe the fort was attacked on the morning of the sixteenth.
14. Reuben T. Durrett, *Bryant's Station,* Filson Club Publications No. 12 (Louisville: Morton, 1897), 42. Some claim that Elijah Craig was in charge of the fort, but if John Craig was not the leader, En. Jeremiah Craig would have had military seniority.
15. John Hammon was an ancestor of coauthor Neal Hammon.

16. DM 17CC144–8; Billey Buchanan was probably related to John Floyd's wife.

17. CCRF, Fayette County Complete Book A, 679; *Nathaniel Hart's heirs v. Samuel Estill et al.,* June 24, 1805, deposition of Thomas Allen, July 28, 1803. Daniel Boone did not make the survey in question but only pointed out the site to another surveyor who did the work. The heirs of Nathaniel Hart lost this law suit on appeal.

18. Durrett, *Bryant's Station,* 23–24. Durrett used the name Bryant rather then Bryan, according to his statement, because Cave Johnson and several other pioneers had spelled the name Bryant. The Bryan family had first settled at this location but had gone back to North Carolina two years before the attack.

19. Haldimand Papers, Ser. B, Vol. 123, 297, Capt. William Caldwell to Major DePeyster, August 26, 1782.

20. Estimated by the author, based upon the location of the northern-most ravine, now partly filled in by the state for construction of a lodge. Levi Todd said the battleground was three-quarters of a mile from the ford and Daniel Boone said one mile.

21. Some sources say that Silas Harlin's men charged on horseback.

22. Hammon, *My Father: Daniel Boone,* 78.

23. DM 12CC134.

24. DM 6S154.

25. DM 6S163–4; Netherland quotation by Olive Boone.

26. AWL, 265. Abernethy believes that this was the beginning of a campaign to discredit the popular military leader.

27. William Kincheloe (1736–1797) was born in Prince William County, Virginia, the son of John Kincheloe and Elizabeth Canterbury. He married Mary White and moved to Kentucky about 1779. The station was constructed on the preemption of William Polke, who began construction of a cabin on the property in 1776.

28. DM 52J40.

29. WF, entry of January 4, 1783; DM 2ZZ69. The exact date of the attack was not mentioned.

30. *CVSP,* 3: 332.

31. Virginia State Archives, 131.

32. *MilRec,* 158–97. All of the companies except three were identified by county. One company was left to guard a salt lick and did not participate in the raid. The total militia that took part in the campaign was 1,106 men, according to these lists, but a few stayed at the crossing place to guard the boats, etc.

33. DM 52J53.
34. TB*KH,* 316, quotation from Illinois Historical Collection, 19: 157–58.
35. DM 52J55, Gen. William Irvine to Clark, November 7, 1782.

CHAPTER 9
1783: WHO OWNS WHAT?

1. Many of the same men, mostly from New England, also opposed President Thomas Jefferson's purchase of Louisiana in 1802.
2. DM 52J69, James Monroe to G. R. Clark, January 5, 1783.
3. The census of 1790 would indicate that approximately one-third of the population of the United States was then located in North Carolina and Virginia.
4. Merrill Jenson, *The New Nation* (New York: Vintage, 1950), 307. The debt problems of other colonies are also covered in the text.
5. Virginia State Archives, Executive Documents, G. R. Clark to William Davies, January 1, 1783.
6. DM 52J73, Benjamin Harrison to G. R. Clark, January 13, 1783.
7. *CVSP,* 3: 437.
8. DM 11CC226.
9. *CVSP,* 3: 327–28.
10. DM 51J99.
11. The Fishpools were a series of sinkholes that had an underground stream running exposed through their bottoms. White, eyeless fish were caught in the sinkholes by pioneers. About 1965 these holes were filled up by a subdivision developer and houses built over them. The sinkholes were about a mile southwest of the present quarry in Oklalona.
12. DM 52J28.
13. WF, entry of April 7, 1783; DM 2ZZ69; WW, 196. These accounts tell about the same story and say the incident occurred at Crab Orchard. Apparently those inside the house were Mr. Michael Wood and his wife, both elderly, their grown daughter, Hannah, and an unidentified Negro, who was, according to William Whitley, "very much disabled."
14. The Colonial and State Records of North Carolina, 16: 457–58, Harrison to Martin, November 12, 1782.
15. *CVSP,* 3: 376–77, Martin to Harrison, November 21, 1782.

16. Phillip Lee Phillips, *A Rare Map of the Northeast, 1785* (Washington, D.C.: Lowdermilk, 1916), 6. A cider press was generally used to squeeze the juice from apples.
17. Ibid., 16–18.

CHAPTER 10
1784–86: VIRGINIA'S LAST CAMPAIGNS

1. The large house called Spring Station was built by Samuel Beall, and Farmington was the plantation of James Speed. Both dwellings are still in existence. "Farmington," managed by the Louisville Historic Homes Foundation, is open to the public.
2. "Locust Grove," now managed by the Louisville Historic Homes Foundation, is open to visitors. It was built almost on the boundary line between the 1774 surveys made for Hancock Eustace and William Peachey. The privately-owned Taylor house, northwest of the Zachary Taylor military cemetery, is also still standing.
3. The Abraham Chaplin grant, for example, originally consisted of 1,400 acres, but three small tracts were sold, and the remainder went to his five children, so by the early 1800s the largest farm contained fewer than 200 acres.
4. The U.S. Bureau of the Census estimated the Kentucky population in 1780 at 45,000, with an increase to 73,677 at the census of 1790; thus the increase would have averaged 2,867 people per year during this period. In the author's opinion the original estimate was too high and the rate of increase was greater.
5. VAHS, William Christian to Elizabeth Christian, November 4, 1785.
6. Ibid., William Christian to William Fleming, September 25, 1785.
7. Ibid., Ann Christian to Ann Fleming, November 3, 1785.
8. Ibid., William Christian to William Fleming, November 4, 1785.
9. According to John Bakeless, *Daniel Boone* (New York: Morrow, 1939), the original of this letter, dated August 16, 1785, has been lost, but there is a good forgery in the New York Public Library, Rare Books and Manuscript Division, Emmet Collection, no. 6277. This copy was furnished to the author by Nancy O'Malley, University of Kentucky, Lexington. Spelling revised by the authors.
10. Lula Porterfield Givens, *Highlights in the Early History of Montgomery County Virginia* (Christianburg, Va.: Givens, 1975), 98, letter from John May to Patrick Henry.

11. Mary B. Kegley and F. B. Kegley, *Early Adventures on the Western Waters* (Orange, Va.: Green, 1980), 1: 341, letter from William Christian to James McCorkle, September 25, 1785.

12. DM 14C81.

13. Beall-Booth Family Papers, manuscript department, the Filson Club, letter to John May from Samuel Beall "at Williamsburg," December 9, 1782.

14. Talbert, *Logan,* 207.

15. DM 9CC; statement of Solomon Clark, reprinted in R*KHS* (July 1938), 207–8. Lyman C. Draper disagrees with this version, saying that one of the Negroes was shot a few days after reaching Piqua.

16. Talbert, *Logan,* 209.

17. Ibid., both quotes from page 210.

18. Hammon, *My Father: Daniel Boone,* 81. The fact that Daniel Boone was on this campaign is confirmed by the militia pay records; see Kentucky Historical Society, Military Certificates, photocopy book of original documents, no. 976.903/M644i.

19. John Mack Faragher, *Daniel Boone: The Life and Legend of an American Pioneer* (New York: Holt, 1992), 255.

20. National Archives, Washington D.C., Revolutionary War Pension File S9559, Affidavit of John Hammon, September 5, 1832; also Talbert, *Logan,* 214.

21. DM 19C99–101. According to Moses Boone, the men came upon a party of Indians preparing to camp, some not yet dismounted. "These latter dashed away when Hardin's men rushed up. The whites endeavored by dividing to surround the Indians & effected it, though most of the Indians got off. Ten Indians were killed and two Indian girls taken prisoners." Others in the company included surveyors William Shannon and Dan Sullivan.

22. Department of State, Washington D.C., Bureau of Indexes and Archives, Accounts Involved in the Settlement of Virginia's Claims against the United States, May 15, 1788.

EPILOGUE

THE FEDERAL GOVERNMENT TAKES COMMAND

1. Freeman Cleavers, *Old Tippecanoe: William Henry Harrison and His Time* (New York: Scribner's, 1939), 28–30.

2. James Thomas Flexner, *George Washington and the New Nation* (Boston: Little, Brown, 1965–1972), 3: 264.

3. WFP, manuscript WF12, William Fleming to his wife, December 3, 1789.
4. Ibid., manuscript 009–M9, Harry Innes to William Fleming, May 13, 1790.
5. Ibid., manuscript O15, Harry Innes to William Fleming, August 14, 1791.
6. The site of this battle was at Fort Recovery, Ohio, near the Indiana state line, southeast of Fort Wayne.
7. John C. Fitzpatrick, ed., *Calendar of Correspondence of George Washington* (Washington: Government Printing Office, 1931–1944), 3: 62.
8. DM 19C110–111.
9. TB*HK,* 532–33 and 406–7, quotation from General Wayne's report from Western Annals.
10. Wiley Sword, *President Washington's Indian War* (Norman: University of Oklahoma Press, 1995), 334, quote from William L. Stone's *Life of Joseph Bryan.*
11. Ibid., 335, quote from Calvin M. Young, *Little Turtle,* 125.
12. Ibid.
13. Ibid.

BIBLIOGRAPHY

BOOKS

Abernethy, Thomas Perkins. *Western Lands and the American Revolution.* New York: D. Appleton-Century, 1937.

Adams, James Truslow, ed. *Atlas of American History.* New York: Scribner's, 1943.

Alden, John Richard. *The American Revolution.* New York: Harper and Brothers, 1954.

———. *A History of the American Revolution.* London: MacDonald, 1969.

Allen, William B. *A History of Kentucky.* Louisville: Bradley and Gilbert, 1872.

Anderson, William G. *The Price of Liberty: The Public Debt of the American Revolution.* Richmond: Banta, 1983.

Andrews, Charles M. *The Colonial Background of the American Revolution.* New Haven: Yale University Press, 1924.

Bakeless, John. *Daniel Boone.* New York: Morrow, 1939.

———. *Background to Glory.* Philadelphia: Lippincott, 1957.

———. *Turncoats, Traitors, and Heroes.* Philadelphia: Lippincott, 1959.

Bardsley, Charles W. *English Surnames: Their Source and Significations.* London: Chatto and Windus, 1875.

Barnhart, John D. *Henry Hamilton and George Rogers Clark in the American Revolution.* Crawfordsville, Ind.: Banta, 1951.

Bass, Robert D. *The Green Dragoon.* Columbia, S.C.: Sandlapper, 1973.

Bidwell, Bruce W. *History of the Military Intelligence Division: Department of the Army General Staff, 1775–1941.* Frederick, Md.: University Publications of America, 1986.

Bodley, Temple. *George Rogers Clark: His Life and Public Services.* Boston: Houghton, Mifflin Co., 1926.

———. *History of Kentucky.* 2 vols. Chicago: Clarke, 1928.

———. *Our First Great West.* Louisville: Morton, 1938.

Brookes-Smith, Joan E. *Master Index: Virginia Surveys and Grants, 1774–1791.* Frankfort: Kentucky Historical Society, 1976.

Buckley, Thomas G. *Church and State in Revolutionary Virginia.* Charlottesville, Va.: University Press of Virginia, 1977.

Butler, Mann. *Valley of the Ohio.* Edited by G. Glenn Clift and Hambleton Tapp. Frankfort: Kentucky Historical Society, 1971.

Caruso, John A. *Appalachian Frontier.* Indianapolis: Bobbs-Merrill, 1959.

Chapelle, Howard L. *The History of the American Sailing Navy.* New York: Bonanza, 1959.

Chief of Engineers of the U.S. Army. *The Ohio River.* Washington, D.C.: U.S. Printing Office, 1935.

———. *Kentucky River.* Louisville: U.S. Printing Office, 1968.

Chinn, George Morgan. *Kentucky: Settlement and Statehood.* Frankfort: Kentucky Historical Society, 1975.

Clark, George Rogers. *Sketches of His Campain in the Illinois in 1778–9, with an Introduction by Hon. Henry Pirth of Louisville and an Appendix Containing the Public and Private Instructions to Col. Clark and Major Bowman's Journal of the Taking of Post St. Vincents.* Cincinnati: Clarke, 1869.

Clark, Jerry E. *The Shawnee.* Lexington: University Press of Kentucky, 1977.

Clark, Thomas D. *A History of Kentucky.* Lexington: Bradford, 1954.

———. *Frontier America.* New York: Scribner's, 1959.

Cleavers, Freeman. *Old Tippecanoe: William Henry Harrison and His Time.* New York: Scribner's, 1939.

Clement, Maud Carter. *Pittsylvania County Virginia.* Lynchburg, Va.: Bell, 1929.

Clift, G. Glenn. *Kentucky in Retrospect.* Frankfort: Kentucky Historical Society, 1967.

Coke, Ben H. *John May, Jr., of Virginia, His Descendants, and Their Land.* Baltimore: Gateway, 1975.

Collins, Lewis. *History of Kentucky.* Cincinnati: Collins and James, 1847.
———. *History of Kentucky.* Edited and revised by Richard H. Collins. Louisville: Richard H. Collins, 1877.

Cotterill, R. S. *History of Pioneer Kentucky.* Cincinnati: Johnson and Hardin, 1917.

Crabb, Anne. *And the Battle Began Like Claps of Thunder: The Siege of Boonesboro—1778, As Told by the Pioneers.* Richmond: n.p., 1998.

Davis, Burk. *The Campaign That Won America: The Story of Yorktown.* New York: Dial, 1970. Reprint, Eastern Acorn Press, 1982.

Derleth, August. *Vincennes: Portal to the West.* Englewood Cliffs, N.J.: Prentice-Hall, 1968.

Draper, Lyman C. *The Life of Daniel Boone.* Edited by Ted Franklin Belue. Mechanicsburg, Pa.: Stackpole Books, 1998.

Drimmer, Frederick, ed. *Captured by the Indians.* New York: Dover, 1961.

Durrett, Reuben T. *Bryant's Station.* Filson Club Publications No. 12, Louisville: Morton, 1897.

Eckert, Allan W. *The Frontiersmen: A Narrative.* Boston: Little, Brown, 1967.
———. *The Court-Martial of Daniel Boone.* Boston: Little, Brown, 1973.

Elliott, Lawrence. *The Long Hunter: A New Life of Daniel Boone.* New York: Reader's Digest, 1976.

Faragher, John Mack. *Daniel Boone: The Life and Legend of an American Pioneer.* New York: Holt, 1992.

Faust, Albert B. *The German Element in the United States.* 2 vols. Boston: Houghton Mifflin, 1909.

Filson, John. *The Discovery, Settlement, and Present State of Kentucke.* Wilmington, Del.: James Adams, 1784.

Fleming, Thomas. *1776: Year of Illusions.* Edison, N.J.: Castle, 1976.

Flexner, James Thomas. *George Washington and the New Nation.* 4 vols. Boston: Little, Brown, 1965–1972.

Freeman, Douglas Southall. *George Washington.* 6 vols. New York: Scribner's, 1948–1954.

Friend, Craig Thompson, ed. *The Buzzell about Kentucky: Settling the Promised Land.* Lexington: University Press of Kentucky, 1999.

Givens, Lula Porterfield. *Highlights in the Early History of Montgomery County Virginia.* Christianburg, Va.: Givens, 1975.

Gwathmey, John H. *Twelve Virginia Counties: Where the Western Migration Began.* Richmond: Dietz, 1937.

Hamilton, Edward P. *The French and Indian Wars.* New York: Doubleday, 1962.

Hamilton, Holman. *Zachary Taylor: Soldier of the Republic.* 2 vols. Indianapolis: Bobbs-Merrill, 1941.

Hammon, Neal O. *Early Kentucky Land Records, 1773–1780.* Louisville: Filson Club, 1992.

———. *My Father: Daniel Boone.* Lexington: University Press of Kentucky, 1999.

Harper, Josephine L., ed. *Guide to the Draper Manuscripts.* Madison: State Historical Society of Wisconsin, 1983.

Harrison, Henry. *Surnames of the United Kingdom: A Concise Etymological Dictionary.* 2 vols. London: Eaton, 1912.

Harrison, Lowell H., and James C. Klotter. *A New History of Kentucky.* Lexington: University Press of Kentucky, 1997.

Hirst, Francis W. *Life and Letters of Thomas Jefferson.* New York: MacMillan, 1926.

Isaac, Rhys. *The Transformation of Virginia.* Chapel Hill, N.C.: University of North Carolina Press, 1982.

James, James Alton. *George Rogers Clark Papers, 1781–1784.* Springfield: Illinois State Historical Library, 1924.

Jennings, Francis. *Empire of Fortune.* New York: Norton, 1988.

Jensen, Merrill. *The New Nation.* New York: Vintage, 1950.

Jillson, Willard Rouse. *Pioneer Kentucky.* Frankfort: State Journal, 1934.

Johnson, Patricia Givens. *James Patton and the Appalachian Colonist.* Verona, Va.: McClure, 1973.

Johnson, William. *Sketches of the Life and Correspondence of Nathanael Greene, Major General of the Armies of the United States in the War of the Revolution: Compiled Chiefly from Original Materials.* 2 vols. Charleston: Miller, 1822.

Johnston, J. Stoddard, ed. *Memorial History of Louisville.* 2 vols. Chicago: American Biographical, 1896.

Kegley, Mary, and F. B. Kegley. *Early Adventures on the Western Waters.* 2 vols. Orange, Va.: Green, 1980.

Kincaid, Robert L. *The Wilderness Road.* Middlesboro, Ky.: Bobbs-Merrill, 1966.

Kleber, John E., ed. *The Kentucky Encyclopedia.* Lexington: University Press of Kentucky, 1992.

————. *The Encyclopedia of Louisville.* Lexington: University Press of Kentucky, 2001.

Kramer, Carl E. *Capital on the Kentucky.* Frankfort: Thomson-Shore, 1986.

Lee, Henry. *Memoirs of the War in the Southern Department of the United States.* New edition with revisions and biography by Robert E. Lee. New York: University, 1780.

Lofaro, Michael A. *The Life and Adventures of Daniel Boone.* Lexington: University Press of Kentucky, 1978.

Mason, Kathryn Harrod. *James Harrod of Kentucky.* Baton Rouge: Louisiana State University Press, 1951.

Meuter, Maria Kitty. *The Long Rifle, The Bow, and the Calumet.* Louisville: McClanahan, 2000.

Middlekauff, Robert. *The Glorious Cause.* Oxford: Oxford University Press, 1982.

Monmonier, Mark. *Drawing the Line.* New York: Holt, 1995.

Montross, Lynn. *War through the Ages.* 3rd ed. New York: Harper and Brothers, 1960.

Moore, Arthur K. *The Frontier Mind.* Lexington: University of Kentucky Press, 1957.

O'Donnell, James H., III. *Southern Indians in the American Revolution.* Knoxville: University of Tennessee Press, 1973.

O'Malley, Nancy. *Stockading Up.* Lexington: Kentucky Heritage Council, 1987.

————. *Searching for Boonesborough.* Rev. ed. Lexington: University of Kentucky Press, 1990.

Perkins, Elizabeth A. *Border Life: Experience and Memory in the Revolutionary Ohio Valley.* Chapel Hill and London: University of North Carolina Press, 1998.

Peterson, Harold L. *Arms and Armor in Colonial America, 1526–1783.* New York: Bramhall House, 1956.

Phillips, Phillip Lee, *A Rare Map of the Northeast, 1785.* Washington, D.C.: Lowdermilk, 1916.

Ranck, George W. *Boonesborough.* Louisville: Morton, 1901.

Rice, Otis K. *The Allegheny Frontier.* Lexington: University Press of Kentucky, 1970.

————. *Frontier Kentucky.* Lexington: University Press of Kentucky, 1975.

Schmidt, Martin F. *Kentucky Illustrated: The First Hundred Years.* Lexington: University Press of Kentucky, 1992.

Stevens, Phillip H. *Artillery through the Ages.* New York: Franklin Watts, 1965.

Stone, Richard G., Jr. *A Brittle Sword: The Kentucky Militia, 1776–1912.* Lexington: University Press of Kentucky, 1977.

Sword, Wiley. *President Washington's Indian War.* Norman, Okla.: University of Oklahoma Press, 1985.

Talbert, Charles Gano. *Benjamin Logan: Kentucky Frontiersman.* Lexington: University of Kentucky Press, 1962.

Taylor, Richard. *Girty.* Frankfort: Gnomon, 1977, 1990.

Thornely, Samuel, ed. *The Journal of Nicholas Cresswell, 1774–1777.* New York: Dial, 1924.

Thwaites, Reuben Gold, and Louise Phelps Kellogg. *Documentary History of History of Dunmore's War, 1774.* Madison: Wisconsin Historical Society, 1905.

———. *The Revolution on the Upper Ohio, 1775–1777.* Madison: Wisconsin Historical Society, 1908. Reprint, Port Washington, N.Y.: Kennikat Press, 1970.

Usner, Daniel H., Jr. *Indians, Settlers, and Slaves in a Frontier Exchange Economy.* Chapel Hill: University of North Carolina Press, 1992.

Van Every, Dale. *A Company of Heroes.* New York: Morrow, 1962.

Ward, Christopher. *The War of the Revolution.* 2 vols. New York: Macmillan, 1952.

Wilson, Samuel M. *First Land Court of Kentucky, 1779–1780.* Lexington: n.p., 1923.

———. *Battle of the Blue Licks, August 19, 1782.* Lexington: n.p., 1927.

Wingfield, Marshall. *A History of Caroline County, Virginia, from Its Formation in 1727 to 1925.* Richmond: Trevvet Christian, 1924.

Wooley, Carolyn Murray. *The Founding of Lexington, 1775–1776.* Lexington: Lexington-Fayette County Historic Commission, 1975.

Wrobel, Sylvia, and George Grinder. *Isaac Shelby: Kentucky's First Governor and Hero of Three Wars.* Danville, Ky.: Cumberland, 1973.

Yater, George H. *Two Hundred Years at the Falls of the Ohio.* Louisville: Heritage Corporation of Louisville and Jefferson County, 1979.

Young, Chester Raymond, ed. *Westward into Kentucky: The Narrative of Daniel Trabue.* Lexington: University Press of Kentucky, 1981.

ARTICLES

Akers, Vincent, "The Low Dutch Company: A History of the Holland Dutch Settlements of the Kentucky Frontier." *de Halve Maen* 55 (1980).

Bate, R. Alexander. "Colonel Richard Callaway, 1722–1780." *Filson Club History Quarterly* 29 (1955).

Beckner, Lucien. "John Findley: The First Pathfinder." *Filson Club History Quarterly* 43 (1969): 206–15.

Belue, Ted Franklin. "Olive's Gift." *Muzzleloader Magazine* (March 1991): 58–61.

———. "Terror in the Canelands: The Fate of Daniel Boone's Salt Boilers." *Filson Club History Quarterly* 68 (January 1994): 3–34.

———. "Did Daniel Boone Kill Pompey, the Black Shawnee, at the 1778 Siege of Boonesborough?" *Filson Club History Quarterly* 69 (1994): 5–22.

Brown, William Dodd. "The Capture of Daniel Boone's Saltmakers: Fresh Perspectives from Primary Sources." *Register of the Kentucky Historical Society* 83 (winter 1985): 1–18.

Carstens, Kenneth C. "George Rogers Clark's Fort Jefferson, 1780–1781." *Filson Club History Quarterly* 71 (July 1997): 259–84.

Haffner, Gerald O. "Colonel Henry Hamiliton: A Famous POW of the American Revolution." *Filson Club History Quarterly* 29 (1955): 339–48.

Hagy, James William. "The First Attempt to Settle Kentucky: Boone in Virginia." *Filson Club History Quarterly* 44 (1970): 227–34.

Hall, Richard H. "Callaway Family Data." *Filson Club History Quarterly* 29 (1955): 331–38.

Hammon, Neal O. "Early Roads into Kentucky." *Register of the Kentucky Historical Society* 68 (April 1970): 91–131.

———. "The First Trip to Boonesborough." *Filson Club History Quarterly* 45 (July 1971): 249–63.

———. "Captain Harrod's Company, 1774: A Reappraisal." *Register of the Kentucky Historical Society* 72 (1974): 224–42.

———. "Legend of Daniel Boone's Cabin at Harrodsburg." *Filson Club History Quarterly* 48 (1978): 241–52.

———. "Early Louisville and the Beargrass Stations." *Filson Club History Quarterly* 52 (April 1978): 147–65.

———. "Land Acquisition on the Kentucky Frontier." *Register of the Kentucky Historical Society* 78 (1980): 297–321.

———. "John Filson's Error." *Filson Club History Quarterly* 59 (1985): 462–63.

———. "Settler, Land Jobbers, and Outlyers." *Register of the Kentucky Historical Society* 84 (1986): 241–62.

———. "Clark and the Land Office." *Filson Club History Quarterly* 70 (July 1996): 317–25.

———. "Pioneer Routes in Central Kentucky." *Filson Club History Quarterly* 74 (spring 2000): 125–43.

Hargreaves, Reginald, Maj. "The Fabulous Ferguson Rifle and Its Brief Combat Career." *American Rifleman* (August 1971): 34–37.

Harris, James Russell, and Neal O. Hammon. "Letters of Col. John Floyd, 1774–1783." *Register of the Kentucky Historical Society* 83 (1985): 202–36.

Henderson, Archibald. "Transylvania Company Personnel." *Filson Club History Quarterly* 21 (1947): 3–21.

Hoyt, William D., Jr. "Colonel William Fleming: County Lieutenant of Botetourt, 1776–1779." *Americana* 35 (1941): 405–34.

———. "Colonel William Fleming: Commissioner to Examine and Settle the Public Accounts in the Western Country, 1782–1783." *Americana* 36 (1942): 175–210.

———. "Colonel William Fleming in Dunmore's War, 1774." *West Virginia History* 3 (1942): 99–119.

Igleheart, Ted. "Squire Boone: The Forgotten Man." *Filson Club History Quarterly* 44 (1970): 357–66.

McDonald, Forrest, and Helen McDonald. "The Ethnic Origins of the American People, 1790." *William and Mary Quarterly* 37 (1980): 179–87.

Sanderlin, John B. "Ethnic Origins of Early Kentucky Land Grantees." *Register of the Kentucky Historical Society* 85 (1987):103–10.

Switlik, Matthew C. "Shooting the Famous Ferguson Rifle." *American Rifleman* (August 1971): 38–41.

Talbert, Charles G. "A Roof for Kentucky." *Filson Club History Quarterly* 29 (1955): 145–62.

DOCUMENTS AND MANUSCRIPTS

Akers, Vince. *The American Revolution in Kentucky, 1781.* Manuscript. Columbus, Ind.: 1982.

American Archives. Ser. 4, Vol. 1, 707. William Preston to Governor Dunmore, July 1774.

Beall-Booth Family Papers. Manuscript department. The Filson Club, Louisville, Kentucky.

Bentley, James, director. *Early Kentucky Settlers: Records of Jefferson County, Kentucky.* From *Filson Club History Quarterly.* Baltimore: Genealogical, 1988.

Canadian Archives. Colonial Office Records. Ser. 2, Vol. 20, 288. Alexander McKee to Major De Peyster, August 28, 1782.

Cook, Michael L., and Bettie A. Cummings Cook. *Fayette County Kentucky Records.* 2 vols. Evansville: Cook, 1985.

Crumrine, Boyd. *Virginia Court Records in Southwestern Pennsylvania.* Baltimore: Genealogical, 1974.

Draper, Lyman. Draper Manuscripts. 480 vols. State Historical Society of Wisconsin, Madison.

Early Kentucky Settlers: Records of Jefferson County, Kentucky. From *Filson Club History Quarterly.* Baltimore: Genealogical, 1988. Copied for publication by Alvin L. Prichard.

Fitzpatrick, John C., ed. *Calendar of Correspondence of George Washington.* 40 vols. Washington: Government Printing Office, 1931–44.

Fleming, William. Papers. Special Collections. Leyburn Library. Washington and Lee Univeristy, Lexington, Virginia.

Ford, Carol Lee, indexer. *Early Kentucky Tax Records.* Baltimore: Genealogical, 1987.

Hammon, Neal O. *The Daniel Boone Papers.* Manuscript. Shelbyville, Ky.: 1998.

———. *No Stranger to Difficulty: Letters and Journals of Dr. William Fleming.* Manuscript. Shelbyville, Ky.: 1999.

Hammon, Neal O., and Nelson Dawson. *The Letters of James John Floyd, 1774–1783.* Manuscript. Shelbyville, Ky.: 1996.

Hammon, Neal O., and Charles T. Long. *Pioneer Depositions 1795–1810.* Manuscript. Shelbyville, Ky.: 1998.

Harding, Margery Heberling, ed. *George Rogers Clark and His Men: Military Records, 1778–1784.* Frankfort: Kentucky Historical Society, 1981.

Heinemann, Charles B., ed. *First Census of Kentucky, 1790.* Baltimore, 1956.

Hening, William W. *The Statutes at Large of Virginia.* 13 vols. Richmond: 1810–23. Reprint, New York: AMS Press, 1970.

Hopping, Charles Arthur. *The Washington Ancestry and Records of the McClain, Johnson, and Forty Other Colonial American Families.* 3 vols. Greenfield, Ohio: Privately Published, 1932.

McChesney, H. V., ed. "Certificate Book of the Virginia Land Commission of 1779–80." In *Register of the Kentucky Historical Society,* 1923.

Palmer, William P., et al., eds. *Calendar of Virginia State Papers and Other Manuscripts Preserved in the Capitol at Richmond, 1652–1869.* 11 vols. Richmond: R. F. Walker, superintendent of printing, 1875–1893.

Stevens, Frank E. *Illinois in the War of 1812–4.* In transactions of the Illinois State Historical Society. Springfield, 1904.

PUBLISHED LEGAL REVIEWS

Bibbs, George M. *Reports of Cases at Common Law and in Chancery Argued and Decided in the Court of Appeals of the Commonwealth of Kentucky.* 3rd ed. 4 vols. Cincinnati: Clarke and Russel, 1909.

Hardin, Martin D. *Reports of Cases Argued and Adjudged in the Court of Appeals, 1805–1808.* Cincinnati: Clarke, 1869.

Hughes, James. *A Report of the Causes Determined by the Late Supreme Court for the District of Kentucky and by the Court of Appeals, 1786–1801.* Louisville: Fetter, 1898.

Littell, William. *Reports of Cases at Common Law and in Chancery Decided by the Court of Appeal of the Commonwealth of Kentucky.* 5 vols. Louisville: Amos and Kendall, 1822–1824.

Marshall, Alexander K. *Decisions of the Court of Appeals of Kentucky.* 3 vols. Louisville: Fetter, 1899.

INDEX

Jarboe, Elizabeth, second wife of
    Kenton, 224
Jared, Eli, killed, 63
Jefferson, Thomas, xxxv, 23, 33,
    98, 102, 138, 142, 183
Jefferson's proposal, 35
Jennings, Jonathan, 20
Jeptha's Mountain, 18
Johnson, Andrew, 70
Johnson, Benjamin, 19
Johnson, Richard M., vice
    president of the United
    States, 155
Johnson, Robert, 155, 181
Johnson, Samuel, 164
Johnson, Thomas, 3
Jones, John Gabriel (Jack), 24,
    31, 33, 46
Jordan, Garrett, 18
Jordan, Patrick, 11, 15
Jouett, Jack, 142
Jouett, Matthew, 11

Kaskaskia, captured 1778, 76
Kaumanaugh, Joseph, 177
Kellar, Isaac, killed, 190
Kelly, James, 30
Kemp, Joseph, 140
Kennedy, John, 59
Kenton, Simon, 19, 30, 49, 57,
    76, 78, 90, 223
Kentucky became state, 213
Kentucky, population in 1777,
    53; in 1784, 186
Kincade, Joseph, 164
Kincheloe Station, 167
Kincheloe, William, 167
King Louis XVI of France, 75,
    101

King, John, 50
King's Mountain, battle of, 132
Knight, Edward, 202
Knob Lick, 19
Knox, James the Secretary of
    War, 206, 208–9, 216
Knox, James, 11, 12
Knox, James, marries Logan 223
Knox, James, xiv, xxiv, xxvii

Lain, William, 18
Land awarded to settlers, 126
Land claims in 1781, 139
Land companies, Indiana and
    Vandalia, 37
Land law, 102, 104
Land speculators, 111
Land for Virginia veterans of the
    Revolutionary War, 139
Land, Military surveys & settlers
    claims, xvii
Land, waste and ungranted lands
    open to settlement, 45
Langlade, Charles, 123
lead mines, fortified, 40–41; See
    Chiswell lead mines
Lecompt, Charles, 17
Lee, John, 18
Lee, Richard Henry, 23
Lee, Willis, xviii, xxii, xxvi, xxix
Leeper, Hugh, 79
Leestown, established, 19
Lewis, Andrew, xiv, xvii, xxx,
    102, 228
    first Kentucky entry, xv
Lewis, Charles, xxx, xxxi
Lewis, John, 140
Lewis, Samuel, 72
Lexington named, 18